BASIC
GRAMMAR
IN MANY
VOICES

D0169531

CONTENTS

v

CHAPTER EIGHT

Punctuation   167

Basic Grammar in Many Voices is designed to help you understand how the English language works. You will learn about the words that provide content—the nouns, verbs, adjectives, and adverbs—and about the words that help the content words make sense, the function words known as articles, pronouns, prepositions, and conjunctions. You will also learn how these words arrange themselves in English sentences to make meaning. You will come to recognize phrases and clauses and their uses in the writing of others and in your own writing. In short, you will learn about English grammar.

Grammar is interesting in itself, but understanding it can also help you become a better writer. In the hopes of showing you what good writers do when they are working, I have selected for study sentences taken from novels, short stories, essays, and biographies written by many different authors. Probably none of these writers had any idea that the structure of the sentences they were putting on paper would be examined in such a detailed way. Nevertheless, good grammar guided their work, even though they may not have been conscious of it. That is, good writers learn to put the rules of grammar in action, and they don't usually have to think about them. In some ways, learning to write is like learning to drive a car. At first, you have to think about what you are doing, but after a while, you know what to do without having to pay conscious attention to all the steps. Eventually, you will be able to operate in the same way when you write. You will incorporate the rules of grammar into your writing.

ORGANIZATION

In order to help you think about the rules of English grammar, I have provided a step-by-step approach to grammar in eight chapters. Each of the chapters assumes that you have worked through the previous chapters. Thus, it is important that you begin with the first chapter and continue working through the chapters in the order in which they are presented.

Each chapter includes a number of exercises for you to do that will help you learn specific grammar concepts. I have provided an answer key at the back of the book for checking your work. I encourage you to complete these exercises on your own *before* consulting the answers. Having you get the right answers in a particular exercise isn't the primary goal of this book; helping you develop an understanding of the principles underlying English grammar is its true objective. So, if after doing an exercise, you find you have made some mistakes, reread the portion of the text that the exercise addresses so that you can fully understand the concept. Think of mistakes as your friend—they tell you what you need to work on. Then you can focus your energy in that area and make your learning more efficient.

In every chapter you will find terms printed in **boldface** type. The boldface tells you that the term is important in grammar and that it appears in the glossary at the end of the book. Any time you meet with a grammar term whose meaning you are unsure of, look it up in the glossary for clarification. The index can also help you locate previous discussions about specific terms.

At the end of each chapter, you will find a list of projects that require you to go outside of the text to enhance your learning. Sometimes you will be asked to read material of your choosing in order to find certain kinds of grammar elements. Other times you will be asked to write something of your own and to examine the grammar elements that occur. Try to do as many of these projects as you can. In addition to being fun, they serve as a wonderful learning tool and provide practice in writing.

ACKNOWLEDGMENTS

I am indebted to my editor, Marisa L'Heureux, whose encouragement and insightful criticism helped me through this project. I also am grateful to my husband and colleague, Dan Alford, who commented on drafts of the manuscript and helped me proofread. Lucille Alford deserves special thanks; without her help in dealing with family matters as the deadline approached, this book might not have been completed. I also thank all the students I have ever taught. They have taught me how to teach them.

Marilyn N. Silva

Recognizing Nouns and Pronouns

NOUNS

A **noun** is a word for a living being or lifeless thing. Words such as *Bob, Jane, woman, student,* and *dog* (living beings) and *Chicago, city,* and *handkerchief* (lifeless things) are all nouns. In addition, words naming groups of living beings (for example, *army*) and names of qualities (*goodness*), states (*happiness, gout*), and ideas (*belief*) also are nouns.

Articles

If you are uncertain about whether a particular word is a noun, a good way to decide is to look at the way the word is used in a given sentence. The word is a noun if you find in front of it a function word like *the, a,* or *an*. These three words are called **articles.** *The* is called a **definite article;** that means it is used when both speaker/writer and hearer/reader are familiar with what is being discussed. For example, if you and a friend together were taking a gift to a birthday party, and your friend were in charge of wrapping it, you might ask, "Did you bring *the* present?" That would mean that you had a specific present in mind, and both of you knew what it was. *A* is an **indefinite article,** and we use it when we do not have a specific item in mind. For example, if you and your friend were not buying a gift together, and you were uncertain that your friend had purchased one, you might ask, "Did you bring *a* present?" That would mean that you were not thinking of a specific present.

An is a variant of *a*. When the next word begins with a consonant sound such as *p*, you should use the indefinite article *a*; when a vowel sound such as *o* follows, *an* should be used. Thus we say *an orange*. However, it is the sound, not the spelling, that determines whether the beginning of the word is a vowel. Notice that we say *a one-shot deal*, even though *one* begins with *o*. The choice of *a* or *an*, then, depends on the sound of the following word, and not on any difference in meaning.

Noun Phrases

Articles may occur in a grouping of words called a **noun phrase,** and they never appear in any other place. (A noun phrase is a unit that includes a noun and any elements that modify that noun in some way. We will discuss those modifying elements later.) Articles are therefore a very powerful identifier of nouns, because if you find an article, you will find a noun. What makes articles all the more useful in identifying nouns is that the list of articles is so limited: *the, a,* and *an*. You don't have to memorize a long list of elements or even a definition. You simply need to remember that finding any one of these three words will tell you that a noun phrase is present.

Exercise 1.1

 The following sentences come from *The Diary of Anais Nin, Volume One, 1931–1934*, edited by Gunther Stuhlmann. Circle every article you find and underline the noun that it introduces.

1. The street runs down unevenly towards the Seine.

2. By the Seine there is a tavern and a restaurant.

3. The dogs bark at night.

4. The fountain emerges like the headstone of a tomb.

5. The day begins always with the sound of gravel crushed by the car.

6. The shutters are pushed open by Emilia, and the day admitted.

7. Below the rug, I felt, was the earth.

8. The fountain was gay and sprightly.

9. He would have passed anonymously through a crowd.

10. Then I slipped down into the seat and went to sleep.

Adjectives

Often an article is not followed immediately by a noun but by one or more words that describe the noun by limiting or qualifying it. For example, the indefinite article in Sentence (1) from *The Diary of Anais Nin* begins a noun phrase that includes such descriptive words:

1. Behind the house lies a vast wild tangled garden.

The noun phrase in Sentence (1) is *a vast wild tangled garden*. In that phrase, the words *vast*, *wild*, and *tangled* all describe the noun *garden*. The general term for words that fine-tune the meaning of other words is *modifier*, and the descriptive modifiers in Sentence (1) above are all **adjectives**. Adjectives typically occur in noun phrases and ordinarily precede the noun they modify.

Exercise 1.2

 Underline the noun phrases introduced by articles in the following sentences from *The Diary of Anais Nin*. Circle the adjectives you find.

1. When [the bell] rings, the Spanish maid, Emilia, swings open the large gate and the cars drive up the gravel path, making a crackling sound.

2. There are eleven windows showing between the wooden trellis covered with ivy.

3.   Every room is painted a different color.

4.   I seek only the high moments.

5.   The big garden is in the back of the house.

Other Identifiers of Nouns

Articles are not the only words that help to identify nouns. In fact, they are part of a larger group of function words called **determiners.** Determiners are noun modifiers that always precede any adjectives modifying the same noun. Unlike adjectives, determiners do not describe. They do not provide a characteristic of the noun. Instead, they "determine" the kind of reference a noun phrase has—for example, whether the noun phrase refers to a specific or nonspecific person or thing. The most important members of this class, in addition to the articles *the, a,* and *an,* are *another,* the **demonstratives** *this* and *that* and their plural forms *these* and *those,* and quantifying words such as *each, enough, every, all, some, many, more, much, few, any, no,* the numbers (*one, two,* and so on), and the **possessive pronouns** that precede nouns (*my, our, your, his, her, its, their*). These determiners are listed in Table 1.1.

Table 1.1. English Determiners

Articles	Demonstrative Determiners	Quantifying Words	Possessive Pronouns	Numbers
the *a, an*	*this, these* *that, those*	*all* *another* *any* *each* *enough* *every* *few* *many* *more* *much* *no* *some*	*my, our* *your* *his, her, its* *their*	*one* *two* *three,* etc.

Exercise 1.3

Circle each determiner you encounter in the following sentences from Robert Fulghum's *It Was on Fire When I Lay Down on It*. Then underline the noun phrase it begins, including any adjectives that may come between the determiner and the noun.

1. No adrenaline was left in her body.

2. On the tenth anniversary of this disastrous affair, a party was held.

3. I don't have any pets.

4. Yes, I know, there is an old lady up in that tree over there.

5. At some point your genetic code presses a switch in your head.

6. Your life becomes like your old car—just as long as as it runs and gets you there, who cares how it looks?

7. Sometimes the old geek asks another lady to dance.

8. After the dishes are washed and the sink rinsed out, there remains in the strainer at the bottom of the sink what I will call, momentarily, some "stuff."

9. A willingness to do your share of cleaning up the mess is a test.

10. The sons leave, kick away and burn all bridges, never to be seen again.

11. But sometimes they come back in their own way and in their own time and take their own fathers in their arms.

12. The ultimate source of this information was the snake in the Garden of Eden.

13.   There is no water.

14.   She was anchored to her seat by her own dignity.

15.   A new religion could be founded on this one
      sacrament.

Possessive Noun Phrases

In addition to the function words we call determiners, a noun phrase
may begin with another noun or noun phrase that is possessive in form.
Sentence (2) from *It Was on Fire When I Lay Down on It* has such a possessive noun:

2.   I tore open Molly's bag and shook out the contents.

In this sentence, *Molly's* has an *-'s* suffix, which shows possession.
Notice that *Molly's* begins a noun phrase, *Molly's bag.* Thus, finding a
possessive noun can help you find other nouns.

The suffix *-'s* attaches only to freestanding nouns or entire noun
phrases. When we use expressions like *the Queen of England's children,*
the possessive suffix is found on the end of the noun phrase *the Queen
of England,* even though we mean that it is the Queen who has the children, not England. (We will study modifiers that come after the noun,
such as *of England,* in Chapter 4.) We do not say **the Queen's of England
children* (the asterisk [*] in front of a phrase or sentence means that it
is unacceptable).

Compound Nouns

Some English nouns are actually made up of two or more nouns
used together. We call such nouns **compound nouns.** In particular, the
noun phrases *the police dog, the church bells,* and *a prison gate* in the following sentences from Anais Nin's *Diary* provide examples of compound nouns:

3. With the first crushing of the gravel under wheels comes the barking of <u>the police dog</u>, Banquo, and the carillon of <u>the church bells</u>.

4. When I look at the large green iron gate from my window it takes on the air of <u>a prison gate</u>.

In the noun phrase *the police dog*, the words *police* and *dog* are both nouns; combining them in *police dog* results in a compound noun.

The difference between a compound noun and an adjective-noun combination typically is easy to identify. There are two ways to tell them apart. One way is to listen to the accent pattern in the phrase. When you say the phrase aloud, does the main emphasis fall on the first of the two words following the article or on the second? In an adjective-noun combination such as *the heavy gáte*, the emphasis is always on the noun, not on the adjective. So if the accent falls on the second word, then in all likelihood that word is a noun and the word preceding it is an adjective. If, on the other hand, the accent falls on the first of the two words, as it does in the phrase *the chúrch bells*, the pair constitutes a compound noun, which behaves just like any single noun.

A second way to recognize a compound noun is to try to turn it into a sentence of its own. As you will see, you cannot turn a compound noun into a sentence; only an adjective-noun combination will allow this process to occur. For an example, let's look at some of the adjective-noun combinations we found in Exercise 1.2: *the Spanish maid, the large gate, the wooden trellis.* In each case, we can make a simple sentence involving the noun, the verb *is* or *are*, and the adjective. Thus, we get the following:

5. The maid is Spanish.

6. The gate is large.

7. The trellis is wooden.

As you can see, Sentences (5) through (7) represent what we understand when we express phrases such as *the Spanish maid, the large gate, the wooden trellis.*

Compound nouns such as *the police dog, the church bells,* and *a prison gate,* on the other hand, behave quite differently. If we try to make a sentence out of the two words that comprise a compound noun, we come up with gibberish:

8. *the dog is police

9. *the bells are church

10. *a gate is prison

Though these three compound nouns—*police dog, church bells, prison gate*—are all written as two words, many ordinary compounds are conventionally spelled as single words. When a compound is written as one word, it is easy to tell that it functions as a single noun: *birthday, bookstore, slaughterhouse, firemen, toothpaste, cheesecake, headache, doorway, fireplace, drawstring, paperweight, ashtray, workplace, sidewalk, stockboy, cannonball, redwood.*

Because compound nouns function as ordinary single-word nouns, they may be preceded by determiners and adjectives, just like any noun. In Sentence (11), from Jerry Seinfeld's *SeinLanguage*, the compound noun is *entertainment town* and *the* and *ultimate* are the determiner and adjective modifying it:

11. Las Vegas is still the ultimate entertainment town to me.

Compound nouns also may include more than two elements, as the following sentences, also from *SeinLanguage*, demonstrate:

12. The tuxedo is a <u>wedding safety device</u>, created by women, because they know that men are undependable.

13. The clearest indication of the complexity of modern relationships is that <u>greeting card companies</u> are forced to put out cards that are blank on the inside.

14. I felt bad for the <u>traffic school instructor</u>.

15. The <u>soda commercial people</u>—where do they get this enthusiasm?

Exercise 1.4

Each of the following sentences from *SeinLanguage* has at least one compound noun. Underline every compound noun you find. Remember that the accent falls on the first of the two words in a compound and that we cannot make a reasonable sentence with the two words by using *is* or *are*.

1. What is a date really, but a job interview that lasts all night?

2. Don't get me wrong, the wedding ceremony is a beautiful thing.

3. For men, the transplant is the hair procedure of choice.

4. The hair plug is an interesting process.

5. One of the most popular procedures today is the nose job.

6. I was in the drug store the other day trying to get a cold medication.

7. The other day I was watching women in a department store looking at clothes.

8. To me nothing matches the phone machine as a modern technological accomplishment.

9. Somebody just gave me a shower radio.

10. I also love the gift certificate.

11. Wouldn't it be nice if you could have a car alarm that was a little more subtle?

12. I don't know why people always have the same reaction when they hear about a plane crash.

13. You go up to the ticket agent.

14. I hate the waiting room because it's called the waiting room so there's no chance of no waiting.

15. Do the security guards in the art museums ever stop anybody from taking the paintings?

16. Little Jimmy here needs an organ transplant.

17. I'd like once for a sweepstakes company to have some guts, come out with the truth, just be honest with people one time.

18. A person suffering from fear of success is scraping the bottom of the fear barrel.

19. Whenever you ask for the doggie bag at a restaurant, there's a certain sense of failure there, isn't there?

20. I've never really understood the importance of the orchestra conductor.

21. The thing about L.A. that kind of threw me was the smog alerts.

22. But the health clubs are a little too strict.

23. I don't even know where the wall outlets are anymore.

24. When I was a kid, my favorite ride was the bumper cars.

25. I always preferred a machine ride to anything live, like a pony ride.

Nouns without Determiners

Though determiners are a reliable indicator of nouns, they are not *necessary* ones. That is, a word can still be a noun even if it is not introduced by a determiner. However, only certain kinds of nouns can occur without determiners (see Table 1.2).

Many of the nouns we have seen so far have been **count nouns,** words for any one individual of a class of living creatures or inanimate objects—for example, *bell, body, car, chair, child, dog, donkey, father, fountain, fuse, garden, gate, head, house, maid, path, restaurant, shutter,*

Table 1.2. Nouns Occurring without Determiners

Kind of Noun Phrase	Kind of Noun	Example
definite	*proper*	Jane: <u>Jane</u> is my friend.
indefinite	*plural common count*	dogs: <u>Dogs</u> make good pets.
indefinite	*mass*	rice: <u>Rice</u> is a tasty side dish at any meal.
indefinite	*abstract*	happiness: <u>Happiness</u> is often difficult to attain.

son, street, supermarket, switch, tavern, trellis, wife. All of these nouns can occur with both the definite and indefinite articles—for example, *the bell, a bell; the body, a body; the car, a car.* But this fact is true only if the noun is singular, indicating only one of whatever the noun names. However, if the noun is plural, indicating more than one and typically shown on the noun by the suffix -*s* or -*es*, then only definite noun phrases can take a determiner. If the noun phrase is both indefinite and plural, no determiner may appear; *a/an* can introduce only singular nouns. As a result, we will find noun phrases such as *the bells*, or simply *bells*, but never **a bells; the cars* and *cars* are both possible but not **a cars.*

Count nouns are typically **common nouns,** because they indicate any one member of a class of individuals. In contrast to the common noun, there is the **proper noun,** a noun that always begins with a capital letter. A proper noun names a particular, unique entity, either living or inanimate, and by virtue of this quality, it is definite but takes no determiner in most circumstances. Your name is a proper noun, as is the name of the city, state, or country where you live. *Marilyn, San Francisco, Indiana,* and *Canada* are all proper nouns.

A third kind of noun may also appear without a determiner, but only when the noun phrase is indefinite. This type is often called a **mass noun** and typically indicates a formless substance, such as *water, flour, sand.* Mass nouns generally do not have plural forms (except in special circumstances). Nonetheless, they can occur as freestanding nouns (perhaps modified by adjectives) without any article whatsoever. We find noun phrases such as *the water* and *water,* but not **a water; the flour* or *flour,* but not **a flour,* and so on.

A fourth class of potentially determiner-less nouns is the **abstract noun**. An abstract noun designates a quality, action, or idea, such as *warmth, exercise,* or *music*. Some of these nouns may have plural forms (for example, *exercises*) and take the indefinite article (for example, *a strenuous exercise*) when indicating an activity with boundaries, but when they refer to a general idea, they typically take no determiner at all, as in the following sentences:

16.   <u>Warmth</u> is a wonderful quality in a friend.

17.   Aerobic <u>exercise</u> is good for the heart.

18.   <u>Music</u> calms the spirit.

Exercise 1.5

The following passage from Robert Fulghum's *It Was on Fire When I Lay Down on It* contains several nouns that occur without determiners. Find them and underline them. Can you say why they occur without determiners in this instance?

Chaos Science has led researchers back to the most fundamental

everyday matters—the formation of clouds, the mixing of paint, the

flow of traffic, the spread of disease, and the freezing of water in

pipes. The cycle of earthquakes and the eruption of volcanoes fits into

Chaos Science, too, which is pretty important these days if you live in

California or in the Cascade Mountains.

PRONOUNS

Pronouns serve to replace a freestanding noun or a noun phrase, typically when the original word or phrase must be repeated in a sentence or paragraph. There are four types of pronouns: personal, possessive, demonstrative, and indefinite.

Personal Pronouns

Some pronouns are **personal pronouns** (see Table 1.3). The term *personal* refers to the grammar notion **person.** Three persons are relevant in English grammar: first person is the speaker or writer (*I, me, we, us*), second person is the listener or reader (*you*), and third person is whoever or whatever is discussed (*he, she, it, him, her, they, them*).

Personal pronouns are distinguished by **number;** they can be singular, pointing to one individual (*I, he, she, it*), or plural, pointing to more than one (*we, they*). Third-person singular pronouns, unlike first and second person, also show **gender.** That means that they change form depending on whether the noun or noun phrase they replace points to a male being, a female being, or something that is taken to be neither male nor female, such as *a bug, a whale, a tree, a house.*

Most personal pronouns have one form for a pronoun serving as a subject (subject form) and another form for a pronoun serving as an object (object form). However, the third-person neuter singular pronoun (*it*) does not vary, nor does the second-person pronoun (*you*). We will discuss the distinction between subjects and objects in Chapter 3.

Table 1.3. Personal Pronouns

	Subject Form	Object Form
First Person (speaker)		
Singular	*I*	*me*
Plural	*we*	*us*
Second Person (spoken to)	*you*	*you*
Third Person (spoken about)		
Masculine singular	*he*	*him*
Feminine singular	*she*	*her*
Neuter singular	*it*	*it*
Plural (all genders)	*they*	*them*

Possessive Pronouns

Closely related to the personal pronouns are the **possessive pronouns** (see Table 1.4), which typically show possession between the pronoun and a noun in the sentence. Like the personal pronouns, possessive pronouns change for person, and the third-person singular has gender. We have encountered many of the possessive pronouns in our discussion of determiners (for example, *my, his, her*). However, there are other personal pronouns that are used alone, as freestanding pronouns (for example, *mine, yours, hers*). In the sentence *That book is mine*, the pronoun *mine* is a possessive pronoun, though it does not precede a noun. Whether a possessive pronoun is a determiner or a freestanding pronoun, an apostrophe is *never* used.

To see how pronouns work, examine the passage below from Jane O'Reilly's *The Girl I Left Behind*. Pay particular attention to the words in italics; they are personal pronouns. In brackets next to each pronoun, I have given the person and number. *My*, a possessive pronoun, is not underlined. Because *my* is a determiner, *my son* is a noun phrase:

19a. My son is addicted. Last night *he* [third, singular] asked
me [first, singular] to serve dinner on a tray in front of

Table 1.4. Possessive Pronouns

	Determiner Form	Freestanding Form
First Person		
Singular	*my*	*mine*
Plural	*our*	*ours*
Second Person	*your*	*yours*
Third Person		
Masculine singular	*his*	*his*
Feminine singular	*her*	*hers*
Neuter singular	*its*	(no form)
Plural (all genders)	*their*	*theirs*

"Star Trek." Last night *I* [first, singular] unplugged *him* [third, singular]. *He* [third, singular] has been the fourth Stooge long enough.

Antecedents

Personal and possessive pronouns have **antecedents,** the nouns or noun phrases for which they substitute and which they must match in certain ways. The process of making pronouns match their antecedents is called **agreement,** and you will study it in detail in Chapter 7. But for now, let's take another look at Sentence (19a) to see in a general way how pronouns and antecedents work. Let's focus on *he* and *him* and the noun phrase they replace, which is now underlined in (19b):

19b. <u>My son</u> is addicted. Last night *he* asked me to serve dinner on a tray in front of "Star Trek." Last night I unplugged *him*. *He* has been the fourth Stooge long enough.

If we were to rewrite (19b) with the full noun phrase *my son* appearing wherever we find one of the italicized pronouns, we would have the following awkward rendition:

19c. <u>My son</u> is addicted. Last night <u>my son</u> asked me to serve dinner on a tray in front of "Star Trek." Last night I unplugged <u>my son</u>. <u>My son</u> has been the fourth Stooge long enough.

I doubt you need convincing that the original passage is better than my reworking of it; you intuitively know that English uses pronouns to replace noun phrases on subsequent mention. However, notice that although the phrase *my son* does not change form no matter where it appears in a sentence, the pronoun that replaces it does. We will see why this is so in Chapter 3.

Exercise 1.6

 Underline the pronoun or pronouns in each of the following sentences from Margaret Atwood's novel *The Handmaid's Tale*. Then in the space below each sentence give the person, number, and form of each pronoun (subject, object, or possessive). If the pronoun is third-person singular, give the gender as well. Consult the pronoun charts in Tables 1.3 and 1.4 for help.

1. We folded our clothes neatly and laid them on the stools at the ends of the beds.

2. The Guardian from the previous posting brought me to the front door.

3. The Guardian set down the bag and saluted her.

4. She waited until the car started up and pulled away.

5. I looked at the cigarette with longing.

6. We stole extra paper packets of sugar for her, from the cafeteria at mealtimes.

7. He pulls a chair out for me, sets it in front of his desk.

8. I simply look at him.

9. The Commander and I have an arrangement.

10. They get sick a lot, these Wives of the Commanders.

11. It adds interest to their lives.

12. As for us, the Handmaids and even the Marthas, we avoid illness.

13. Deftly he adds up our final scores on his pocket computer.

14. "You ran away with it," he says.

15. She plunges her big hand down, selects a match, hands it over to me.

Demonstrative Pronouns

The demonstrative determiners *this* and *that* and their plural forms *these* and *those* can appear by themselves, without any accompanying nouns. When they do, they are called **demonstrative pronouns.** Demonstrative pronouns indicate physical or emotional closeness (*this, these*) or distance (*that, those*) between the speaker or writer and the antecedent of the pronoun. Sometimes the closeness or distance can be of time, as in *this morning* and *those days.* The following sentences illustrate the use of demonstrative pronouns, which are underlined. These examples are taken from *Always Running—La Vida Loca: Gang Days in L.A.*, a memoir by Luis J. Rodriguez:

20. The refrain "<u>this</u> is not your country" echoed for a lifetime.

21. <u>These</u> were the familiar aromas: the funky earth, animal and mechanical smells which were absent from the homes my mother cleaned.

22. I turned around, and beneath my breath, mumbled something about how I didn't have time to argue with them. I shouldn't have done <u>that</u>.

23. [My dad] bought a house in Reseda. In those days, <u>this</u> made us the only Mexican family around.

Indefinite Pronouns

Words such as *someone, somebody,* and *something,* as well as many of the quantifying words listed in Table 1.2, can serve as freestanding pronouns. When they do, they are called **indefinite pronouns** (see Table 1.5)

Table 1.5. Common Indefinite Pronouns

everyone, everybody	*everything*
someone, somebody	*something*
no one, nobody	*nothing*
anyone, anybody	*anything*
all, any, both, each, neither, none, one, some	

because they point to antecedents that are not specific and that may even be implied rather than expressed.

The following sentences from *Always Running* provide examples of indefinite pronouns, which are underlined:

24. Inevitably, <u>somebody</u> used brass knuckles and some dude would end up with cracked ribs.

25. <u>Everyone</u> called me Chin because of my protruding jaw bone.

26. Suddenly <u>everything</u> slowed down. I just couldn't do <u>anything</u> fast enough.

27. I wanted to be untouchable: <u>Nobody</u> could get to me.

28. But he couldn't be challenged that way either. He had to do <u>something</u>.

29. Police officers, <u>some</u> in uniform and others in plainclothes with walkie talkies, walked two abreast down the aisles of booths.

30. <u>Nothing</u> would have come of <u>any</u> of this. We were bored. <u>Everyone</u> else soon watched the game, the cheering and roaring—<u>something</u> we weren't a part of.

Exercise 1.7

 Underline all the pronouns in the following passages from *Always Running*. State whether the pronoun is personal, possessive, demonstrative, or indefinite.

1. Suddenly everything around me exploded.

2. She didn't say anything, just turned around and left.

3. The driver of the DeSoto tried to pull out, but somebody threw a brick at his head.

4. But he also knew it might involve crossing Puppet, and he wanted to avoid this more than anything.

5. Puppet looked intently at everyone, especially Toots in a corner with Lourdes.

6. In fact, Puppet didn't care about anybody.

7. I felt edgy, my muscles straining, my leg striking a beat against the back of the seat.

8. Everybody got out safely, but the back of the house went up in flames and the rest of it sustained irreparable water damage from the fire hoses.

9. Everything lost its value for me: Love, Life and Women.

10. We yelled: *You can't touch this!*, but *Come kill me!* was the inner cry.

11. One day at lunch time, I passed a number of hefty dudes in lettered jackets.

12. One of them said something.

13. Maybe it had nothing to do with me.

14. "I don't know about any of this; all I know is you did wrong. You stole from me. You have to pay something for it."

SUMMARY

Though nouns typically express the name of a living being or lifeless thing, it is sometimes difficult to decide on this basis alone whether a particular word is a noun. Observing the function words (determiners) that may introduce them and recognizing the kinds of nouns that may have no determiners at all will help you make a decision.

A freestanding noun or a noun phrase can be replaced by a pronoun. Nouns, noun phrases, and pronouns constitute a very important part of English grammar. However, they cannot operate by themselves. In particular, they need verbs, which we will study in Chapter 2.

Projects for Chapter One

1. Find a passage in your daily newspaper or in a favorite book and circle all of the determiners you find. Then underline the rest of the noun phrase introduced by each determiner.

2. Find a passage in your newspaper or in a favorite book (different from the one you used in #1 above), and circle all the pronouns you find. For each pronoun, give the type (personal, possessive, demonstrative, or indefinite), and for each personal or possessive pronoun, indicate person, number, gender (where applicable), and form. Give the antecedent for each pronoun that has one.

3. Write a brief description of a member of your family or of a friend. When you have finished, find all of the determiners and all of the pronouns (if any), and proceed as in #1 and #2 above. What adjectives did you use in your noun phrases?

4. The following terms appeared in this chapter. Be sure you are familiar with all of them. Use the index and/or the glossary in the back of this book to help you.

abstract noun	definite article	mass noun
adjective	demonstrative	modifier
antecedent	determiner	number
common noun	gender	personal pronoun
compound noun	indefinite article	possessive pronoun
count noun	indefinite pronoun	proper noun

Recognizing Verbs and Verb Phrases

VERBS

A verb is a word that expresses action, being, or condition and that changes form to show time. Words such as *run, be,* and *sit* are verbs. In English, because many words can be either nouns or verbs depending on how they are used in a sentence, the suffixes and function words that appear with a particular word will help you decide whether that word is a noun or a verb. For example, in Sentence (1), the word *walk,* which expresses action, actually is a noun because it is introduced by the indefinite article *a:*

1. We took a <u>walk</u> through the countryside.

However, in Sentences (2) and (3), *walk* is a verb because it changes form when the sentence changes from present time (2) to a past time, such as *last summer* (3):

2. We <u>walk</u> around the lake every afternoon.

3. Last summer, we <u>walked</u> around the lake every afternoon.

In Chapter 1, you learned that a reliable way to decide whether a particular word is a noun is to look at the words that occur with it. In Chapter 2, you will learn to identify verbs by looking at some specific words and suffixes that can help you decide.

Subjects and Verbs

Though we will not focus on subjects in detail until Chapter 3, learning a bit about them now will help you recognize verbs, in particular present-tense verbs, which often have no suffixes at all. The **subject** is the part of the sentence, usually a noun, noun phrase, or pronoun, that performs the activity expressed by the verb. The pronoun *we*, which occurs in each of the three examples above, is the subject of each of the sentences. When you find a pronoun in subject form, such as *I, we, he, she, they,* you would be typically correct in believing it to be the subject of its sentence.

Tense

Unlike a noun, a verb can change form to show time, for example by taking the *-ed* suffix found on *walk* in Sentence (3). We call such indicators of time **tense.** English has two tenses, *present* and *past.* The *-ed* suffix on the verb in Sentence (3) above expresses past tense, but only the past tense is always indicated by the addition of a suffix or by some change inside the verb. The verb in Sentence (2) expresses present tense, but it has no suffix. If, however, we alter this sentence by changing the pronoun subject from *we* to *she,* we find that a suffix appears on *walk, -s,* as in Sentence (4):

4.   She <u>walks</u> around the lake every afternoon.

In Chapter 1, you learned that a pronoun is a short way of stating a noun phrase. Only *third-person singular* pronouns (*he, she, it,* and so on) and the nouns and noun phrases they can replace can serve as subjects of present-tense verbs having the *-s* suffix. Other kinds of subjects—all other personal pronouns and all plural nouns and noun phrases—require a verb with no suffix added to express present tense. For example, in Sentences (5) through (8), the present-tense form of the verb has no suffix, despite the different kinds of subjects:

5.   I <u>walk</u> around the lake every afternoon. [first-person singular pronoun subject]

6.   You <u>walk</u> around the lake every afternoon. [second-person pronoun subject]

7. They <u>walk</u> around the lake every afternoon. [third-person plural pronoun subject]

8. The girls <u>walk</u> around the lake every afternoon. [plural noun phrase subject]

If the subject of the sentence is a singular noun or noun phrase and the verb is in the present tense, the *-s* suffix appears on the verb:

9. The girl <u>walks</u> around the lake every afternoon. [singular noun phrase]

The *-s* suffix is the *third-person, singular, present tense* suffix. The *-ed* suffix is a *past-tense* suffix, and it appears with all kinds of subjects—singular and plural, and first, second, and third person.

Exercise 2.1

The following sentences come from *Moon Passage*, a novel by Jane LeCompte. Underline each of the verbs you find, and in the space below each sentence, write whether the verb is present tense or past tense.

1. I avoid her for a day.

2. She gazes at the tabletop.

3. Ellen looks at me.

4. I followed her, five steps behind, to the orchard.

5. Yellow apples glowed among the leaves.

6. I frowned up at her, sticky with apple juice and dizzy with heat.

7. I stare at her across the chasm between our frames of reference.

8. Adrenaline buzzes in my ears and veins.

9. You startled me.

10. Only the gulls break the silence.

11.   She turns away from me.

12.   My voice surprised me.

13.   I gazed at him.

14.   Jay shifted uneasily.

15.   We groped slowly and painfully back to equilibrium.

16.   Ellen wants something from me.

17.   She stands still and silent.

18.   Ellen's eyes widen.

19.   Jay's shoulders twitched.

20.   Her smile offends me.

PRINCIPAL PARTS OF VERBS: REGULAR VERBS

Verbs that follow the pattern of *walk* are **regular verbs;** they form the past tense by adding *-d* or *-ed* to the "base" form of the verb, which is called the **infinitive.** The infinitive is the verb form that has no suffixes to indicate tense or anything else; for example, the infinitive form of *walk* is, indeed, *walk.*

A useful way to present English verbs is to give their four **principal parts:** the infinitive, the past tense, the past participle, and the present participle. The principal parts of some common regular verbs are presented in Table 2.1. The past participle of regular verbs is identical to the past-tense form; the present participle is formed by adding *-ing* to the infinitive form. Though participle forms are called "present" and "past," they do *not* express tense. We will discuss some of the uses of the past and present participles in a later section of this chapter.

Table 2.1. Principle Parts of Some Regular Verbs

Infinitive	Past	Past Participle	Present Participle
walk	walked	walked	walking
jump	jumped	jumped	jumping
wash	washed	washed	washing
search	searched	searched	searching
talk	talked	talked	talking
open	opened	opened	opening
study	studied	studied	studying
start	started	started	starting
settle	settled	settled	settling

PRINCIPAL PARTS OF VERBS: IRREGULAR VERBS

A number of verbs do not follow the pattern of regular verbs, and so we call them **irregular verbs.** Though they nearly all add -s or -es to the infinitive for the third-person singular, present tense, and they all form the present participle by adding -ing to the infinitive, they express past tense in several different ways, but not by adding -d or -ed. In addition, though the past participles and past-tense forms of some irregular verbs are identical, many irregular verbs have unique past participle forms. A list of irregular verbs, organized by type, is presented in Table 2.2.

Table 2.2. Irregular Verbs

Type I: These verbs have different forms for the infinitive, the past tense, and the past participle. The vowel inside the infinitive changes from *i* to *a* to *u*.			
Infinitive	**Past**	**Past Participle**	**Present Participle**
begin	began	begun	beginning
drink	drank	drunk	drinking

ring	rang	rung	ringing
shrink	shrank	shrunk	shrinking
sing	sang	sung	singing
sink	sank	sunk	sinking
spring	sprang	sprung	springing
stink	stank	stunk	stinking
swim	swam	swum	swimming

Type II: Verbs of this type form the past tense in several ways; however, for all of them, the past participle usually ends in *-en* or *-n*.

Infinitive	Past	Past Participle	Present Participle
arise	arose	arisen	arising
awake	awoke	awoken	awaking
beat	beat	beaten	beating
bite	bit	bitten	biting
blow	blew	blown	blowing
break	broke	broken	breaking
choose	chose	chosen	choosing
do	did	done	doing
draw	drew	drawn	drawing
drive	drove	driven	driving
eat	ate	eaten	eating
fall	fell	fallen	falling
fly	flew	flown	flying
forbid	forbade	forbidden	forbidding
forget	forgot	forgotten	forgetting
forgive	forgave	forgiven	forgiving
forsake	forsook	forsaken	forsaking
freeze	froze	frozen	freezing
get	got	gotten	getting
give	gave	given	giving
grow	grew	grown	growing
hide	hid	hidden	hiding
know	knew	known	knowing
lie	lay	lain	lying
ride	rode	ridden	riding

rise	rose	risen	rising
see	saw	seen	seeing
shake	shook	shaken	shaking
slay	slew	slain	slaying
speak	spoke	spoken	speaking
steal	stole	stolen	stealing
strive	strove	striven	striving
swear	swore	sworn	swearing
take	took	taken	taking
tear	tore	torn	tearing
throw	threw	thrown	throwing
wear	wore	worn	wearing
weave	wove	woven	weaving
write	wrote	written	writing

Type III: Verbs of this type have identical forms for two of the principal parts. Most often, the past tense and the past participle are identical, but not always.

Infinitive	Past	Past Participle	Present Participle
beat	beat	beaten	beating
become	became	become	becoming
bleed	bled	bled	bleeding
breed	bred	bred	breeding
bring	brought	brought	bringing
build	built	built	building
catch	caught	caught	catching
come	came	come	coming
dig	dug	dug	digging
feed	fed	fed	feeding
feel	felt	felt	feeling
fight	fought	fought	fighting
find	found	found	finding
flee	fled	fled	fleeing
fling	flung	flung	flinging
grind	ground	ground	grinding
hang	hung	hung	hanging

have	*had*	*had*	*having*
hear	*heard*	*heard*	*hearing*
hold	*held*	*held*	*holding*
keep	*kept*	*kept*	*keeping*
kneel	*knelt*	*knelt*	*kneeling*
lead	*led*	*led*	*leading*
leave	*left*	*left*	*leaving*
lend	*lent*	*lent*	*lending*
lose	*lost*	*lost*	*losing*
make	*made*	*made*	*making*
mean	*meant*	*meant*	*meaning*
meet	*met*	*met*	*meeting*
read	*read*	*read*	*reading*
	[sound		
	changes]		
run	*ran*	*run*	*running*
say	*said*	*said*	*saying*
seek	*sought*	*sought*	*seeking*
sell	*sold*	*sold*	*selling*
send	*sent*	*sent*	*sending*
shoot	*shot*	*shot*	*shooting*
sit	*sat*	*sat*	*sitting*
sleep	*slept*	*slept*	*sleeping*
slide	*slid*	*slid*	*sliding*
sling	*slung*	*slung*	*slinging*
spend	*spent*	*spent*	*spending*
spin	*spun*	*spun*	*spinning*
stand	*stood*	*stood*	*standing*
stick	*stuck*	*stuck*	*sticking*
sting	*stung*	*stung*	*stinging*
strike	*struck*	*struck*	*striking*
string	*strung*	*strung*	*stringing*
sweep	*swept*	*swept*	*sweeping*
swing	*swung*	*swung*	*swinging*
teach	*taught*	*taught*	*teaching*
tell	*told*	*told*	*telling*
think	*thought*	*thought*	*thinking*

win	*won*	*won*	*winning*
wind	*wound*	*wound*	*winding*
wring	*wrung*	*wrung*	*wringing*

Type IV: Verbs of this type have identical forms for the infinitive, the past tense, and the past participle. These are all verbs of one syllable whose infinitive ends in *-t* or *-d*.

Infinitive	Past	Past Participle	Present Participle
bet	*bet*	*bet*	*betting*
bid	*bid*	*bid*	*bidding*
burst	*burst*	*burst*	*bursting*
cast	*cast*	*cast*	*casting*
cost	*cost*	*cost*	*costing*
cut	*cut*	*cut*	*cutting*
hit	*hit*	*hit*	*hitting*
hurt	*hurt*	*hurt*	*hurting*
let	*let*	*let*	*letting*
put	*put*	*put*	*putting*
quit	*quit*	*quit*	*quitting*
rid	*rid*	*rid*	*ridding*
set	*set*	*set*	*setting*
shed	*shed*	*shed*	*shedding*
shut	*shut*	*shut*	*shutting*
slit	*slit*	*slit*	*slitting*
split	*split*	*split*	*splitting*
spread	*spread*	*spread*	*spreading*
wet	*wet*	*wet*	*wetting*

Type V: This is a rare type. Forms for the past bear no resemblance to the infinitive.

Infinitive	Past	Past Participle	Present Participle
go	*went*	*gone*	*going*
be	*was/were*	*been*	*being*

Exercise 2.2

Find and underline the past-tense verb or verbs in each of the following sentences from *Farewell to Manzanar* by Jeanne Wakatsuki Houston and James D. Houston. Then in the space below each sentence give the infinitive form of the verbs you find. These sentences are a little more challenging than those for Exercise 2.1. Many of the sentences have more than one verb, and some verbs are regular and some irregular.

1. We watched until the boats became a row of tiny white gulls on the horizon.

2. Mama shook her head.

3. And, in the case of my older brothers and sisters, we went with a certain amount of relief.

4. The bus felt very secure to me.

5. We rode all day.

6. No one waved or spoke.

7. They just stared out the windows, ominously silent.

8. I slept with her every night after that until Papa came back.

9. An old seamstress took a peacoat of mine, tore the lining out, opened and flattened the sleeves, added a collar, put arm holes in and handed me back a beautiful cape.

10. When she stood, only her head showed over the top.

11. We ate in shifts, and I yearned all the more for our huge round table in Ocean Park.

12. He kept that cane for years, and it served him well.

13. He reached Honolulu in 1904, with a letter of introduction to a cousin who taught school on Oahu.

14. She met Papa early one summer morning at a wholesale market where her family sold produce.

15. The next morning I awoke long after sunup.

16. Woody, Chizu, and Mama knew the tune, so they hummed along while Papa and the other woman sang the words.

17. In Japan, before the turn of the century, outside my father's house there stood one of those stone lanterns, with four stubby legs and a small pagoda-like roof.

18. He hauled stones in off the desert and built a small rock garden outside our doorway, with succulents and a patch of moss.

19. Because they came from wealthy families and spoke and understood both English and Japanese, they had high opinions of themselves.

20. One night the local PTA held an awards dinner for all the students in the scholarship society.

AUXILIARY (HELPING) VERBS

Not all verbs are main verbs; some verbs appear together with main verbs to form **verb phrases** that indicate certain shadings of action or time. We call such verbs **auxiliary** (or *helping*) **verbs.** Though some verbs that can be auxiliaries (*be, have,* and *do*) sometimes act as main verbs, when they combine with another verb to form a verb phrase, they are auxiliary verbs. The verb phrases *is running, have eaten,* and *didn't finish* include auxiliary verbs. These verb phrases express continuing action, completed action, and negation. You will learn more about these notions in the following sections of this chapter.

Table 2.3. Auxiliary Verbs

Be Family	*Have* Family	*Do* Family	Modals
am, is, are was, were be, being, been	have, has had	do, does did	can, could will, would shall, should may, might must

Auxiliary verbs come in families: the *be* family, the *have* family, the *do* family, and the modal verbs. Modal verbs are function words that express the "mood" of the speaker or writer (thus the word *modal*) about the necessity, possibility, or intention of doing the action expressed in the main verb. Table 2.3 above lists the auxiliary verb families.

Exercise 2.3

Circle the auxiliary verbs in each of the following sentences from Barbara Neely's mystery novel *Blanche on the Lam*. Then underline the entire verb phrase that it introduces. Consult Table 2.3 for help.

1. His eyes were boring a hole in the opposite wall.

2. She was smoothing down the skirt of her dress.

3. The matron was standing to the left of the door, almost in front of the men's room.

4. You can take care of that tomorrow.

5. Aunt Sarah had continued her turkey-smoking instructions even while Blanche and one of the bag boys were hoisting her to her feet.

6. As for worry, Miz Cora has handled a whole lot worse than this!

7. The door was moving slowly inward.

8. Blanche was staring up at the cupids painted on the ceiling.

9. He was pushing a wheelchair.

10. A long black limousine was waiting for them at the bottom of the wide front stairs.

11. Aunt will want her dinner around five.

12. She could feel it in the house, too, a kind of dour restlessness.

13. Grace was breathing through her mouth in short, quick bursts.

14. She could see their round, plump faces, replicas of their daddy's sloe-eyed Geechee good looks.

15. She was carrying Mumsfield's automobile tools under her left arm.

16. She could hear three different birds' songs, none of which she could identify.

17. Somehow she would convince her mother to give up the children.

18. Rosalie had loved her children dearly.

19. Dr. Haley is expecting you.

20. Either Emmeline or that husband of hers is driving this girl's blood pressure right on up there!

Aspect

An important feature that can be expressed in a verb phrase with the help of an auxiliary is the time notion called **aspect.** Like tense, aspect is indicated in the main verb by a suffix or some other change in form. Unlike tense, aspect indicates whether an event is continuing or completed. The expression of aspect is not always necessary, but the verbs or verb phrases of sentences *must* express tense, which also is indicated by a suffix. English does not allow suffixes that express tense and aspect to pile up at the end of the same word. So, if a verb has a suffix for aspect, that verb must be accompanied by an auxiliary verb to express the tense. Members of the *be* family occur with a present participle of a main verb to show **progressive aspect** (a continuing or regular event: Jenny *is eating* lunch), and members of the *have* family occur with a past participle of a main verb to show **perfect aspect** (a completed event: Jenny *has eaten* lunch).

Progressive Aspect with Present Tense

At the beginning of this chapter, we examined the difference between the present and past tenses. In particular, we noted that Sentence (2), repeated here as Sentence (10), has a present-tense verb:

10. We <u>walk</u> around the lake every afternoon.

The activity expressed in (10) is not actually happening as the speaker says the sentence; Sentence (10) describes an action that the subject of the sentence performs on a regular basis. In fact, in ordinary conversation and writing, most main verbs in the present tense express not an action occurring right now, but either a habitual activity as in (10) or a state that holds across time periods, such as the verbs *know* and *believe* in Sentences (11) and (12):

11. I <u>know</u> the answer.

12. I <u>believe</u> him.

If we are talking about an action that is in progress right now, we are likely to use progressive aspect along with present tense to express that action. For example, if someone telephones you while you are reading this book and asks you what you are doing, you might answer with (13). The progressive aspect is indicated in the main verb (*studying*) by the suffix *-ing*; the auxiliary *am* from the *be* family supplies the tense:

13. I <u>am studying</u> grammar.

In (13), *am* is a present-tense form of *be*. Unlike other verbs, *be* has present and past-tense forms that differ on the basis of the kinds of subject

Table 2.4. Forms of Be

Present Tense				Past Tense	
uncontracted		contracted		uncontracted only	
singular	plural	singular	plural	singular	plural
I am	*we are*	*I'm*	*we're*	*I was*	*we were*
you are	*you are*	*you're*	*you're*	*you were*	*you were*
he/she/it is	*they are*	*he's/she's/it's*	*they're*	*he/she/it was*	*they were*

that occurs with them. In addition, a pronoun subject and the present tense of *be* can be combined in shortened forms, called **contractions**, that use apostrophes. These forms are presented in Table 2.4.

Progressive Aspect with Past Tense

A verb phrase with progressive aspect may also show past tense. A past progressive verb phrase typically expresses a continuing event whose starting and ending points are not given, whereas a past-tense verb generally indicates an event that begins or ends. This contrast is evident in Sentence (14), a passage from Walter Mosley's novel *Devil in a Blue Dress*:

14. I went over to the bar and ordered two ales. . . . People were shouting and talking, kissing and laughing.

In (14), the narrator tells us that he <u>*went*</u> over to the bar and <u>*ordered*</u> two ales. These past-tense actions show that the narrator changed from not doing these things to doing them. They also show that he reached his destination (the bar) and that he finished placing his order. However, the past progressive verb phrase *were shouting and talking, kissing and laughing* shows that these events continued during the entire time that the narrator was going to the bar and ordering. The beginnings and endings of *shouting and talking, kissing and laughing* are not provided. Similarly, in Sentence (15), also from *Devil*, Corretta begins and ends her statement during the time that she and the narrator are *dragging Dupree from the car to her door*:

15. "They done throwed him outta his place cuz he missed the rent," Coretta said. We were dragging Dupree from the car to her door.

The auxiliary *were* provides the past tense; the main verb *dragging* provides progressive aspect.

Exercise 2.4

Underline the verbs or verb phrases in each of the following passages from *Devil in a Blue Dress*. In the space below each of the passages, identify the verbs or verb phrases as: present tense; past tense; present tense with progressive aspect; or past tense with progressive aspect.

1. A small boy climbed over the seat. He was wearing soiled briefs and dirty white socks.

2. He was holding a few damp bills in his hand.

3. "I am calling you about a problem with a friend of yours."

4. "Yeah," Curtis Cross said. He was sitting in front of a plate of rice at the dining table.

5. The short woman and two big-bellied Mexican men were coming our way. One of the men was swinging a nightstick. They stopped a foot from me.

6. A grizzled old man in overalls and a tee-shirt was sitting in an aluminum chair at the foot of the stairs.

7. I'm looking for somebody, for a friend.

8. He was smiling at me.

9. He was staring into someplace far from that dirty basement.

10. He was wearing a woolly brown suit and bright blue shoes.

Perfect Aspect with Present Tense

In addition to progressive aspect, English has perfect aspect, which is expressed through a verb phrase that pairs a form from the *have* family with the past participle of the main verb. Table 2.5 provides the present- and past-tense forms of *have*, along with their contracted forms.

Perfect aspect indicates an event that may be completed, yet still is relevant to an event that may be present. For example, in (16), the activity expressed in the past-tense verb could have happened at any past time, even long ago:

16. I <u>ate</u> lunch.

However, a verb phrase expressing perfect aspect is more appropriate if the action of eating recently happened; for example, if after having lunch at noon, you visit a friend who offers you some food, you might turn down the offer, saying:

17. No, thank you. I have <u>eaten</u> lunch.

The main verb *eaten* in (17) is the past participle of *eat;* the auxiliary verb *have* is actually present tense. Thus, the verb phrase of (17) is present tense, perfect aspect. The action is complete (perfect), but it is relevant to the moment of speaking (present).

Perfect Aspect with Past Tense

A verb phrase also may express perfect aspect in the past tense. A past perfect verb phrase is appropriate when one event in a story precedes another and the earlier event has some bearing on the later one.

Table 2.5. Forms of Have

Present Tense				Past Tense			
uncontracted		contracted		uncontracted		contracted	
singular	plural	singular	plural	singular	plural	singular	plural
I have	*we have*	*I've*	*we've*	*I had*	*we had*	*I'd*	*we'd*
you have	*you have*	*you've*	*you've*	*you had*	*you had*	*you'd*	*you'd*
he/she has	*they have*	*he's/she's*	*they've*	*he/she had*	*they had*	*he'd/she'd*	*they'd*

For example, in Sentence (18), from *Devil in a Blue Dress*, the narrator describes his past experience in a jail cell, where he pondered the death of a mouse whose corpse he had discovered:

18. I <u>speculated</u> [past tense] that another prisoner <u>had killed</u> [past perfect] the mouse by stamping it. He probably <u>had tried</u> [past perfect] in the middle of the floor at first but the quick rodent <u>had swerved</u> [past perfect] away two, maybe even three times.

The alternation between the past tense of the verb *speculated* and the past perfect of *had killed, had tried*, and *had swerved* assists us in understanding which events happened earlier. Moreover, the past perfect indicates that the earlier events are connected to the past event of *speculated*, if only in the speaker's mind. The auxiliary verb provides the tense; the main verb provides the aspect.

Perfect Progressive Aspect

It is also possible to indicate in the verb phrase an action that begins at a prior time but is not complete. Sometimes the present perfect can express this idea. For example, in (19), the verb phrase indicates that the work began prior to the time of speaking (perfect) and that it has not ended (present):

19. I <u>have worked</u> at my present job for five years.

However, you can also express continuing activity begun at an earlier point by combining the perfect and progressive aspects. Sentences (20) through (22) from *Devil* demonstrate how the perfect and progressive together can express an earlier action that continues. The tense in (20) is present (*have*); the tense in (21) and (22) is past (*had*):

20. I'<u>ve been calling</u> you all night.

21. He <u>had been standing</u> to the side of the door, where Junior couldn't see, but then he stood out in plain sight.

22. Dupree <u>had been crying</u> and upset the whole evening.

In such verb phrases, the *have* auxiliary precedes the *be* auxiliary. Each auxiliary treats the verb that follows it as its "main verb." Thus, since

Table 2.6. The Meanings of Progressive and Perfect Aspect

Aspect	Tense	Meaning	Example
Progressive	*present*	continuing event in present	I *am looking* for somebody.
	past	continuing event in past	He *was smiling* at me.
Perfect	*present*	completed event in present	I *have worked* at my present job for five years.
	past	completed event in past	I speculated that another prisoner *had killed* the mouse.
Perfect Progressive	*present*	event begun at earlier time and continuing into present	I *have been calling* you all night.
	past	event begun earlier than some past event and continuing	When I found her, she *had been crying* for some time.

have or *had* requires a past participle, *be* appears in its past participle form, *been*. *Been* requires the next verb to have the present participle form, and so we find *calling*, *standing*, and *crying* in the verb phrases in the last three examples. The first auxiliary always carries the tense.

Table 2.6 above summarizes tense and aspect combinations expressed in verb phrases.

Exercise 2.5

Underline the verbs or verb phrases in each of the following passages from Anne Lamott's nonfiction book, *Operating Instructions: A Journal of My Son's First Year*. In the space under each of the passages, identify the verbs or verb phrases as present tense or past tense. In addition, if aspect is indicated in the verb phrase, write whether the aspect is progressive, perfect, or perfect progressive. Some sentences have more than one verb or verb phrase. Consult Table 2.6 for help.

1. Pammy drove and I was bellowing at the top of my lungs the entire way.

2. Even the oldest black people at my church had been laughing when they saw me the week before.

3. He sounds like a baby dolphin.

4. Big Sam was drawing a picture of dolphins and whales and an octopus for baby Sam.

5. My friend Armistead called the other day.

6. The baby is sleeping.

7. This has become my specialty.

8. The kitty is lying beside me asleep.

9. My mother lives about twenty minutes up the highway.

10. Yesterday we took a fabulous Polaroid of Pammy and Sam.

11. The sun was pouring in through the tops of the redwoods.

12. People have been inviting me and Sam to their parties lately.

13. They have lived in the same home for forty years.

14. Pammy is coming for a pool party this afternoon.

15. Emmy and Bill came by with some groceries.

16. He inches around the living room like a spy.

17. All of the birds were singing, and Sam fell asleep in my arms.

18. Pammy has gone to Morocco for a month.

19. "Hey, babe, you've been working too hard."

20. Alice had been cooking a roast all afternoon.

The Modals

The modal auxiliaries indicate whether the action of the main verb is possible, likely, demanded, or permitted. Sometimes, as in the case of *will*, a modal may indicate future time, even though a modal is *not* a tense. Table 2.7 provides the present and past tenses of the modal auxiliaries. However, the past-tense forms of the modal are often used not to indicate past time, but to imply that some action is desirable. In particular, the modal *should* works in this way, as in *Students should study every day.*

The present-tense forms provided in Table 2.7 take no suffixes whatsoever. We never find the third-person singular, present-tense singular suffix on a modal verb.

Modal auxiliaries require the main verb to appear in the infinitive form. The following examples from Kyoko Mori's novel *Shizuko's Daughter* illustrate verb phrases with modal auxiliaries:

23. But I <u>can practice</u> the same pieces another week.

24. From the window, she <u>could see</u> the tall white buildings of downtown Kobe and the mountains to the north.

25. You <u>should wait</u> for your lesson.

Table 2.7. Modal Auxiliaries

Present Tense	Past Tense
can	*could*
shall	*should*
will	*would*
may	*might*
must	[no past form]

26. Somebody else <u>will finish</u> the skirt for her.

27. The ceremony <u>would start</u> in a few minutes, when the bride came in.

28. You <u>may stay</u> there overnight.

29. You <u>must have</u> a pen in your purse, Mother.

Sentence (30) shows us that a verb phrase with a modal auxiliary may express aspect as well. In (30), the modal *might* begins a verb phrase with perfect aspect, as does the modal *would* in Sentence (31):

30. If her mother had lived, she <u>might have worn</u> it to Yuki's graduation from high school, a week ago.

31. "You almost hurt me, Yuki," Hanae said. "You <u>would have pushed</u> me down the stairs."

A modal may also introduce a progressive verb phrase, as Sentence (32) shows:

32. Soon they <u>would be running</u> against each other for the first time.

And a modal may begin a perfect progressive verb phrase:

33. He got on one stop after mine, so he <u>might have been looking</u> for me.

When a verb phrase that expresses aspect begins with a modal, the verb phrase must also include the auxiliary that goes with that aspect. Remember that progressive aspect has the *be* auxiliary, and perfect aspect has the *have* auxiliary. The modal takes the next auxiliary in line as its main verb, and so *be* or *have* appears in the infinitive form. The verb that follows *be* is a present participle (for example, *running*); the verb that follows *have* is a past participle (for example, *pushed*).

Exercise 2.6

Each of the passages below from *Shizuko's Daughter* has a verb phrase introduced by a modal auxiliary. Underline all the verb phrases that begin with a modal.

1. She would be so unhappy.

2. Your things should arrive on the truck next week.

3. You must understand how awkward it would be otherwise.

4. Through the open gate, in the background, she could imagine the green leaves of the trees in the temple garden.

5. Maybe we should leave them.

6. "Somebody will notice them," her mother said.

7. Maybe we can meet in Uzumoridai Park.

8. He must go to the boys' high school in eastern Kobe.

9. "You must give me back my clothes."

10. Besides, she can get to the woods and back faster than any of us.

11. Nobody could see the frogs under the bushes.

12. Soon, a door slammed. Her stepmother must have walked out.

13. Soon, her own room would look the same.

14. If we leave them outside, the neighbors' children might pull things out, and then their parents might talk.

15. I should have seen him more often.

Asking Questions and Making Negative Statements

All of the sentences we have examined so far have been statements, known as **declarative sentences,** and they have all been affirmative declarative sentences. That is, the sentences have not denied or rejected an idea, nor have they asserted that someone or something doesn't exist. Clearly there are other possibilities; we can ask questions, and we can make negative statements. Auxiliary verbs play an important role both in questions and in negative sentences. Questions and negative statements always have an auxiliary verb, even if they derive from affirmative statements that have no auxiliary at all.

The following affirmative declarative sentences have appeared in the exercises in this chapter. Below each of the examples, you will find a question form of the same sentence, followed by a negative form. In the question, the first auxiliary verb appears not in front of the main verb or the next auxiliary, but at the very front of the sentence. In the negative form of the sentence, the adverb *not* (or its contracted form -*n't*) follows the first auxiliary verb:

34. **Declarative sentence:** The baby is sleeping.
    Question: Is the baby sleeping?
    Negative: The baby is not [isn't] sleeping.

35. **Declarative sentence:** They have lived in the same home for forty years.
    Question: Have they lived in the same home for forty years?
    Negative: They have not [haven't] lived in the same home for forty years.

36. **Declarative sentence:** Pammy is coming for a pool party this afternoon.
    Question: Is Pammy coming for a pool party this afternoon?
    Negative: Pammy is not [isn't] coming for a pool party this afternoon.

37. **Declarative sentence:** Pammy has gone to Morocco for a month.
    Question: Has Pammy gone to Morocco for a month?
    Negative: Pammy has not [hasn't] gone to Morocco for a month.

38. **Declarative sentence:** We should leave them.
    Question: Should we leave them?
    Negative: We should not [shouldn't] leave them.

39. Declarative sentence: She can get to the woods and back faster than any of us.
Question: Can she get to the woods and back faster than any of us?
Negative: She cannot [can't] get to the woods and back faster than any of us.

The Do *Auxiliary in Questions and Negatives*

Some affirmative declarative sentences have no auxiliary. Nevertheless, their question and negative counterparts must use the *do* auxiliary. Forms of the *do* auxiliary appear in Table 2.8.

When *do* is used in questions and in negative statements, *do* carries the tense and the main verb appears in the infinitive form. Because of this feature, *do* behaves much like the modals; however, unlike the modals, *do* has a special form for the third-person singular, present tense, *does*.

The following affirmative statements appeared in Exercise 2.4. I have provided the question and negative form of each by using the *do* auxiliary:

40. Declarative sentence: He sounds like a baby dolphin. [present tense]
Question: Does he sound like a baby dolphin?
Negative: He does not [doesn't] sound like a baby dolphin.

41. Declarative sentence: My friend Armistead called the other day. [past tense]
Question: Did my friend Armistead call the other day?
Negative: My friend Armistead did not [didn't] call the other day.

Table 2.8. Forms of Do

Base	Third-Person Singular, Present Tense	Past
do	*does*	*did*

42. **Declarative sentence:** My mother lives about twenty minutes up the highway.
    Question: Does my mother live about twenty minutes up the highway?
    Negative: My mother does not [doesn't] live about twenty minutes up the highway.

43. **Declarative sentence:** Emmy and Bill came by with some groceries.
    Question: Did Emmy and Bill come by with [any] groceries?
    Negative: Emmy and Bill did not [didn't] come by with [any] groceries.

Emphatic Do

In addition to its use as an auxiliary in questions and in negative statements, *do* also is used to show emphasis, to show, for example, that contrary to what one may think, a particular circumstance is true. The following passage from *Shizuko's Daughter* illustrates this use:

44. Mrs. Murai began to rummage through her purse. "But I can't find a pen," she said after a while. "It's very strange. I usually <u>do carry</u> one around."

BE, HAVE, AND DO AS MAIN VERBS

Unlike the modals, which serve only as auxiliaries, *be, have,* and *do* can be main verbs. When any of these three is a main verb, it will be either the only verb or the last verb in the verb phrase. The following sentences from Tom Sullivan's autobiography *If You Could See What I Hear* provide examples:

45. Yet on other occasions my father <u>could be</u> gentler than a nun.

46. Poor Tucky <u>had had</u> enough of Dad's curses.

47. I <u>can't do</u> that.

48. One evening when I <u>was</u> about eight years old, the gang was creating mayhem in Greaton Road.

When *have* and *do* appear as main verbs without auxiliaries, like any other main verb, they require the *do* auxiliary to express negation or to form questions:

49a. Jake <u>didn't have</u> any sense.

49b. <u>Do</u> you <u>have</u> the time?

50a. They <u>didn't do</u> anything to help.

50b. <u>Did</u> you <u>do</u> your homework?

Be, however, is exceptional. Even when it is a main verb, it behaves like the *be* auxiliary. That is, the *be* verb appears at the beginning of questions without any additional auxiliary, as in Sentence (51) from *Devil in a Blue Dress:*

51. <u>Is</u> this some sort of joke?

And in a negative statement, *not* immediately follows the form of *be*, as in Sentence (52) from Susan Cheever's family memoir, *Treetops:*

52. Even the metaphysical world <u>was not</u> immune to the advancing frontiers of human understanding.

Exercise 2.7

Underline the verbs or verb phrases in the following sentences from Tom Sullivan's autobiography *If You Could See What I Hear.* In the space below each sentence, give the tense and aspect (if aspect is given in the verb phrase). Be careful; some sentences have more than one verb/verb phrase.

1. Beyond the hedge a truck was rumbling down the road.

2. She has grown an inch or two.

3. I can hear the squeak of her crayons across a sheet of paper.

4. Porky Sullivan had waited fourteen years for a son.

5. Dad did not coo.

6. She could not understand my whining reluctance.

7. I had not held a pane of glass before.

8. Dad and a friend had bought a pony.

9. We continued our walk and were crossing a parking lot.

10. I may have learned the rudiments of the art and the Queensberry rules from Tussey Russell.

11. Sheila didn't reject his friends.

12. Our new neighbors did not speak in Boston Irish but in the accents of blue-blooded New England Yankees.

13. He did not answer immediately, and for a while we listened to the crickets and the frogs.

14. Cynicism and love cannot be companions in one human heart, for they are mortal and eternal enemies.

15. The face can be a mask.

ADVERBS IN THE VERB PHRASE

Just as an adjective modifies a noun, an **adverb** modifies a verb or verb phrase. An adverb may also modify an adjective or another adverb, thereby creating an adjective phrase or an adverb phrase (for example, *really small, quite suddenly*). When an adverb modifies a verb or verb phrase, it typically expresses ideas such as time, frequency, location, and manner and generally appears at the end of the sentence. However, it is important to know that an adverb may occur within a verb phrase, often between the auxiliary and the main verb. We have already met such an adverb, *not*. In addition, *never, always, even, then, hardly, just*, and *already* sometimes will occur. The following sentences from *If You Could See What I Hear* provide good examples:

53. But in 1947 pediatrics <u>had *just* taken</u> a quantum jump.

54. The doctors, the scientists, the nurses on twenty-four-hour duty at the Faulkner Hospital in West Roxbury, Massachusetts, <u>did not *then* understand</u> nature's delicate balance of air.

55. Though probably no more than twelve, he <u>had *already* developed</u> a degree of compassion.

56. The twins and even older children <u>would *never* have ventured</u> down the weed-covered path.

Exercise 2.8

 Underline the entire verb/verb phrase in each of the following sentences from *Treetops*. In the space below each sentence, write the tense and aspect.

1. The late nineteenth century in Boston was a fertile time for dreams.

2. The city had named itself the "Athens of America."

3. Longfellow was teaching at Harvard.

4. Electric trolleys and trains provided fast, clean transportation.

5. Elias Howe had just invented the sewing machine.

6. Anything seemed possible.

7. He had done definitive work on war gases as a captain in World War I.

8. My mother doesn't talk very much about her mother.

9. They didn't like her high society manner.

10. Buff's story is not part of our family myth.

11. Buff could match her father's insincerity.

12. She had never worked for money.

13. [Polly] had always favored my mother.

14. He was wearing his overalls and those high-top sneakers.

15. Every family has its own cast of characters—the pretty and the plain, the weak and the strong, the bright and the dull, the cop and the rebel.

16. He lives in a house at the edge of a thick pine grove on a lake in the Alabama woods.

17. Tom could never get anything quite right.

18. The researchers at Bell Labs can't tell me much.

19. Tom has been working in top secret military communications all these years.

20. My father was just telling stories.

21. He writes for readers.

22. Of course he couldn't take care of himself.

23. My brother Ben and I are sitting on a wooden bench in a windowless room in the federal courthouse of the Southern District Court in White Plains.

24. Judge Goettel interrupts the questioning of my mother.

25. Iole had always scolded our family for our disdain for physical comforts.

SUMMARY

A verb is a word whose form can be altered to show changes in time by expressing tense and aspect. There are two kinds of verbs, auxiliary verbs and main verbs; an auxiliary combines with a main verb in a verb phrase. Each auxiliary requires its main verb to have a particular form. Sometimes more than one auxiliary appears in a verb phrase. In this case, the form of the second auxiliary depends on what the first requires. That is, a modal requires the infinitive form of the verb that comes next, *have* requires the past participle, and *be* requires the present participle, even when that verb is another auxiliary. In addition to auxiliaries and main verbs, verb phrases sometimes include adverbs. *Not* is the most important of these adverbs, and in the absence of any other auxiliary, appears with a form of *do*. Other adverbs that may appear in the verb phrase include *never, even, just, already,* and *then.*

Projects for Chapter Two

1. Find ten different words that can be used as either a noun or a verb. Then for each word, write two sentences, one using the word as a noun, the other using the word as a verb. When you have finished writing your sentences, write a brief report describing how you were able to differentiate between the two uses, i.e., what did you do that made the use of the word a noun use on the one hand and a verb use on the other?

2. Find ten sentences from today's newspaper, and for each sentence, describe as much as you can about the verbs and verb

phrases that occur in those sentences. That is, list each verb/verb phrase and give the tense, aspect, and any adverbs that may appear in the verb phrase. Is the main verb regular or irregular?

3. Describe, in precise terms, the difference among the following sentences with respect to tense and aspect.

    I drove to the library.
    I have driven to the library.
    I was driving to the library.

4. The following terms appeared in this chapter. Be sure you are familiar with all of them. Use the index and/or the glossary in the back of this book to help you.

adverb	perfect aspect
aspect	perfect progressive
auxiliary verb	present participle
common noun	principal parts
contraction	progressive aspect
infinitive	regular verb
irregular verb	subject
main verb	tense
past participle	verb phrase

The Basic Sentence

A simple sentence has at a minimum a noun or noun phrase, called the subject, and a **predicate phrase.** A predicate phrase always includes a verb or verb phrase expressing tense; it often includes other elements that complete the verb, such as a noun or noun phrase, an adverb or adverb phrase, or another kind of phrase that behaves like an adverb although it may have no adverbs in it.

THE SUBJECT

In the previous chapters, you learned that the subject is the part of the sentence, usually a noun, noun phrase, or pronoun, that performs the activity expressed in the verb. You learned that certain pronouns—subject-form pronouns—reliably could be identified as subjects. Not all sentences, however, have pronoun subjects, yet every sentence has a subject.

One way to identify the subject of a sentence is to turn that sentence into a yes/no question, the kind of question that requires for an answer either a yes or a no. We hear many questions of this type in our daily lives: *Did you eat yet? Have you finished your homework? Would you come to my party on Saturday? Is it raining?* In the yes/no question, the first auxiliary verb appears at the very front of the sentence, and the subject of the sentence *always* follows the first (and perhaps only) auxiliary. Since a statement and its yes/no question counterpart have the same subject, turning a statement into a question will allow you to find the subject of both sentences. In the question form, the subject will appear between the auxiliary and the rest of the verb phrase, which often is just the main verb itself.

The general rule for forming a yes/no question is to take the first (often the only) auxiliary and move it to the front of the sentence. If there is no auxiliary verb, *do* will be the auxiliary, and it will carry the tense. The main verb appears in its infinitive form. If the main verb is a form of *be*, the verb itself is moved. Let's try this procedure with some sentences from Bill Cosby's autobiographical book *Childhood:*

1a.   A hum ran through the class.

2a.   I flung my hand into the air.

Sentences (1a) and (2a) are statements that have no auxiliary, so we use *do:* Notice that the main verbs in these sentences are irregular (the past tense verbs have no -*ed*), and so we must find the appropriate infinitives, using Table 2.2, if necessary. Then we underline the material that comes between the *do* auxiliary and the rest of the verb phrase:

1b.   Did <u>a hum</u> run through the class?

2b.   Did <u>I</u> fling my hand into the air?

A hum is the subject of Sentence (1), as *I* is of Sentence 2 (we could have predicted this finding because of the subject-form pronoun).

Sentence (3a) already has an auxiliary, so all we need to do is move it (3b):

3a.   The bed had become a boxing ring with two feebleminded flyweights.

3b.   Had <u>the bed</u> become a boxing ring with two feebleminded flyweights?

Again, this process accurately identifies *the bed* as the subject of the sentence.

Exercise 3.1

The following sentences are taken from James Finn Garner's *Politically Correct Bedtime Stories*. Construct a yes/no question for each sentence and insert your question in the space below it; find the auxiliary and main verb in the question, and then underline the subject in your question and the corresponding word or phrase in the *original* sentence.

1. Red Riding Hood walked on along the main path.

2. The parade began with great hoopla.

3. The emperor is naked.

4. The parade stopped.

5. The emperor paused.

6. The emperor is merely endorsing a clothing-optional lifestyle!

7. The frightened pigs ran to the house of sticks, with the wolf in hot pursuit.

8. The tinker and his wife lived in a little hovel next to the modest estate of a local witch.

9. The wife of the tinker was pregnant.

10. They named the baby Rapunzel, after a type of lettuce.

11. The witch was Rapunzel's only companion.

12. Papa Bear had prepared big bowls of all-natural porridge for them to eat.

13. The rogue biologist had been watching the cottage for some time.

14. They moved into the bedroom with growing alarm.

15. Baby Bear watched with astonishment.

THE PREDICATE PHRASE

A predicate phrase includes a verb or verb phrase and often other elements that complete the verb. Some sentences have only a verb in the predicate phrase; in Sentence (4), the verb *stopped* comprises the entire predicate phrase:

4. The parade stopped.

More often, however, the predicate phrase includes other elements in addition to the verb. Some verbs and verb phrases are followed by a noun, noun phrase, or pronoun that is acted upon by the subject, such as the underlined noun phrase in Sentence (5):

5. He locked <u>the cell door</u>. (From Ernest J. Gaines, *A Lesson Before Dying*)

Yet other verbs or verb phrases are followed by a noun or noun phrase (Sentence 6) or an adjective or adjective phrase (Sentence 7) that identifies or describes the subject:

6. The face can be <u>a mask</u>. (Tom Sullivan, *If You Could See What I Hear*)

7. His hair was <u>white and long</u>. (*A Lesson Before Dying*)

Any verb or verb phrase, whether it is followed by a noun phrase or adjective phrase or by neither, may be modified by a word or phrase that gives details of time, location, direction, manner, and purpose. Such elements are called **adverbials.**

Adverbials

Many kinds of words and phrases do the work that adverbs do, but typically they include no adverbs at all. We call these elements adverbials. In this chapter, you will learn about two kinds of adverbials, the **prepositional phrase** and the adverbial noun phrase. In Chapter 4, you will learn about some other kinds of adverbials.

Prepositional Phrases

A prepositional phrase has a **preposition** followed by the **object of the preposition**—a noun or noun phrase or a pronoun. A preposition is a function word that indicates a relationship of time, location, direction, or association between the word or phrase that follows it (its object) and another element in a sentence, usually a verb or a noun. Adverbial prepositional phrases modify verbs and verb phrases and sometimes entire predicate phrases.

To find a prepositional phrase, you must learn to locate the preposition and its object. Because prepositions do not vary in form and are limited in number, you can learn to spot them by familiarizing yourself with the words listed in Table 3.1.

Many sentences include adverbial prepositional phrases. Sentence (8), which appeared in the last exercise, has a prepositional phrase that is an adverbial:

8. The parade began <u>with great hoopla</u>.

With great hoopla tells *how* the parade began. Though it expresses manner (that is, *how*), this phrase is not an adverb. However, because it behaves like an adverb, we call it an adverbial.

Table 3.1. Common English Prepositions

about	*besides*	*on*
above	*between*	*on account of*
across	*beyond*	*onto*
after	*by*	*on top of*
against	*by means of*	*out of*
along	*down*	*over*
alongside (of)	*during*	*since*
along with	*except*	*to*
around	*for*	*toward*
as	*from*	*through*
as for	*in*	*under*
at	*inside (of)*	*underneath*
because of	*in spite of*	*until*
before	*instead of*	*up*
behind	*into*	*upon*
below	*like*	*with*
beneath	*of*	*within*
beside	*off*	*without*

Sometimes, a verb or verb phrase is followed by a lone preposition instead of a prepositional phrase. In such cases, the preposition expresses the direction of action. For instance, in Sentences (9) and (10), the prepositions *up* and *down* express the direction in which the subject looked. Though these words are not adverbs, they are adverbials because of the work they do in the sentence:

9. She looked up.

10. She looked down.

Exercise 3.2

Underline the prepositional phrase in each of the following sentences from *A Lesson Before Dying*, a novel by Ernest J. Gaines. Consult Table 3.1 for help.

1. The big black iron pots still hung against the wall.

2. A black patent-leather purse hung from her right shoulder.

3. He was waiting for his drink.

4. We danced for a while.

5. He fidgeted with his hat.

6. The four white men split into pairs.

7. The thin, brown-skinned man nodded at me.

8. The program began at seven o'clock.

9. They were looking at the fire.

10. We had stopped for a moment.

Adverbial Noun Phrases

Some noun phrases are not subjects, they are not acted upon by the subject, and they do not identify the subject. Instead, these noun phrases provide information about the event in the sentence regarding time (point of time or length of time) or space (usually place or distance). Such noun phrases are adverbials. An adverbial noun phrase of time (underlined) occurs in Sentence (11), from Mona Simpson's novel *Anywhere But Here:*

11. My mother had given me choices <u>all my life</u>.

Such adverbial phrases can begin as well as end a sentence, as in Sentence (12). Notice that in (12), the subject-form personal pronoun *we* serves as the subject of the sentence:

12. <u>Most nights</u> we stayed in those motels.

In Sentence (13), an adverbial noun phrase expressing location appears:

13. <u>Next door</u>, someone was mowing their lawn.

Not all noun phrases expressing time or space are adverbials, however. Sentence (14), for example, has no noun phrase but the one expressing time to serve as subject. Thus, the underlined phrase cannot be an adverbial since a word or phrase cannot be both a subject and an adverbial at the same time:

14. <u>That last time in Nevada</u> was different, too.

Exercise 3.3

 Underline each adverbial noun phrase in the sentences below, taken from *Anywhere But Here.*

1. That summer, Ben and I sat in the fields outside.

2. [The perfume] would last me five years probably.

3. She bought things all the time.

4. A lot of times, I've thought about it.

5. I've heard my mother say that fifty times.

6. She only had me six more years.

7. You said it this afternoon.

8. All day the air conditioners in the arena hummed like the inside of a refrigerator.

9. A minute later, I was in trouble in the kitchen.

10. Tim drew all the time, on everything.

11. A few seconds later, she called from the back of the house.

12. A week later, my mother ran to my room.

13. All of a sudden, I was starving.

14. Every mile or so he would lazily turn back and circle around to us.

15. Then, a few squares of sidewalk later, he looked back and stood there.

16. They never went to bed that night.

17. They had been married three years but they never had any furniture.

18. The next morning my mother came in and sat on the edge of my bed.

19. The first week in June the weather turned.

20. We were going over the bridge; the steel underneath roared every ten feet.

The Direct Object

As you have seen, some verbs or verb phrases require nothing to follow them in the predicate phrase, and some are followed only by adverbials; these verbs are called **intransitive verbs.** Some other verbs or verb phrases must be followed by a noun, noun phrase, or pronoun—called the **direct object**—that is acted upon by the subject of the sentence; these verbs are called **transitive verbs.** Sentence (5), repeated below as Sentence (15), has a transitive verb (underlined) followed by a direct object (in square brackets):

15. He <u>locked</u> [the cell door].

Direct objects can follow many different verbs. The verb or verb phrase can express any tense or aspect because tense and aspect do not affect whether a verb can take a direct object. Sentence (16), from *Politically Correct Bedtime Stories*, has a present progressive verb phrase. This verb phrase is transitive and takes a direct object:

16. The emperor <u>is merely endorsing</u> [a clothing-optional lifestyle]!

Because adverbials may appear with any kind of verb, an adverbial prepositional phrase can accompany the direct object in the predicate phrase. In Sentence (17), the adverbial prepositional phrase *for some time* tells the duration of the action *watching.* The adverbial is in parentheses:

17. The rogue biologist <u>had been watching</u> [the cottage] (for some time).

Some transitive verbs include in the verb phrase a **verbal particle** that is selected from the set of prepositions but functions to alter the meaning of the verb in a particular way. A particle does not behave like a preposition; unlike a preposition, it can "hop" over the noun phrase that follows it. The particle belongs to the verb phrase, and so it becomes part of the verb. Sentence (18) has a transitive verb phrase with a verbal particle that is then followed by the noun phrase that is the direct object:

18. Elaine <u>put on</u> [her coat].

Because *on* in (18) is a particle and not a preposition, it can hop over the direct object, *her coat*, as Sentence (19) shows:

19. Elaine <u>put</u> her coat <u>on</u>.

When the direct object is a pronoun, a particle *must* hop over it, as shown in Sentence (20a). Sentence (20b) clearly is unacceptable:

20a. Elaine put it on.

20b. *Elaine put on it.

You can use "hopping" to help you decide whether a preposition-like word is a particle and to determine whether an accompanying noun, pronoun, or noun phrase is a direct object.

Exercise 3.4

The following sentences were taken from *A Lesson Before Dying*. Underline the verb or verb phrase (be sure to include auxiliaries and particles in your underlining, if they occur) and bracket the direct object.

1. The two old men had continued their conversation.

2. The fat man shrugged his shoulders.

3. He did not answer her.

4. Miss Emma dished up the food.

5. He would not open his mouth.

6. The audience appreciated the singing.

7. Vivian put on her galoshes.

8. I put down my fork.

9. An old automobile tire surrounded each flower.

10. A white sharecropper must have been plowing the ground.

11. Paul stuck out his hand.

12. He wore a black pin-striped suit.

13. Vivian lowered her head.

14. Dr. Joseph acknowledged their greeting.

15. The old man nodded his head emphatically.

Direct Object with Indirect Object

Some transitive verbs have two objects, one direct and one indirect. In general, the verbs that belong to this class have subjects that give or tell something (the direct object) to someone (the **indirect object**). Each of the following sentences from *A Lesson Before Dying* has a transitive verb (underlined) that is followed by two separate noun-type elements (nouns, noun phrases, or pronouns); the first one (in parentheses) is the indirect object, and the second (in square brackets) is the direct object:

21a. The deputy behind the desk <u>was giving</u> (the prisoner) [instructions].

22a. I <u>passed</u> (her) [the basket].

23a. I <u>will never tell</u> (him) [another lie].

24a. Claude <u>handed</u> (him) [the safety razor].

There is a handy test for recognizing this "double object" predicate phrase. In general, you can rewrite a sentence having a "double object" by putting the preposition *to* (and sometimes *for*) in front of the first object—the indirect object—and then moving the resulting prepositional phrase to the end of the sentence. If this operation causes no change in meaning, then you know that the moved element is the indirect object of the original sentence. When this test is applied to Sentences (21a) through (24a), the results are as follows:

21b. The deputy behind the desk <u>was giving</u> [instructions] (to the prisoner).

22b. I <u>passed</u> [the basket] (to her).

23b. I <u>will never tell</u> [another lie] (to him), no matter what.

24b. Claude <u>handed</u> [the safety razor] (to him).

Exercise 3.5

Underline the transitive verb or verb phrase in each of the following sentences from Mona Simpson's novel *Anywhere But Here*. Then put parentheses around each indirect object and brackets around each direct object. (Not all the sentences have an indirect object.) In the space below each sentence in which you have found an indirect object, write the test sentence you used to show that the sentence has an indirect object.

1. The woman in the gray dress had offered them tea.

2. She gave me a five-dollar bill.

3. She put down her spoon.

4. I passed her the salad.

5. She also gave us each a plate-sized salad.

6. She served us protein snacks.

7. She made us steak tartare for breakfast.

8. We told her little bits.

9. She gave me her old Sears jacket.

10. I lifted up the chrome door handle.

11. Benny kicked me with a wet foot.

12. She made me cinnamon toast.

13. My mother handed him the receiver.

14.   I gave her the marbles.

15.   The men wore V-necked T-shirts.

Direct Object with Complement

Some transitive verbs take a direct object followed by a **complement** that describes or identifies the object. The complement may be a noun, noun phrase, or pronoun, or it may be an adjective or adjective phrase. Sentence (25a), from *A Lesson Before Dying*, provides examples of a direct object (in square brackets) followed by a complement (in curly brackets) that is a noun:

25a.   Her husband, who was dead now, <u>had called</u> [her] {Miss Emma}, and she <u>had called</u> [him] {Mr. Oscar}.

Sentence (26a) has a complement that is an adjective, *guilty:*

26a.   The jury of twelve white men <u>found</u> [Jefferson] {guilty}.

A handy test can help you identify the direct object and complement construction. When a direct object is followed by a complement, you can make another sentence out of the two elements by using a form of the verb *be*. The first element is the subject of *be*, and the second follows *be*. If the first element is an object-form pronoun, you must change it to subject-form to apply this test. Trying this test on (25a) and (26a), we get the results shown in (25b) and (26b):

25b.   She *was* Miss Emma. He *was* Mr. Oscar.

26b.   Jefferson *was* guilty.

Since (25b) and (26b) have nearly the same meaning as (25a) and (26a), the test shows that *Miss Emma* and *Mr. Oscar* are the complements in (25a) and that *guilty* is the complement in (26a).

Exercise 3.6

Underline the transitive verb or verb phrase in each of the following sentences from *Anywhere But Here*. Then put square brackets around each direct object and curly brackets around each complement. (Not all sentences have a complement.) In the space below each sentence in which you have found a direct object followed by a complement, write the test sentence you used to show that the sentence has a complement.

1. I'd have just left it dirty.

2. I crossed my arms over my chest.

3. She must have found me terribly plain.

4. The waiter left us alone.

5. That made me exhausted.

6. Her bright voice made me angry.

7. We painted my bedroom floor white.

8. My mother rested her chin on her hands.

9. My mother loved that car.

10. Milton shook me awake.

Reflexive Pronouns

Sometimes the direct or indirect object of a transitive verb is a pronoun that points to the same real-world individual as the subject noun or noun phrase. In this case, the object pronoun must be **reflexive** in form, as in Sentence (27). A reflexive pronoun always ends in the suffix *-self* (singular form) or *-selves* (plural form):

27. George shaved himself.

Table 3.2. Reflexive Pronouns

	Singular	Plural
First Person	*myself*	*ourselves*
Second Person	*yourself*	*yourselves*
Third Person	**masculine:** *himself* **feminine:** *herself* **neuter:** *itself*	*themselves*

If an object-form personal pronoun appears as direct object instead, as in Sentence (28), the sentence means that George shaved someone else:

28. George shaved him.

An indirect object may also be a reflexive pronoun if the pronoun points to the same real-world person as the subject. Sentence (29), from *Anywhere But Here,* has such an indirect object, shown in parentheses:

29. She bought (herself) [a new one].
(*Compare:* She bought a new one *for* herself.)

The reflexive pronouns are listed in Table 3.2 above. They *never* serve as sentence subjects.

Exercise 3.7

Underline the transitive verb or verb phrase in each of the following sentences. Then put square brackets around each direct object, parentheses around each indirect object, and curly brackets around each complement. All of the sentences come from Robert Fulghum's *All I Really Need to Know I Learned in Kindergarten.*

1. I like my work.

2. She flings her baggage in all directions.

3.   The waitress gave me a kiss.

4.   I left her a two-dollar tip.

5.   I gave her the clock.

6.   I told her the story.

7.   They bought themselves an 18-speed mountain bicycle.

8.   Elias Schwartz repairs shoes.

9.   With regret in his voice he pronounced them unworthy.

10.   I accepted the unwelcome judgment.

Linking Verb with Complement

Another kind of verb or verb phrase, called a **linking verb,** connects the element that follows it—usually a noun, noun phrase, or pronoun, or an adjective or adjective phrase—to the subject. This element describes or identifies the subject by assigning it to a class of individuals (for Sentence 30, *student*) or giving a characteristic (for Sentence 31, *studious*). Sentences (30) and (31) have linking verbs (underlined) followed by complements (in curly brackets):

30.   Elaine <u>is</u> {a student}.

31.   Elaine <u>seems</u> {studious}.

The most common linking verb is *be* when it is used as a main verb. Other verbs are linking insofar as they do the kind of work that *be* does in describing the subject. *Seem*, for example, used in Sentence (31) above, makes a weaker claim than does *be*. Sentence (30) asserts that it is a fact that Elaine is a student. On the other hand, Sentence (31) merely expresses the *impression* that Elaine is studious.

A list of common linking verbs is provided in Table 3.3. Only *be* and *seem* are always linking. Each of the others is linking only when the element that follows it describes the subject in some way.

Table 3.3. Linking Verbs

appear	become	grow	remain	taste
be	feel	look	seem	turn

Be is special among the linking verbs. Not only is it the most frequently used among them and is always linking, but it can also be followed by an adverb or adverbial phrase that locates the subject. Sentence (32) demonstrates this use:

32. Elaine is in the library.

In the library gives the location and not a characteristic of the subject, and the verb itself has the sole purpose, not of expressing action, condition, or state, but of carrying tense (in Sentence 32, the present tense). The real work of the predicate phrase is carried out in the adverbial prepositional phrase.

Exercise 3.8

Underline the linking verb in each of the following sentences from *A Lesson Before Dying*. Then put curly brackets around each complement (noun or noun phrase or adjective or adjective phrase), and parentheses around any adverbial prepositional phrase that may complete the verb.

1. The deputy was looking very mean.

2. The three of them were in the kitchen.

3. Miss Emma looked tired.

4. She was tired.

5. His breakfast was two homemade biscuit sandwiches.

6. His godmother became immobile.

7. The store was empty.

8. Jefferson became frightened.

9.   The prosecutor's story was different.

10.   The Rainbow Club was quiet.

VARYING THE BASIC SENTENCE

Basic English declarative sentences typically follow a particular word order that depends on the functions of the words and phrases in a given sentence. That is, the subject comes first, followed by the verb or verb phrase, and then the indirect object (if one occurs), the direct object (if the verb is transitive), the complement (if the verb is linking or transitive with complement), and finally any adverbs or adverbials, and there may be more than one. Using abbreviations for these sentence functions and parentheses to show that an element may or may not occur, we can write the following formula:

S V (IO) (DO) (C) (A)

S = subject, **V** = verb, **IO** = indirect object, **DO** = direct object, **C** = complement, and **A** = adverbial.

If every English sentence followed this pattern, however, English sentences would be dull and repetitious. Therefore, English has a way of varying this basic pattern; it allows adverbs and adverbials to appear first from time to time, and it allows sentences with transitive verbs to be expressed in the passive voice.

Putting Adverbials First

Since adverbs and adverbials typically express time, location, manner, or other background details, it often is useful to present them first in the sentence, as a guidepost to the main event. In English, the end of the sentence is reserved for the most important information, so it makes sense to put the background details at the beginning. In Sentence (33), for example, from John Steinbeck's novel *Cannery Row,* the main point is that everyone owed money to a particular character; that this circumstance came to be "over the course of years" is simply background information expressed in an adverbial prepositional phrase. Thus, it appears first in the sentence:

> **33.** <u>Over the course of years</u> everyone in Cannery Row owed him money.

Usually, introductory adverbials are set off from the main part of the sentence by commas, as in Sentence (34):

> **34.** <u>On the exposed rocks out of water,</u> the barnacles bubble behind their closed doors.

No adverbial nor any part of it is the subject of the sentence. The subject of (33) is *everyone in Cannery Row;* the subject of (34) is *the barnacles.* The yes/no question test for finding the subject can still be used if we ignore the adverbial or move it to the end of the sentence. If we apply the test to (33), the result is (35):

> **35.** Did <u>everyone in Cannery Row</u> owe him money (over the course of the years)?

Exercise 3.9

Each of the following sentences from *Cannery Row* has at least one introductory adverb or adverbial phrase, either a prepositional phrase or an adverbial noun phrase. Put parentheses around each introductory adverb or adverbial, and then underline the sentence subject.

1. That afternoon he had come into the grocery.

2. In fine weather they lived in the shadow of the black cypress tree at the top of the lot.

3. During the depression she was hardest hit.

4. After a while William went disconsolately back to the Bear Flag.

5. In the evening just at dusk, a curious thing happened on Cannery Row.

6.   In his hand he carried a covered wicker basket.

7.   To the left the office opens into a library.

8.   Over a period of years Doc dug himself into Cannery Row.

9.   In the laboratory the girls from Dora's heard the Plain Songs and Gregorian music for the first time.

10.   On the reef the whistling buoy bellows like a sad and patient bull.

11.   Quite often he went collecting with Doc.

12.   On a good night Eddie got three-quarters of a gallon.

13.   In April 1932 the boiler at the Hediondo Cannery blew a tube for the third time in two weeks.

14.   In a few minutes Hazel came damply up the chicken walk to the Palace.

15.   For a week or so he just stood outside the basement door and looked in.

16.   Then one day he stood inside the door.

17.   Ten days later he was in the basement.

18.   Finally Frankie got to the work bench.

19.   One afternoon he did a desperate thing.

20.   For a moment Frankie stood still.

21.   One morning elderly Mr. Carriaga was walking from his house on the hill down toward Alvarado Street.

22.   In those days little boys were courteous.

23.   Some time before dawn Eddie came back.

24.   Over the hill a fox was barking sharply.

The Passive Voice

Basic sentences having transitive verbs may be varied by putting the transitive verb in the **passive voice.** All of the sentences with transitive verbs you have studied so far have had **active voice** verbs. That is, the noun phrase that is the subject of the sentence is also the noun phrase that performs the action. However, some sentences have subjects that do *not* perform the action but have actions performed on them. Such a sentence appears in Sentence (36), from *Cannery Row:*

> **36.** Without effort, confusion, or much thought, four round
> stones were rolled together on the little beach.

The introductory prepositional phrase in (36), *without effort, confusion, or much thought,* is an adverbial. The subject is the noun phrase *four round stones.* The verb phrase is *were rolled,* formed from the auxiliary *be* accompanied by the past participle of the main verb, a combination we have not seen before. The verb phrase is said to be in the passive voice. The subject is affected by the action and does not bring the action about. Someone or something else, not specified in the sentence, is responsible.

There is a relationship between the active and passive voice of transitive sentences—the object of the active voice version becomes the subject of the passive voice version. Let's use Sentence (36) for illustration. To simplify matters, I will remove the introductory adverbial from the sentence and repeat it here as Sentence (37a):

> **37a.** Four round stones were rolled together on the little beach.

Someone must have caused these four round stones to be piled together, but (37a) does not provide this information, perhaps because the narrator does not know, or because it is not important for the reader to know. It is possible to state (37a) in the active voice as in Sentence (37b):

> **37b.** Someone rolled four round stones together on the little
> beach.

In (37b), *someone* is the subject of the sentence, and *four round stones* is the direct object. However, a sentence such as (37b) might lead the reader to expect that knowing *who* rolled the stones together is important. Thus Steinbeck uses the passive voice to do the job. In that way, he allows us to see the result of someone's action without giving importance to the identity of the character. In the passive voice, what was the direct object of the active voice becomes the subject of the passive: *four round stones*. The verb phrase undergoes a change as well; the *be* auxiliary is used, along with the past participle of the main verb, *roll*. The tense is held constant, but as is true for any verb phrase having an auxiliary, the tense in the passive voice is carried by the auxiliary. Thus *were rolled* is the passive form of *rolled*, and it is past tense.

It is possible, however, for a passive verb phrase to include a modal auxiliary, the *have* auxiliary, even another *be* auxiliary, if the passive verb phrase is progressive. In any of these instances, the last auxiliary in the chain of auxiliaries is always a form of *be*, and the main verb always appears in the past participle form. Sentences (38) and (39), from Susan Cheever's memoir *Treetops*, have passive verb phrases with more than one auxiliary (underlined):

38.   All problems <u>could be solved</u> by human ingenuity.

39.   A sound-shaped current <u>had been carried</u> through the wires.

Sentence (38) also provides an example of a second feature of passive sentences; sometimes the noun-type element that brings about the action is still expressed, but as the object of the preposition *by*. Writers may use a passive verb with a *by*-phrase to shift the focus of the sentence. In (38), for example, *human ingenuity* appears at the end, the point of prominence in the sentence. They may also use a passive verb with a *by*-phrase if the object of *by* is not a person with the intention of performing the action of the main verb. Such a use is demonstrated by Bill Cosby in Sentence (40), from *Childhood*, in which *one unwritten rule* governs school fights, and not a human being:

40.   In those old-fashioned days, school fights often <u>were governed</u> by one unwritten rule.

Exercise 3.10

All of the following sentences from Brent Staples's memoir, *Parallel Time*, have either active transitive verbs or verb phrases or passive verb phrases. Underline the verb or verb phrase in each sentence, and in the space below write *active* or *passive*. Remember that a passive voice verb phrase *must* include the *be* auxiliary *and* the past participle of the main verb. Review the forms of *be* in Table 2.4 if necessary.

1. The deceased, twenty-two-year-old Negro male, was allegedly shot by another person on the premises of a night club.

2. No weapon was found on or near his body.

3. The jury turned back the prosecution's request for a conviction of murder in the first degree.

4. Mark was found guilty of second-degree murder.

5. The coroner describes the wounds in detail.

6. The surgical incision and its grisly clamps are dismissed in a single sentence.

7. The six bullet holes receive one full paragraph each.

8. Blake and I were making small talk.

9. For him, everything about the killing had been said.

10. In bed, I was shocked awake by groaning timbers or voices.

11. Downtown, near the police station or the courthouse, he could have been stopped at any time.

12. The ceremony was performed in the log house.

13. The way for this marriage was smoothed by a previous union between the Pattersons of Hollins and the Staples of Troutville.

14.   My mother's uncle Blaine had married my father's aunt, Ruby.

15.   I visited the log house in Hollins as a small boy in the 1950s.

16.   I remember Hollins as a place of women.

17.   My father was not included in these trips.

18.   Enormous tins of lard were lined up around the smokehouse walls.

19.   My father missed the luck of the draw.

20.   He was raised in the home of Ada's father, Tom Perdue, a brown-skinned version of Simon Legree.

SUMMARY

The basic English sentence has a subject, which typically is responsible for the action, and a predicate phrase, which includes the verb or verb phrase and, depending on the verb, objects and a complement. A sentence can be varied in several ways. The predicate phrase may include adverbial prepositional phrases and noun phrases that add details, and these modifiers can be moved to the front of the sentence. In addition, transitive sentences—sentences whose verbs are completed by direct objects—may be expressed in the passive voice in order to change the focus of the sentence or to eliminate the need to specify who is responsible for the state of affairs presented in the sentence.

Projects for Chapter Three

1.   Find a passage in your daily newspaper and circle all of the prepositions you find. If you can, underline the objects of the prepositions you find (this can be tricky).

2. Rewrite the passive sentences of Exercise 3.10 in the active voice, keeping the tense and aspect constant. You may have to supply a subject for the active voice, such as *someone* or *the jury*.

3. Rewrite the active sentences of Exercise 3.10 in the passive voice, keeping the tense and aspect constant.

4. There is no passive counterpart for intransitive and linking verbs. Can you say why not? Think carefully. What does a transitive sentence have that an intransitive or linking sentence does not? How does this fact relate to the active/passive distinction? You will need some examples of the different types of sentences to reach your conclusions. Write a paragraph detailing your findings and providing examples to illustrate your points.

5. The following terms appeared in this chapter. Be sure you are familiar with all of them. Use the index and/or the glossary in the back of this book to help you.

active voice	passive voice
adverbial	predicate phrase
complement	preposition
direct object	prepositional phrase
indirect object	reflexive pronoun
intransitive verb	transitive verb
linking verb	verbal particle
object of the preposition	

Adding Details with Modifiers

The basic sentences you thus far have studied represent only a small portion of the kinds of sentences found in everyday writing activities. Most sentences that occur in written English are more complex, varied, and interesting. One essential way to supply the details that add this interest is to use modifiers. You have already studied two types of modifiers, the adverbial prepositional phrase and the adverbial noun phrase. In Chapter 4, you will learn about modifiers of nouns and noun phrases, as well as new kinds of adverbial modifiers.

MODIFIERS THAT FOLLOW NOUNS AND NOUN PHRASES

In Chapter 1, you learned that determiners and adjectives modify nouns and that they precede the nouns they modify. Some modifiers of nouns, particularly those that are phrases rather than single words, follow rather than precede nouns. These modifiers include prepositional phrases, participle phrases, relative clauses, and appositives. In the following sections, we will explore how these modifiers are used to add details that make sentences more precise and often more interesting.

Expanding Noun Phrases with Prepositional Phrases

Though prepositional phrases often modify verbs, verb phrases, and predicate phrases, they also may modify nouns, and when they do, they follow the nouns they modify. Sentences (1) through (5), from John Cheever's novel *Oh What a Paradise it Seems*, have noun phrases that include prepositional phrases. The entire expanded noun phrase is underlined, with the prepositional phrase given in parentheses:

1. The shadow (of a hill) had darkened half the ice.

2. The main entrance (to the church) was dark and locked.

3. The parish-house door (around the corner) was lighted and unlocked.

4. Sears had taken many business trips (to the Balkans).

5. The corridor (for soaps) was a great distance (from the entrance).

Of a hill, to the church, around the corner, to the Balkans, for soaps, and from the entrance are all prepositional phrases; each begins with a preposition that is followed by the noun phrase that is its object.

Though *any* noun phrase in a sentence can include a prepositional phrase modifier, Sentences (1), (2), (3), and (5) have subjects that are such noun phrases. To illustrate, let's convert Sentence (1) into a yes/no question to find its subject; remember that the subject will fall between the moved auxiliary and the main verb:

6. Had the shadow of a hill darkened half the ice?

As you can see, *the shadow of a hill* is the subject of the sentence.

Sentence (4), repeated below as Sentence (7), shows us that a noun phrase that includes a prepositional phrase can be a direct object. I have underlined the verb phrase and bracketed the direct object. The prepositional phrase is given in italics:

7. Sears <u>had taken</u> [many business trips *to the Balkans*].

Sentences (8) through (10), from *Oh What a Paradise*, also have such noun phrases as direct objects:

8. The mill owner's house with its four Corinthian columns still <u>crowns</u> [the only hill *in town*].

9. She <u>had prophesied</u> [an accident *at their New Mexico mines*].

10. Chisholm <u>had saved</u> [the life *of her son*].

Sometimes, a prepositional phrase occurs within a noun phrase that is itself the object of a preposition. Sentences (11) and (12) from *Oh What a Paradise It Seems* include such noun phrases. In (11), *of Buster* modifies *assassination*, and *to the assassination of Buster* modifies *witness*:

11. <u>The only other witness (to the assassination *of Buster*)</u> had been Betsy Logan.

Can you say how the modifiers work in Sentence (12)?

12. <u>Sear's lack (of interest *in the occult*)</u> was genuine.

Exercise 4.1

 Find the prepositional phrases in the following sentences from *Oh What a Paradise it Seems*. Put parentheses around each one and then underline the entire noun phrase that includes it.

1. These mixtures of blood had made them a highly spirited pack.

2. She was the daughter of sainted Amelia.

3. Sears then remembered a scene with Estelle.

4. His feeling for Renee was confused and profound.

5. The loveliness of the landscape had been restored.

6.   Maybelle was the name of the checkout clerk.

7.   His doctor had given him a list of psychiatrists.

8.   The politics in this profession are absolutely indescribable.

9.   This turn of thought troubled Chisholm.

10.   The tape of an operatic soprano's voice led them on.

Other Post-Noun Modifiers and the Restrictive/Nonrestrictive Distinction

Prepositional phrases are not the only elements that modify nouns by following them. Nouns also may be modified by appositives, relative clauses, and participle phrases, all of which follow the noun or noun phrase. An example of each of these modifiers appears in Sentence (13), from Gary Soto's collection of stories *Small Faces*. The appositive and the relative clause are underlined, but because the participle phrase appears *inside* the relative clause, it is given in italics:

13.   For my childhood friend <u>Jackie</u> and me, there was no recognition of animal life, other than cats and dogs and an occasional squirrel <u>that from a distance looked like a base-ball mitt *nailed to a tree*</u>.

The noun *Jackie* modifies the compound noun *childhood friend* by limiting the reference of the compound to the particular individual, *Jackie*. Nouns or noun phrases such as *Jackie* that modify nouns or noun phrases are called **appositives**. We assume that a person has more than one friend, so by modifying *friend* with an appositive, Soto lets his readers know which friend he means. The second modifier is *that from a distance looked like a baseball mitt nailed to a tree*. This modifier is called a **relative clause**. Just like a sentence, it has its own subject and predicate phrase, but it cannot stand alone; rather it assists Soto in describing the squirrel so that readers imagine not just any squirrel, but one so motionless that it looks like a thing rather than an animal. The third modifier, the phrase *nailed to a tree*, is called a **participle phrase** because it begins with the past participle *nailed* (which, as a participle, has no tense) and includes the adverbial prepositional phrase *to a tree*. This participle phrase modifies *baseball mitt* and helps readers imagine something they are not likely to see in the real world—a baseball mitt not on a shelf, nor on someone's hand, but one that has been nailed to a tree! Notice the description: *one that <u>has been nailed</u> to a tree*. The verb phrase *has been nailed* is passive, so the past participle phrase *nailed to a tree* implies a passive meaning. Someone has "nailed" that mitt, but that someone is not mentioned in the phrase.

The three modifiers highlighted in Sentence (13) are said to be **restrictive** because each narrows (or *restricts*) the reference of a very general noun (such as *friend, squirrel, mitt*) so that the resulting noun phrase can point to a particular individual or a specific case. Notice that no punctuation comes between a noun and a restrictive modifier.

Not all modifiers are restrictive, however. Some modifiers, called **nonrestrictive** modifiers, follow nouns or noun phrases that are already quite specific; they do not limit a general noun to a specific case. In general, a nonrestrictive modifier is separated from the noun or noun phrase it modifies by a comma. If the appositive in Sentence (13), *Jackie*, had been set off with commas so that the noun phrase having the appositive was *my childhood friend, Jackie,* Soto would have implied that he had only one childhood friend, who happened to be named Jackie.

Additional examples of nonrestrictive modifiers are underlined in (14), a brief passage from "Channelled Whelk," an essay included in *Gift from the Sea*, by Anne Morrow Lindbergh:

14. The shell in my hand is deserted. It once housed a whelk, <u>a snail-like creature</u>, and then temporarily after the death of the first occupant, a little hermit crab, who <u>has run away, leaving his tracks behind him like a delicate vine on the sand</u>.

The first modifier is *a snail-like creature*. This noun phrase, a nonrestrictive appositive, modifies the noun phrase *a whelk*, and it does so by identifying it. The second modifier is *who has run away*. This nonrestrictive relative clause provides additional information about the noun phrase it modifies, *a little hermit crab*. The third modifier is the nonrestrictive participle clause *leaving his tracks behind him like a delicate vine on the sand*. This modifier begins with an -*ing* verb (the participle *leaving*) along with its object (*his tracks*) and adverbial prepositional phrases. It provides additional information about that same *hermit crab*.

A modifier is nonrestrictive when it adds detail to the noun or noun phrase it modifies, but because the noun or noun phrase points to a specific individual, the modifier does not help to narrow the reference of the noun to a specific case. In fact, nonrestrictive modifiers provide details that could appear in separate sentences. In (15) below, you will find the passage from (14) rewritten with separate sentences wherever one of the nonrestrictive modifiers appears. Brackets appear around the words that were added to make the separate sentences possible. The underlined words are those that appeared in the modifiers of the original example. As you can see, the result is much less effective than the original:

15. The shell in my hand is deserted. It once housed a whelk. A whelk is <u>a snail-like creature</u>. And then temporarily after the death of the first occupant, [the shell housed] a little hermit crab. [The little crab] <u>has run away</u>. [He has left] <u>his tracks behind him like a delicate vine on the sand</u>.

Whereas the original passage had only two sentences and forty-six words, the revision has six sentences and fifty-six words. The added length is no improvement, however, because the extra words add no information, and the additional sentences give the impression of disconnectedness among the ideas. Thus, (14) is preferable to (15). You will continue to study the restrictive/nonrestrictive distinction as you work through the sections dealing specifically with each type of modifier.

Appositives

An appositive is a noun or noun phrase that modifies another noun or noun phrase and typically follows what it modifies. When an appositive is nonrestrictive, it is separated from the rest of the sentence by a comma, or sometimes a dash (—) or a colon (:). If it is restrictive, there is no punctuation mark between the appositive and noun or noun phrase it modifies. Sentences (16) and (17) from Gary Soto's *Small Faces* provide examples of appositives, both nonrestrictive and restrictive, which are underlined. The noun phrases they modify are underlined with a double line:

16. I considered my <u>fiancee</u>, <u>Carolyn</u>, and she didn't look poor. [nonrestrictive]

17. The second time I held my wife's hand was at <u>the movie *Sounder*</u>, on March 19, 1973. [restrictive]

In (16), the nonrestrictive appositive *Carolyn* gives us additional information about *fiancee*. It does not limit or "restrict" *fiancee* because Soto wants the reader to understand that he had just one fiancee. In (17), on the other hand, the reader knows that there are very many movies that one could mention; however, Soto wants us to understand that this movie was the one entitled *Sounder,* and not any other. Thus the appositive "restricts" or limits our understanding of *the movie* to a particular film.

Sometimes a nonrestrictive appositive does not directly follow the noun it modifies; in Sentence (18), the noun phrase *Jon the Estonian and Omar the Mexican* modifies *my friends,* but appears at the end of the sentence.

18. <u>My friends</u> are coming—<u>Jon the Estonian and Omar the Mexican</u>.

In addition, the underlined appositive contains two other appositives: *the Estonian*, which modifies *Jon*, and *the Mexican*, which modifies *Omar.*

Exercise 4.2

Put one line under each appositive in the following passages from *Small Faces*. Then put a double line under the noun or noun phrase that is modified by the appositive. In the space below, write whether the appositive is restrictive or nonrestrictive.

1. The driver, a rancher from Oxnard, bought him burgers and Cokes.

2. My sister, a fight fan from the year one, pounded a fist into her palm and wished Chacon all the luck.

3. We drove to the Ivy Room in Albany, a bar with cable television.

4. Tony Perez, the referee, stepped between them to stop the fight.

5. One summer I heard our three-year-old daughter Mariko say, "The days are filled with air."

Nonrestrictive Adjective Phrases

Another kind of nonrestrictive modifier is the **nonrestrictive adjective phrase,** and it is very similar in function to the nonrestrictive appositive. The nonrestrictive adjective phrase differs from the appositive in that it has no noun. Otherwise, it works the same way as the nonrestrictive appositive does; it typically follows the noun or noun phrase it modifies and provides additional but nonessential information about the noun or noun phrase.

In Chapter 1, you learned that an adjective describes a noun by limiting or qualifying it and that it typically precedes the noun it modifies. However, sometimes a phrase comprising an adjective together with its accompanying modifiers or a phrase comprising several adjectives chained together does not limit the reference of a general noun or noun phrase; instead it provides nonessential descriptive detail. Then the adjective phrase may follow the noun or noun phrase, so long as it is set off by a comma, a dash, or a colon. The result is a nonrestrictive adjective phrase. The following sentences from Candice Bergen's autobiography, *Knock Wood,* illustrate how nonrestrictive adjective phrases (underlined) are used. The noun or noun phrase that is modified has a double underline:

19. They are filming <u>my father,</u> <u>splendid and somber in top hat and overcoat,</u> who holds the Northeastern telephone directory, from which he pretends to read the eulogy.

20. These were people from the land of Ibsen and Strindberg, Munch and Grieg—<u>tall, pale people,</u> <u>stern and strong.</u>

21. The boy's name was Charlie, and he was <u>a bright and brassy kid,</u> <u>confident, cocksure.</u>

Sometimes, as with appositives, the nonrestrictive modifier appears at a distance from the modified noun, even preceding it on occasion, as in Sentence (22):

22. <u>Awkward, silent, socially unsuccessful,</u> <u><u>Edgar</u></u> created someone who caught people's fancies.

The adjective phrase in (22), *awkward, silent, socially unsuccessful,* provides additional detail about *Edgar,* a proper noun naming a unique
individual and thus not open to restrictive modification.

Exercise 4.3

 Put a single line under each nonrestrictive appositive or adjective
phrase in the following sentences from *Knock Wood*. Then put a
double line under the noun or noun phrase that is modified.

1. An only child, she had a less strong bond with her mother, Lillie
    Mae.

2. In Los Angeles, Lillie Mae met and married Parry Boyd, a hand-
    some devil from a fine family.

3. I moved in with my Dutch governess, Dena.

4. Mrs. Grimaldi—round, blond, and fluffy, much like her
    poodles—spoke in strange cooing sounds.

5. Bobby, the Western Union delivery man, lived down the road
    over the Barrymore garage.

6. And so, one Sunday, off I went to a burro ranch with my
    governess, Dee, and her boyfriend, Don.

7. Not a particularly patient man, he was intolerant and short-
    tempered with slowness or stupidity.

8. One of my playmates was Carla Kirkeby, the daughter of a
    hotel magnate.

9. Relentlessly cheerful, infallibly good-hearted, Dee was the
    constant in my life.

10. The two of us became a team of sorts, a prep school Laurel and Hardy.

11. These were all decent people, kind and hard-working.

12. Young and self-absorbed, I scarcely suffered from an excess of sensitivity.

13. My old Montesano roommate, Veronica, had written inviting me to visit her in Rhodesia that summer.

14. His most recent film, *A Man and a Woman*, had been an enormous success.

15. Yves Montand was an idol in France: charming, talented, debonair.

16. The Beach Boys had bought Edgar Rice Burroughs' house, a gracious Mediterranean villa.

17. His seven-hour documentary, *Phantom India*, had been unanimously acclaimed everywhere but in that country.

18. That first meeting was an edgy encounter, awkward and uncomfortable.

19. He entered, breathless from the cold.

20. David Lazer, a family friend, flew in from London.

Participle Phrases

You studied participles of verbs in Chapter 2, where you learned that verbs have two participle forms, the present participle that ends in *-ing* for all verbs, and the past participle that ends in *-ed* for all regular verbs. Despite their names, participles do not show tense and need an auxiliary to do so when they are part of the verb phrase of the sentence.

Participles can do more than be parts of verb phrases. For example, they can serve as simple adjectives that appear to the *left* of the noun. Expressions such as *baked bread, soaring spirits,* and the like are ordinary noun phrases that use participles (*baked, soaring*) as adjectives. Even if the participle is modified by an adverb that precedes it, the participle adjective and its modifier appear to the left of the noun. In Sentence (23), for instance, the adverb *freshly* precedes *baked,* a participle adjective, so the entire phrase *freshly baked* appears to the left of the noun, *bread:*

23. <u>Freshly baked</u> bread smells delicious.

However, if a modifier of *baked,* such as *in brick ovens* in Sentence (24), follows the participle, then the entire phrase—participle and modifier—must *follow* the noun:

24. Bread <u>baked in brick ovens</u> is particularly crispy.

The presence of the past participle implies a passive meaning, as in *The bread was baked in brick ovens by someone.*

Thus, a **participle phrase** consists of a participle verb form along with any associated objects and modifiers. It is like a predicate phrase having a participle but no auxiliary verb. Like any noun modifier, a participle phrase may limit the reference of the noun it modifies—that is, it may be restrictive—or it may provide additional information about the noun or noun phrase—that is, it may be nonrestrictive. The same rules about punctuation followed for appositives apply here: A restrictive participle phrase follows its noun with no punctuation separating the two; a nonrestrictive participle phrase is separated from what it modifies by a comma, a dash, or a colon.

Participle phrases may begin with either a past or a present (*-ing*) participle, and either type may be restrictive or nonrestrictive. As is true for nonrestrictive modifiers in general, a nonrestrictive participle phrase may appear at some distance from the noun or noun phrase it modifies. The modified noun or noun phrase is always the understood "subject" of the participle. That is, a sentence could be written that has the modified noun or noun phrase as subject and the participle phrase—with an added *be* auxiliary—as predicate phrase. Sentences (25) through (29) from Robert Fulghum's book *Uh-Oh* illustrate how participle phrases operate. Each participle phrase is underlined once; what it modifies is underlined twice. Under each sentence I have written whether the participle phrase is restrictive or nonrestrictive, and I have provided the test sentence that shows which noun is the understood subject of the participle. The subject of this sentence is the same noun phrase as the modified noun or noun phrase in the original sentence. In checking your own writing, you must be certain that a participle phrase always finds its modifier in its sentence; using the test sentence I have described can help you avoid a writing error called "a dangling modifier"—a modifier without the noun it modifies appearing in the same sentence:

25. The medical literature is comparatively thin as well—dealing mostly with chronic cases and desperate measures of cure.

Nonrestrictive: The medical literature [is] dealing mostly with chronic cases and desperate measures of cure.

26. Drawn back to the cabin by the yellow glow of a reading lamp in the living room, I stood outside the window for a long time and looked in at my wife.

Nonrestrictive: I [was] drawn back to the cabin by the yellow glow of a reading lamp in the living room.

27. A woman wearing a hard hat hung a little pink card on our front doorknob yesterday.

Restrictive: A woman [was] wearing a hard hat.

There are two participle phrases in (28), one restrictive, one nonrestrictive, but modifying the same noun phrase:

28. A trumpet made from a ram's horn is blown, summoning the people for judgment and self-improvement.

Restrictive: A trumpet [was] made from a ram's horn.
Nonrestrictive: A trumpet [was] summoning the people for judgment and self-improvement.

Nonrestrictive participle phrases can be combined with other nonrestrictive modifiers. In (29), a nonrestrictive present participle phrase, *walking with a slight limp*, is combined with a nonrestrictive adjective phrase, *short, plump, wrinkled:*

29. <u>Short, plump, wrinkled, walking with a slight limp,</u> <u><u>the old man</u></u> ambled on into the morning.

Exercise 4.4

Put a line under each of the participle phrases in the following sentences from *Uh-Oh*. Then put a double line under the noun or noun phrase it modifies. In the space below each sentence, write whether the participle phrase is restrictive or nonrestrictive.

1. Elgar's *Pomp and Circumstance* march, named out of a speech of farewell in Othello, spills its solemn dignity over this scene of passage.

2. Not wanting any kind of heart trouble, I took the cook's advice.

3. I had taken a cable car from Union Square to the foot of Columbus Street, intending to walk back through the old Italian quarter of North Beach.

4. Leaning against a tree, I cut the end off the cigar with my pocketknife and carefully lit up.

5. Placing the lit cigar carefully on the wide brick window ledge of the coffeehouse, I went inside to order.

6. Tossing my briefcase in the closet, I headed for the door without any baggage.

7. Riding home in a thunderstorm, Sarah fell asleep in her car seat beside me.

8. Talking to her father the next day, I inquired of Sarah's report on our excursion.

9. Facing east, they would greet the rising sun with hymns and prayers.

10. In a gesture combining dismissal and blessing, he waved me off to bed.

11. She chases after him, urgently honking her horn.

12. The coffin was brought up from the hearse, carried by sons and grandsons.

13. The superintendent of schools sitting beside me knows.

14. He is sitting very quiet and very still, looking into the mirror that the moving line of seniors is for him.

15. The bowl was painted with a simple curving design representing the four winds.

Relative Clauses

Another type of noun modifier is the **relative clause.** A relative clause is one type of **subordinate clause,** a sentence-like construction that cannot stand on its own as an independent sentence but serves instead as a part of another sentence called the **main clause.** A relative clause is essentially an entire sentence—subject, verb, and object (if one occurs)—that limits or identifies a noun or noun phrase; it is different from an ordinary sentence in that it is generally changed in some way. Usually it begins with a **relative pronoun** that points back to a noun or noun phrase in the main clause, the sentence that includes the modified noun. Though there are no separate masculine, feminine, and neuter relative pronouns, there are different relative pronouns for human and nonhuman entities. Relative pronouns are shown in Table 4.1.

Except for when it is the object of a preposition, the relative pronoun always begins the relative clause, even if it is not the subject of the clause. In Sentences (30) through (34), the relative clause is underlined and the relative pronoun is given in italics. In parentheses below each is the sentence implied by the relative clause. In each example, the

Table 4.1. Relative Pronouns

	Human	**Nonhuman**
Subject form	*who*	*which*
Object form	*whom*	*which*
Possessive form	*whose*	*whose*

relative pronoun has a grammatical function in the relative clause. In (30), the relative pronoun *who* is the subject of the relative clause.

30. Larry was a college friend <u>*who* lived under a tree</u>. [*Small Faces*]
(A college friend [= who] lived under a tree).

In (31), the relative pronoun *whom* is the object of the verb of the relative clause, *love*, and in (32), *which* is the object of the verb *gave:*

31. There are few people <u>*whom* I really love</u>. [Jane Austen, *Pride and Prejudice*]
(I really love few people [= whom]).

32. Edgar passed him every day and then made sketches, <u>*which* he gave to a barkeeper called Mack</u>. [*Knock Wood*]
(He gave sketches [= which] to a barkeeper called Mack).

In (33), the relative pronoun *whom* is the object of the preposition *to* that is part of the relative clause:

33. We both needed one person <u>to *whom* we could tell the truth</u>. [*The Diary of Anais Nin*]
(We could tell the truth to one person [= whom]).

And in (34), the relative pronoun *whose* is a possessive form that appears before the noun *eyes* of the subject noun phrase of the relative clause:

34. I recall a poem of his about an Egyptian cat <u>*whose* eyes were many-cornered diamonds</u>. [*Small Faces*]
(An Egyptian cat's [= whose] eyes were many-cornered diamonds)

Like all of the modifiers we have seen so far, a relative clause may be restrictive or nonrestrictive, and, once again, punctuation usually makes that distinction clear, with a comma or commas setting off the nonrestrictive relative clause. Thus Sentences (30) through (34) above have restrictive relative clauses, except for Sentence (32), repeated below as Sentence (35), which has a nonrestrictive relative clause. Notice that the relative clause *which he gave to a barkeeper called Mack* is separated from the noun it modifies, *sketches*, by a comma:

35. Edgar passed him every day and then made sketches, <u>*which*</u> <u>he gave to a barkeeper called Mack.</u>

However, there are other important differences between restrictive and nonrestrictive relative clauses. Restrictive relative clauses, which restrict or limit the reference of the noun they modify, often do not have the subject and object form relative pronouns shown in Table 4.1, but frequently begin with the function word *that*, particularly when the antecedent of the pronoun is nonhuman. Sentences (36) through (39) from *Small Faces* illustrate this use:

36. And the moon did disappear, for my wife and I married on a night of an eclipse <u>*that* comes every twenty years</u>, a rare treat for the astronomer's wife.
(An eclipse [= that] comes every twenty years.)

37. There we bought penny candies: Tootsie Rolls, Abba Zabbas, jaw breakers, licorice <u>*that* wagged from our mouths like donkey tails</u>.
(Licorice [= that] wagged from our mouths like donkey tails.)

38. We saw leaves and smelled a rudeness <u>*that* puckered our faces</u>.
(A rudeness [= that] puckered our faces.)

39. At the top we rested and scanned the trees for monkeys <u>*that* might drop on us</u>.
(Monkeys [= that] might drop on us.)

Most writers prefer to use *who* when the relative pronoun points to a human being. However, because *who* also can begin a nonrestrictive relative clause, the lack of a comma—and not the pronoun—in Sentences (40) and (41) from *Small Faces* tells us that the relative clauses are restrictive:

40. I joined him and his friends <u>*who* were hunched in old trench coats</u>.

41. I first stole a toy car from the Japanese kid on our block <u>*who* had everything</u>.

In Sentence (42) from Amy Tan's novel *The Kitchen God's Wife*, the relative pronoun *who* begins a relative clause that is set off by commas, and this punctuation indicates that the clause is nonrestrictive:

42. And my mother, <u>*who* was with her at the time</u>, had taken her to the hospital.

Sentence (42) requires the relative clause to be nonrestrictive; since a person has only one mother, it makes no sense to talk about *my mother who was with her at the time*. That phrase implies that the narrator has *another* mother who was *not* there.

In some sentences, the choice between the restrictive and nonrestrictive clause depends upon the writer's point of view. Sentence (43a) from *The Kitchen God's Wife* has a nonrestrictive relative clause:

43a. She was a typical Nanking girl, <u>who had caught a "lightning marriage."</u>

This relative clause implies that the subject of the sentence (*she*) was a typical Nanking girl *and* that she happened to catch a "lightning marriage." If the comma were omitted as it is in Sentence (43b), however, the writer would imply that the subject of the sentence was typical, not of the class of Nanking girls in general, but of those Nanking girls who make such a marriage:

43b. She was a typical Nanking girl <u>who had caught a "lightning marriage."</u>

Sentences may include more than one relative clause. Sentence (44), for example, has three restrictive relative clauses. The relative pronoun for *adults* is *who*, whereas the relative pronoun for *small pay raises* and for *shoes or feathery hats* is *that*. Can you find the beginnings and ends of the relative clauses in (44)? [Hint: one of them includes the other two.]

44. We lose that child of the heart by becoming adults *who* compromise their dreams for jobs, for grades, for small pay raises *that* may buy pants or skirts, shoes or feathery hats *that* cover up the shame.

The relative clauses you have studied in Sentences (36) through (44) all have pronouns that serve as subjects of the relative clause. It is also possible for a relative pronoun to serve as an object in a relative clause. However, there is a special rule that applies to restrictive relative clauses only: When a restrictive relative clause has a relative pronoun that is an *object* in the relative clause, the relative pronoun may be left out entirely, as it is in Sentences (45) and (46). You will see that there is no relative pronoun present in the underlined restrictive relative clauses, though it is possible to insert the word *that* immediately in front of the underlined material. Under each sentence is the implied meaning of the relative clause:

45. We bit into sandwiches, slurped soup, and talked about the secrets <u>we kept from our better halves</u>. [compare: *the secrets that we kept*]
     (We kept secrets from our better halves.)

46. The second thing <u>I stole</u> was a box of maggots—or were they silkworms? [compare: *the second thing that I stole*]
     (I stole a second thing.)

Exercise 4.5

Underline each of the relative clauses you find in the sentences below. Then put a double line under the noun or noun phrase it modifies. In the space below the sentence, write whether the relative clause is restrictive or nonrestrictive. These sentences come from *The Kitchen God's Wife*.

1. And then there's my cousin Bao-bao, whose real name is Roger.

2. At the front of the shop, the only place that gets filtered daylight for a few hours a day, are her "long-lasting bargains."

3. My mother is groping for the piece of string that snaps on the light.

4. Phil offers my mother a good-night kiss, which she cautiously accepts with a stiff upturned cheek.

5. I ran down Columbus, toward the bay, ignoring the tourists who stared at my angry, tear-streaked face.

6. And now I remember the care package my mother gave us.

7. And we have a kind of loyalty that has no word in this country.

8. In my mind, I can still see that steep tunnel of stairs that wound down one floor after another.

9. The servant who brought me my food said nothing.

10. I walked up to Old Aunt, who had arrived that day, and she said, "Don't talk about this anymore."

11. You should have seen Peanut! She huffed like this—hnh! hnh! hnh!—looking as mad as a queen whose servants had run off with her sedan.

12. And Wen Fu's mother, who never liked this servant in the first place, soon came to an angry conclusion.

Relative Clauses That Add Details of Place and Time

When a relative clause is used to describe or limit a noun referring to a place or a time, the function word *where* (for place) or *when* (for time) is used as a relative pronoun. Sentences (47) and (48), from *The Kitchen God's Wife*, demonstrate how *where* is used in both restrictive (47) and nonrestrictive (48) cases. The relative clauses are underlined, with the relative pronouns in italics:

47. That day we also went to all the places <u>*where* the best things in the world could be found.</u>

48. My mother had used the money donated by the First Chinese Baptist Church, <u>*where* my father had served as an assistant pastor.</u>

Sentences (49) and (50) provide examples of restrictive (49) and nonrestrictive (50) relative clauses with *when* as the relative pronoun:

49. The New Year was a time <u>*when* you could change your luck.</u>

50. That was in 1911, <u>*when* my mother was just twenty-one years old.</u>

Exercise 4.6

Underline each of the relative clauses modifying words of place or time in the sentences below. Then put a double line under the noun or noun phrase it modifies. In the space below the sentence, write whether the relative clause is restrictive or nonrestrictive. These sentences come from Amy Tan's novel *The Kitchen God's Wife*.

1. And then we went to Little East Gate, where all the best seafood vendors put up their stands.

2. Lu had been born in Shandong, that place up north of Shanghai where all the good seafood swim.

3. One day, when I was nine or ten, I found a painting of a pretty woman, wearing a plain blue dress, her hair pulled back, looking straight ahead.

4. And later I found a secret place in the greenhouse where Peanut could put on her makeup.

5. She lived in the Japanese section, where buildings curved around corners just like the long body of a dragon.

ADVERBIAL MODIFIERS

In Chapter 3, you learned about adverbials, the words and phrases that do the work of adverbs but may include no adverbs at all. In general, adverbials modify verbs or verb phrases, or entire predicate phrases by supplying details of time, location, direction, purpose, cause, extent, condition, and concession. We have already seen how prepositional phrases can do some of this work. In this chapter, you will learn about adverbial subordinate clauses and adverbial infinitive phrases.

Adverbial Subordinate Clauses

An adverbial subordinate clause is typically easy to recognize because it begins with one of a very small set of function words known as **subordinating conjunctions.** These words can be classified according to the meaning relationship they indicate between the subordinate and main clauses. Table 4.2 provides a list of the most common subordinating conjunctions, the meaning relationships they show, and sentences illustrating their use.

An adverbial subordinate clause specifies a relationship of time, cause, condition, concession, or purpose between the main and subordinate clauses. Like most adverbials, an adverbial subordinate clause can appear at the end or at the beginning of the sentence, usually just before the subject. When an adverbial clause begins a sentence, it is typically set off from the rest of the sentence by a comma; when it occurs at the end, a comma is sometimes used but usually is not necessary.

Table 4.2. Common Subordinating Conjunctions

Meaning	Meaning Relationship Between Clauses	Subordinating Conjunction	Example Sentences (*The Kitchen God's Wife*)
Time	subordinate clause event is simultaneous to or close in time to event of main clause	*when*	<u>When he finally woke up</u>, Wen Fu was fussy and weak. I was ladling out bowls of boiled dumplings <u>when Wen Fu approached me</u>.
	event of subordinate clause is simultaneous to main clause event	*while*	And Gan, the shy man who liked my dumplings so much, played chicken-feather ball with me, <u>while Wen Fu and the others played cards or mah jong in the evening</u>.
	events of subordinate and main clauses are simultaneous or overlapping; the subordinate clause is not a state	*as*	<u>As we left the city</u>, we passed Sorrowfree Lake. We all listened <u>as Old Aunt took a little piece of truth and stretched it in all directions</u>. (Continued on page 100)

Table 4.2. (Continued)

Meaning	Meaning Relationship Between Clauses	Subordinating Conjunction	Example Sentences (*The Kitchen God's Wife*)
Time	main clause event precedes or precludes subordinate clause event	before	Before he could continue, the nurse interrupted him. This will make her hurry before she forgets.
	main clause event follows subordinate clause event	after	After everyone left, I examined Danru's small sleeping face.
	subordinate clause event ends main clause event	until	That last night at the hotel, we talked for many hours, until our eyes could not stay open.
Cause	subordinate event causes main clause event or the subordinate clause provides evidence for statement in main clause	because, since	Because I did not know my father's house that well, I did not notice any other changes, the ones that were later pointed out to me. Wen Fu must have seen my thoughts with his bad eye, because right then

Table 4.2. (Continued)

Meaning	Meaning Relationship Between Clauses	Subordinating Conjunction	Example Sentences (*The Kitchen God's Wife*)
Cause			he reached over and slapped me. "Aiyi," I said, using the polite name for "Auntie," since I did not know this servant's position in the house.
Condition	subordinate clause provides condition under which main clause is possible	*if*	If he married the girl, they would cut him off.
	"if not"	*unless*	How can you blame a person for his fears and weaknesses unless you have felt the same and done differently?
Concession	subordinate clause concedes the point of the main clause but offers some apparently contradictory information; provides contrast	*though, although, even though*	And so no one had used that room in all those years, even though the house was filled with many people. (Continued on page 102)

Table 4.2. (Continued)

Meaning	Meaning Relationship Between Clauses	Subordinating Conjunction	Example Sentences (*The Kitchen God's Wife*)
Concession			And the American advisors did not have their wives or girlfriends with them, <u>although sometimes they brought a bad local girl to their rooms</u>.
Purpose	subordinate clause gives the purpose for the event of the main clause; it implies that the behavior of the main clause was intentional	*so that*	The drawers were lined with cedar, <u>so that the moment you opened them, a good scent flew out</u>.

Exercise 4.7

Underline the adverbial subordinate clause in each of the following sentences from *The Kitchen God's Wife*. In the space below each sentence, write the general meaning relationship that holds between the subordinate and main clause (time, cause, condition, concession, or purpose).

1. All the women in the monastery noticed one another, because there were only six of us.

2. After Gan told me this story, he was trembling hard.

3. When she opened her mouth and cried, I cried too.

4. After the nurse left, I thought about this question she had asked.

5. I turned down an alley, because that was faster.

6. When my senses came together, I was lying with my face to the ground.

7. Just as we reached the place where the bombs fell, the rain started.

8. After we ate, we exchanged addresses.

9. Before we left, Hulan and I held hands.

10. She looked more like someone who cleaned things when no one was looking.

11. When the servant opened the door, she screamed then fainted.

12. Before I married, I had come from a poor family.

13. Because he was Wen Fu's boss, the vice-captain, he was certainly more powerful.

14. Little Yu's mother was still cooking when we went downstairs.

15. The airplane noise became louder, until they were over our backs, roaring like elephants.

16. Hulan's hands were shaking as she held my shoulders.

17. After more money was exchanged, the woman wrote Peanut's name on a piece of red paper, along with her birthdate and the date of the fortune.

18. She knew people in Tientsin, good people who could hide me until I got my divorce.

19.   Old Aunt had kicked them out of the sitting room, because they had been smoking cigars.

20.   And Yau grew more and more dazed with love for this girl, even though she was already his wife.

When *in a Relative Clause vs.* When *in an Adverbial Clause*

You may have noticed that you have learned about two different kinds of clauses that begin with *when*. The first type was the *when* relative clause modifying nouns of time. The second type was the adverbial clause of time, which you learned could appear at the beginning or the end of the sentence. This freedom of position can help you tell the two kinds of clauses apart, since only adverbial clauses are "movable" in this way. A relative clause that begins with *when* must follow the noun it modifies.

In Table 4.2, you found the following sentences:

51a.   When he finally woke up, Wen Fu was fussy and weak.

52a.   I was ladling out bowls of boiled dumplings when Wen Fu approached me.

We can reposition the *when* clauses in both sentences, with the result being completely acceptable:

51b.   Wen Fu was fussy and weak when he finally woke up.

52b.   When Wen Fu approached me, I was ladling out bowls of boiled dumplings.

However, the result is not so good when we move the relative *when* clause of Sentence (49), repeated below as Sentence (53a):

53a.   The New Year was a time when you could change your luck.

53b.   *When you could change your luck, the New Year was a time.

Sentence (53b), if it means anything at all, certainly isn't a rephrasing of (53a). As you can see, moving an adverbial clause from the end to the beginning of a sentence or vice versa does not affect the meaning or the acceptability of the sentence, but moving a relative clause away from its noun results in gibberish.

Adverbial Infinitive Phrases

In addition to adverbial subordinate clauses, we can add details to predicate phrases with infinitive phrases. An infinitive phrase usually begins with the function word *to*, followed by a verb in the infinitive form and any objects and adverbials that complete the verb. Essentially, an infinitive phrase is a predicate phrase without a subject and without an indicator of tense; its verb is the infinitive form. The underlined phrase in Sentence (54), from *Zelda*, a biography of Zelda Fitzgerald by Nancy Mitford, is an example of an infinitive phrase:

> **54.** Her skirts, which were rolled at the waist <u>to shorten them,</u> were uneven, and her slip usually showed.

The infinitive phrase in (54) serves to modify the verb phrase of the relative clause *which were rolled at the waist to shorten them*. It is an adverbial that expresses the purpose for which the skirts were rolled.

Sometimes an adverbial infinitive phrase that expresses purpose begins with *in order*. Sentence (55), from Stephen King's suspense novel *Pet Sematary*,[1] has an infinitive phrase of this type:

> **55.** Looking the other way, he could see the tops of the fir trees they had come through <u>in order to reach the steps.</u>

Exercise 4.8

Underline the adverbial infinitive phrases in the sentences below. Be careful not to mistake a prepositional phrase beginning with *to* for an infinitive phrase; remember that infinitive phrases have infinitive

---

[1] The word *cemetery* is purposely misspelled in the title, which refers to a sign written by young children and posted in an old graveyard.

verbs following *to*, and not a noun or noun phrase. Sentences 1–7 are taken from Nora Ephron's novel *Heartburn*; sentences 8–10 come from Edith Wharton's *The Age of Innocence*.

1. Two days later, the tobacco lobby rented the grand ballroom of the Washington Hilton to celebrate his ouster.

2. A week later, she checked out of the hospital, filed for divorce, and went to New Mexico to find God.

3. We all have stories like that, stories we rely on to establish our charm in the beginning of relationships.

4. Every so often I would fly to New York for one thing or another, and would go by to see Vera.

5. I turned to look behind me.

6. A few days after Mr. Abbey's body was discovered, Homicide Detective Hartman came back to take another crack at my subconscious.

7. Mark deserted me the minute we got to the terminal at La Guardia and went off to buy magazines and newspapers.

8. He and Mrs. Welland and May drove out to old Mrs. Manson Mingott's to receive that venerable ancestress's blessing.

9. She had returned the previous year from a long sojourn in Europe to lay siege to the tight little citadel of New York.

10. She always gave her ball on an Opera night in order to emphasize her complete superiority to household care.

AVOIDING FRAGMENTS

Whenever any of the modifiers discussed in this chapter is written as a separate sentence detached from the noun phrase or predicate phrase it modifies, the result is a writing "fault" called the **fragment**. In speech, and in casual, informal writing, fragments are commonplace and acceptable. In formal writing assignments, such as reports, term papers, letters of application, and the like, fragments should be avoided.

The following passage is taken from an essay by Robert Fulghum included in *All I Really Need to Know I Learned in Kindergarten*. To give a conversational tone to the piece, Fulghum uses a number of fragments, which I have underlined:

56. This is my neighbor. <u>Nice lady. Coming out her front door, on her way to work and in her "looking good" mode.</u> She's locking the door now and picking up her daily luggage: purse, lunch bag, gym bag for aerobics, and the garbage bucket to take out. She turns, sees me, gives me the big, smiling hello, takes three steps across her front porch. <u>And goes "AAAAAAAAAGGGGGGGGGGHHHHHHHHHH!!!"</u> (*That's a direct quote.*) <u>At about the level of a fire engine at full cry.</u> She has walked full force into a spider web.

The partial noun phrase *nice lady* (it is missing an article) is an appositive to *my neighbor*, and *coming out her front door, on her way to work and in her "looking good" mode* is a participle phrase connected to two prepositional phrases. These modifiers could be attached to *nice lady*, which they describe. *And goes "AAAAAAAAAGGGGGGGGGGHHHHHHHHHH!!!"* is a predicate phrase without a subject. *At about the level of a fire engine at full cry* is a prepositional phrase describing the previous fragment. Fulghum uses these devices to good effect in his essay, but if he were writing a formal report, this style would not be acceptable. He would have to connect the modifiers to what they modify, and make certain that every sentence has a subject.

Exercise 4.9

 Here's a little experiment for you to try. Take the paragraph pre-sented in (56) above and rewrite it to eliminate the fragments. Be certain not to change the meaning in any way.

SUMMARY

In this chapter, you have studied several ways of adding details to sen-tences by using modifiers that follow nouns and noun phrases, or that extend the predicate phrase. You have learned about two kinds of sub-ordinate clauses, the relative clause and the adverbial clause. In Chapter 5, you will explore further the use of subordination in English sentences.

Projects for Chapter Four

1. In the Projects for Chapter 1, you were asked to write a description of a member of your family or of a friend. Look at the paragraph(s) you wrote and find and underline every appositive, relative clause, participle phrase, adverbial clause, and infinitive phrase you have written. If you find that you do not have some of these constructions, rewrite the paper to include at least one example of each. After you are finished, underline the modifiers and identify them by name.

2. Here is another passage from *All I Really Need to Know I Learned in Kindergarten*. Underline every fragment you find, identify it by type, and then rewrite the passage so that it no longer has any fragments.

Always wanted a cuckoo clock. A big baroque German job with all kinds of carved foobaz and a little bird that leaps out once an hour and hollers an existential comment about life. So I got one. For my best friend, who also happens to be my wife and lives in the same house with me.

3. The following terms appeared in this chapter. Be sure you are familiar with all of them. Use the index and/or the glossary in the back of this book to help you.

appositive	relative clause
fragment	relative pronoun
infinitive phrase	restrictive modifier
main clause	subordinating conjunction
nonrestrictive modifier	subordinate clause
participle phrase	

Content Clauses
and Verbals

Among the modifiers you studied in Chapter 4 were participle and infinitive phrases and relative and adverbial subordinate clauses. In Chapter 5, you will learn about content clauses, another type of subordinate clause, and about additional functions of participle and infinitive phrases. In this chapter, you will explore their use not as modifiers but as major elements within the sentence—as subjects, objects, and complements.

CONTENT CLAUSES

In Chapter 3, you learned about subjects, direct objects, and complements of basic sentences. All the subjects and objects you examined were nouns, pronouns, or noun phrases, as were many complements of linking verbs. However, entire subordinate clauses having their own subjects, objects, and complements also may serve as subjects, objects, and complements in other sentences. We call such subordinate clauses **content clauses.**

A content clause looks very much like an ordinary declarative sentence, but frequently it begins with the function word *that* appearing just before the subordinate clause subject. For example, Sentence (1), from Stephen King's novel *Pet Sematary*, includes a content clause (underlined) as direct object of the verb *knew:*

1. As a doctor, he knew <u>that death was, except perhaps for childbirth, the most natural thing in the world</u>.

The content clause in (1) could be a sentence in its own right, so long as the word *that* does not appear at the beginning, as in Sentence (2):

2. Death was, except perhaps for childbirth, the most natural thing in the world.

Content Clauses as Direct Objects

The most common function served by a content clause is direct object. Only a small set of verbs can take content clauses as objects. A partial list of these verbs appears in Table 5.1. In general, these verbs express acts of thinking or speaking, such as *know* in Sentence (1) or *say* in Sentence (3):

3. Joan Charlton followed them, saying <u>that the campus police were on their way</u>.

Quite commonly, the function word *that* is left off from content clauses that serve as direct objects. The underlined content clauses in Sentences (4) through (8) appear without *that;* a double underline indicates the verb to which each serves as object:

4. Louis <u><u>thought</u></u> <u>he had just heard the quintessential Yankee understatement</u>.

5. He <u><u>supposed</u></u> <u>she would get over it</u>.

6. Jud looked at him, and for a moment Louis <u><u>thought</u></u> <u>he saw something bright and not completely pleasant in the old man's eyes</u>.

7. For a moment Louis <u><u>wished</u></u> desperately <u>he could see the old man's face again</u>.

8. I <u><u>know</u></u> <u>you were thinking about Gage</u>.

Table 5.1. Common Verbs Taking Content Clauses as Direct Objects

Verbs of Mental and Emotional Experience		Verbs of Speaking	
assume	*learn*	*add*	*joke*
believe	*mean*	*admit*	*maintain*
conclude	*notice*	*agree*	*mention*
consider	*ponder*	*announce*	*object*
decide	*pretend*	*argue*	*persuade*
discover	*prove*	*ask*	*pray*
doubt	*realize*	*bet*	*predict*
dream	*recall*	*boast*	*promise*
fear	*recognize*	*claim*	*protest*
feel	*remember*	*comment*	*remark*
find	*see*	*complain*	*reply*
forget	*sense*	*concede*	*report*
guess	*show*	*contend*	*say*
hear	*suppose*	*declare*	*state*
hope	*suspect*	*deny*	*suggest*
imagine	*think*	*exclaim*	*swear*
intend	*understand*	*explain*	*tell*
judge	*wish*	*hint*	*warn*
know	*wonder*	*insist*	*write*

Sometimes a subordinate clause may include yet another subordinate clause. For example, the content clause in Sentence (9) includes an adverbial subordinate clause (*until his body blew apart under their soft yet implacable pressure*) that modifies the verb phrase of the content clause, *would grow:*

9. The horror, the terror—he <u>felt</u> <u>these things would grow</u>
   <u>in him until his body blew apart under their soft yet</u>
   <u>implacable pressure</u>.

The content clause in (10) includes a restrictive relative clause (*who had more potential than Louis Creed*) that modifies the noun phrase in the content clause, *bums in the gutter:*

10. Goldman <u>said</u> <u>he had seen bums in the gutter who had more potential than Louis Creed</u>.

Some verbs of speaking that take content clauses as direct objects also take an indirect object. The indirect object of such a verb is a noun, noun phrase, or pronoun. In Sentence (11), the verb is underlined twice, the indirect object is given in parentheses, and the direct object—a content clause—is underlined once:

11. The look <u>told</u> (him) <u>that the chill was over</u>.

When the verb that takes a content clause as a direct object expresses asking (a kind of speaking), the content clause may take a special form. Usually it begins with *what, who, if,* or *whether,* thus showing that a question is involved, and the verb may take an indirect object as well, as it does in Sentence (12), but it does not always do so, as Sentence (13) shows:

12. The next morning at breakfast, Ellie saw the new memo on the bulletin board and <u>asked</u> (him) <u>what it meant</u>.

13. The editor of the campus newspaper <u>asked</u> <u>if he could say that Pascow had died of head injuries</u>.

The verb *wonder* is similar to *ask;* when one wonders, one asks oneself. Like *ask, wonder* may take as direct object the special form of content clause you have just seen in Sentences (12) and (13). Unlike *ask, wonder* does not take an indirect object:

14. Louis <u>wondered</u> briefly <u>if Pascow had just ceased to exist</u>.

Exercise 5.1

Each of the following sentences from *Pet Sematary* has a content clause that is a direct object of a verb of thinking or speaking. Underline the content clause once and put a double line under the verb or verb phrase to which it serves as direct object.

1. In the dim light Louis thought the old man looked a hundred and twenty.

2. Louis guessed that the writing on these [gravemarkers] might have been done with chalk or crayon.

3. I'd guess that most men tell their wives a smart of lies.

4. For one moment Louis thought [Jud] had been struck by a sudden pain.

5. Ellie cast a strange, vulnerable glance back over her shoulder, as if to ask them if there might not yet be time to abort this inevitable process.

6. He supposed that even if none of those terrible things had happened, he would have remembered the day forever.

7. After a winter in Maine, most of it in Ludlow, he thought that she needed all the getting out she could lay her hands on.

8. Louis saw that there were no tears in his father-in-law's eyes.

9. Now, as Louis passed the East Room on his way out, he saw that the room was almost empty.

10. By the time Louis had finished three beers, he felt that he had some sort of equilibrium for the first time that day.

11. I don't believe that there's anything new under the sun.

12. And he felt that in truth he was walking along a narrow beam over a gulf of insanity.

13. Suddenly the mist lost its light and Louis realized that a face was hanging in the air ahead of him, leering and gibbering.

14. And in these dreams he would sense that something huge had shrugged by him.

15. He wondered if he had always been within touching distance of such mad irrationalities.

Content Clauses as Indirect Speech

Because content clauses often serve as direct objects to verbs of speaking, they are related to directly quoted speech. Certain content clauses are simply indirect versions of something spoken in a conversation. The indirectness expressed in a content clause allows the writer to present the gist of what was said without having to provide exact words. For example, Sentence (15), from the biography *Zelda*, by Nancy Mitford, reports a statement attributed to Zelda Fitzgerald:

15. Zelda said of herself that she cared for two things: boys and swimming.

We can imagine Zelda saying something like Sentence (16):

16. All I care about is boys and swimming.

If she had chosen to do so—perhaps if she were certain about Zelda's exact words—Mitford could have used direct quotation, such as that in Sentence (17):

17. "All I care about is boys and swimming," said Zelda.

Reported speech presented in content clauses often involves a change of tense and a change in pronouns from the original statement. For example, the following passage from Mona Simpson's novel *Anywhere But Here* includes direct quotation with words (in boldface) that would change in an indirect version:

18. My mother sighed. Whenever my grandmother asked her questions, she sighed and she slumped back into her chair. "Well, Mom, **I don't** like that drive out there every day in **my** old car with the window that **doesn't** roll up."

It is entirely possible to present the quoted dialogue in (18) as indirect speech. It might be given as Sentence (19):

19. She told her mother that **she didn't** like the drive in **her** old car with the window that **didn't** roll up.

When an indirect statement is the direct object of a verb such as *ask*, which takes a content clause of the question form, the content clause does *not* show the subject-auxiliary inversion of the ordinary question. In Sentences (12) and (13), repeated below as (20) and (21), the verb follows the subject, as in an ordinary declarative sentence:

20. The next morning at breakfast, Ellie saw the new memo on the bulletin board and <u>asked</u> (him) <u>what it meant</u>.
(Compare: What did it mean?)

21. The editor of the campus newspaper <u>asked</u> <u>if he could say that Pascow had died of head injuries</u>.
(Compare: Could he say that Pascow had died of head injuries?)

Exercise 5.2

Each of the following sentences from *Anywhere But Here* includes direct quotation. Rewrite each sentence so that a content clause replaces the quoted speech.

1. "We paid seven dollars for that," I said, when I sat down in the car.

2. "I'm just going to cancel," my mother said.

3. "What does your father do for a living?" the taller girl said, her hand on my arm.

4. "You know, you're cuter than Buff," she whispered, looking down hard.

5. "Should I give Peter your coat, Mom?" I whispered.

Content Clauses as Subjects

In addition to serving as a direct object, a content clause may serve as the subject of a sentence. A content clause that is a subject is found in Sentence (22), from *Pet Sematary*:

22. <u>That such events have their own Rube Goldberg absurdity</u> goes almost without saying.

However, it is far more usual to find subject content clauses *at the ends of sentences*. When a content clause that is a subject appears at the end of the sentence, the pronoun *it* takes its place at the beginning, as in Sentences (23a) and (24a):

23a. It occurred to her <u>that she had also been nervous all day</u>. (Compare: That she had also been nervous all day occurred to her.)

24a. It was pretty clear <u>that he had backed her into a corner</u>. (Compare: That he had backed her into a corner was pretty clear.)

The pronoun *it* serves as a substitute subject, and so it behaves as though it were a subject in a yes/no question, for example, where it falls between the auxiliary and the main verb (Sentence 23b) or between the *be* verb and its complement (Sentence 24b):

23b. Did **it** occur to her <u>that she had also been nervous all day</u>?

24b. Was **it** pretty clear <u>that he had backed her into a corner</u>?

Some subject content clauses *must* appear at the end of the sentence. In Sentence (25), the verb *seemed* requires the content clause that serves as its subject to appear at the end:

25. It seemed <u>that a great deal more time had gone by</u>.

The verb *seem* will not allow otherwise, as Sentence (26) demonstrates:

26. *<u>That a great deal more time had gone by</u> seemed.

Content Clauses as Complements

In addition to serving as subjects and objects, content clauses may appear as complements to a linking verb. In Chapter 3, we learned that a complement describes or identifies the subject, and this is exactly what the complement content clause does. The content clauses of (27) and (28), underlined once, identify the subjects of those sentences, underlined twice; the verb of each of these sentences from *Pet Sematary* is *was,* a past tense form of the verb *be:*

27. <u>The main reason he had turned down Steve's offer</u> was <u>that he was a mass of aches and pains.</u>

28. <u>His first thought</u> was <u>that Rachel had been right.</u>

Exercise 5.3

The following sentences from *Pet Sematary* all contain content clauses. Underline each content clause you find, and in the space below the sentence, write whether the clause is a subject, an object, or a complement.

1. Later, Louis would reflect that horses must feel much the same free-floating anxiety when they smell the first smoke of a prairie fire.

2. Tomorrow he would mention casually that he hadn't seen Church around.

3. The day after he would suggest that perhaps Church had wandered off.

4. He felt that he was in his place.

5. It occurred to him that this was very much like a dream.

6. His first guess was that this had not been a grave seizure.

7. It had also occurred to him that the whole adventure had been dangerous.

8. It might be that there was less than a month of really good [days] in any natural man's life in the best of circumstances.

9. Steve saw that Louis had gone insane.

10. I don't think children ever forget the lies their parents tell them.

VERBALS

In Chapter 4, you studied the infinitive phrases and participle phrases that serve as modifiers. However, the present participle phrase and the infinitive phrase also can assume the important grammatical roles of subject, direct object, and complement, and the present participle phrase can serve as the object of a preposition. That is, much like content clauses, they take the roles that are assumed by nouns and noun phrases in basic sentences. Because they fit into the functions typically served by noun phrases, participles and infinitives serving these functions are sometimes called verbal nouns. The modifier *verbal* tells us that though the participle or the infinitive is the chief element in a phrase that may function as a noun phrase, it retains its identity as a verb by taking an object, a complement, and an adverbial. In this chapter, we will call such infinitive phrases and participle phrases **verbals**.

Verbals are predicate phrases that lack tense, though they may express aspect and voice. In particular, present participle phrases express progressive aspect, and infinitive phrases may express passive voice (for example, *to be abandoned*). Some infinitive phrases may express perfect aspect (for example *to have wished*). In the following sections, you will study first verbals serving as direct objects, followed by verbals in the subject function. Finally, you will investigate the use of participle phrases as objects of prepositions.

Verbals as Direct Objects

Like content clauses, both infinitive phrases and participle phrases may serve as direct objects. Many of the verbs that allow infinitive phrases as objects also allow participle phrases, with a slight meaning difference. An infinitive phrase tends to imply merely that the act in question was potentially possible, whereas the participle tends to imply that the act actually happened to some extent.

The Infinitive Phrase as Direct Object

Like content clauses, infinitive phrases commonly appear as direct objects, sometimes in sentences that have certain verbs of mental experience or speaking, though only a small number of the verbs in Table 5.1 take infinitive phrases as objects. Perhaps more importantly, infinitive phrases tend to serve as direct objects of verbs that have no content of their own but instead express whether the action of the infinitive verb is beginning (*begin, start*), in progress (*continue*), or finishing (*cease*), or involves effort (*try, manage, attempt*). Sentences (29) to (33), from Nora Ephron's novel *Heartburn*, have verbs (underlined twice) that take infinitive clauses (underlined once) as direct objects:

29. Julie Siegel and I managed to wangle the recipe from the proprietor of a restaurant in Rome.

30. I tried not to cry.

31. And I had long since ceased to believe in the existence of that mystical sisterly loyalty.

32. I tried to see through a crack below a drawn window shade.

33. I attempted to follow the budget debate.

Other verbs, such as *want* and *need*, also may take infinitive phrases as objects:

34. I don't want to string this part out.

35. You don't really need to hear a blow-by-blow account.

Participle Phrases as Direct Objects

Some verbs that take participle phrases as objects also express whether the action of the participle verb is beginning (*begin, start*), or finishing (*finish, stop*), or in progress (*continue, keep*), or involves effort (*try, attempt*). Sentences (36) to (41) from *Heartburn* provide examples of participle phrases serving as direct objects, underlined once; the verbs they serve as objects are underlined twice:

36. I <u>started</u> <u>crying again</u>.

37. Jonathan put his arms around me and <u>began</u> <u>muttering</u> <u>something about how the economy was in bad shape too</u>.

38. I <u>finished</u> <u>being interviewed by Detective Nolan</u>.

39. I <u>couldn't stop</u> <u>shaking my head</u>.

40. We were lucky. I <u>kept</u> <u>telling myself that</u>.

41. Anyway, just <u>try</u> <u>flying the Eastern shuttle with a baby</u>.

However, these parallels between participle phrases and infinitive phrases are limited. Though some verbs can take either a participle or an infinitive phrase as direct object, many that take participles cannot take infinitives, and a few that take infinitives cannot take participles. (See Table 5.2.) *Continue*, for example, can take either an infinitive phrase (Sentence 42a) or a participle phrase (Sentence 42b) as a direct object:

42a. He <u>continued</u> <u>to talk loudly</u>.

42b. He <u>continued</u> <u>talking loudly</u>.

But *keep*, which also indicates that an activity continues, cannot take an infinitive (43a), although a participle phrase is fine (Sentence 43b):

43a. *He <u>kept</u> <u>to talk loudly</u>.

43b. He <u>kept</u> <u>talking loudly</u>.

The verbs *begin*, *start*, and *cease* take both infinitive and participle phrases as direct objects, but the verbs *finish* and *stop* take only participle phrases. However, whereas it is impossible for *finish* to be followed by an infinitive (44a), *stop* can be followed by an infinitive (Sentence 44b), but the meaning of the sentence is different from what we might expect from the pattern of the other verbs:

44a. *He finished to drink his milk.

44b. He stopped to drink his milk.
    (= He stopped *in order* to drink his milk.)

Table 5.2. Verbs Taking Infinitive and Participle Phrases

Verb Type	Takes Infinitive Phrase as Direct Object	Takes Participle Phrase as Direct Object
Beginning	begin start	begin start
Midpoint	continue	continue keep resume
Endpoint	cease	cease finish quit stop
Difficulty	attempt try manage (implies success)	try

When *stop* is followed by an infinitive phrase, the sentence does not mean that the activity of the infinitive phrase stops, but rather that another activity—not mentioned in the sentence—stops so that the activity of the infinitive phrase can begin. Sentence (44b) means only that the subject of the sentence stopped some activity *in order to drink his milk*. It cannot mean *he stopped drinking his milk*. The infinitive phrase in (44b) is an adverbial (see Chapter 4 to review) and not a direct object.

Another contrast in usage occurs with the verbs *enjoy* and *like*, which are similar in meaning. While *like* can take both infinitive and participle objects, *enjoy* can take only a participle:

45. Normally I <u>enjoy</u> <u>doing food demonstrations</u>—I <u>like</u> <u>giving</u> <u>my speech</u>. [from *Heartburn*]
(Compare: *I enjoy *to do food demonstrations—I like to give my speech.*)

Exercise 5.4

Each of the following sentences from Nora Ephron's novel *Heartburn* contains a verbal as a direct object, either as an infinitive phrase or a participle phrase. Find the verbal, underline it, and then put a double line under the verb or verb phrase to which it serves as object. In the space below the sentence, write whether the verbal is an infinitive phrase or a participle phrase.

1. I kept coming back to that.

2. I never wanted to see him again.

3. Everyone managed to say nice things to me except Diana.

4. I had always meant to write down some of the words.

5. The Secretary of Health, Education and Welfare was preparing to go on the lecture circuit.

6. He said he would stop seeing Thelma.

7. Then she began pasting [plaid stamps] into stamp books.

8. Sam began methodically removing the books from the bookshelves.

9. Mark finished reading to Sam.

10. Maybe you remember reading about it.

Verbals as Subjects

Both infinitive phrases and participle phrases sometimes serve as subjects, as in Sentence (46), where an infinitive phrase is the subject, and in Sentence (47), where a participle phrase has that function:

46. <u>To have your father marry your mortal enemy's older sister</u> is a bit too coincidental for my taste. [from *Heartburn*]

47. Just thinking about the flowers made me want to die. [from *Heartburn*]

As with content clauses, however, an infinitive phrase that is a subject is commonly moved to the end of the sentence, with *it* substituting for the "missing" subject, as in Sentence (48):

48. It [has] never occurred to me to forgo meals. [from *Heartburn*]
     (Compare: To forgo meals has never occurred to me.)

In contrast, when a participle phrase serves as subject, it commonly appears at the beginning of the sentence and not at the end like the infinitive phrase or the content clause. The subject participle phrase of Sentence (49) is underlined:

49. Looking at Church [the cat] made Louis feel sad. [from *Pet Sematary*]

Exercise 5.5

Underline the verbal in these sentences from *Pet Sematary* and *Heartburn* and, in the space below the sentence, write the function of the phrase in the sentence (subject or direct object) and give the verb or verb phrase to which it relates as subject or object. Some sentences have more than one clause, so you may find more than one verbal.

1. He was a young man, age approximately twenty, and it took Louis less than three seconds to make the only diagnosis that mattered.

2. But it was hopeless to resist those eyes.

3. He tried desperately to hold on to the dream idea.

4. Gage began to yell indignantly.

5. It took a good deal longer than seven minutes to shut the machine down that night.

6. The nasty death of Victor Pascow on the first day of the fall semester began to fade in the memory of the student body and in Louis's own.

7. Looking at her made his heart ache.

8. Goldman told him to get out.

9. I started to scream because I knew she was dead.

10. He did not want to be seen at all.

11. It took another ten minutes to pile up the rocks Jud handed him one by one.

12. Having a baby had changed our lives together.

13. Accepting that answer meant accepting that I would never really know what had happened.

14. I might consider coming back under certain circumstances.

15. I remember thinking that no one had ever told me how much I would love my child.

Participle Phrases as Objects of Prepositions

Though an infinitive phrase cannot serve as an object of a preposition, this function is a common one for the participle phrase. Sentence (50) from *Heartburn* has a participle phrase as the object of the preposition *by*, and Sentence (51) has a participle phrase as the object of the preposition *for*:

50. Mark, on the other hand, changes his stories every time he tells them, by <u>making them longer</u>.

51. The next day, their daughter was suspended from school for <u>flushing six gerbils down the lavatory toilet</u>.

Exercise 5.6

 Each of the following sentences from *Heartburn* has a participle phrase that is the object of a preposition. Underline the participle phrase and then put a double line under the preposition for which it is the object.

1.   There's a real problem in dragging a group into a book.

2.   He's known for being chronically perverse about politics.

3.   Sometimes the idea of being single interests me.

4.   Perhaps this is Mark's way of being understated.

5.   I accused Mark of looking at houses.

6.   He accused me of snooping in places I didn't belong.

7.   It was always a little mystifying to me how we had gone from having so much money to having so little.

8.   She responds by having all the feelings I'm refusing to have.

9.   I hated her for turning Mark from the man I had fallen in love with into a cold, cruel stranger.

10.   It was hard enough putting a marriage back together without becoming known publicly as a marriage-in-trouble.

SUMMARY

In this chapter, you have learned new ways of expanding basic sentences by using content clauses and verbals as subjects, objects, and complements. Certain verbs, such as verbs of mental experience and speaking, are likely to have content clauses as direct objects. Verbs that specify the beginning, middle, and endpoints of actions are likely to have verbals as direct objects.

Projects for Chapter Five

1. Imagine the following scene: You have not brought your home-
    work to class. Your teacher accepts no late assignments. However,
    you have a good excuse; your dog ate it (really!). Write a dialog
    between you and your teacher (humor is allowed!). Use the form
    found in scripts for plays. The word *Student* appears, followed by
    a colon (:). Then the exact words spoken by the student are
    written. When the teacher responds, the word *Teacher* appears,
    followed by a colon and the teacher's exact words. When you are
    finished, rewrite the whole script using reported speech. You are
    not allowed to use any direct quotations. Vary your verb choice
    as much as possible. Refer to Table 5.1 for help in selecting
    appropriate verbs.

2. Choose ten verbs from Table 5.1. Then write a sentence for each
    in which the verb or verb phrase takes a content clause as a
    direct object. Can you use the same content clause for each verb?
    Why or why not? Write a brief discussion of your findings.

3. Choose five verbs from Table 5.2 that can take either a participle
    phrase or infinitive phrase direct objects, and write two sentences
    for each, once using a participle phrase, and once using an
    infinitive phrase. Do you sense a meaning difference between the
    two sentences? If so, explain in a paragraph or two what that
    meaning difference is.

4. Get a copy of today's newspaper and select an article from it
    involving local, state, or national news. Find the content clauses
    in it and then make a list of all the verbs with which they occur
    as subjects or objects. What do you notice about these verbs?
    Write a brief report detailing your findings.

5. Collect examples of sentences that include present participle
    phrases from a newspaper or magazine. Write them out, under-

line the participle phrases, and give the function of each phrase in its sentence. Some of them may be modifiers. Review Chapter 4 if you need help.

6. Distinguish between a **verbal** and a **content clause.** Write a brief definition of each and provide examples.

Pulling Ideas Together

In Chapter 4, you learned how to add details with modifiers and therefore how to expand the basic sentence. In this chapter, we turn our attention to connecting words, phrases, and clauses within a sentence through **coordination** and to making connections between sentences within a paragraph with conjunctive adverbs.

COORDINATION

Coordination is the process through which two or more words, phrases, or clauses of the same kind are combined into a single but larger phrase or sentence. This process occurs through the use of the **coordinating conjunctions,** a very small set of function words that "glue" these elements together. An acronym (a word made up of the first letters of a set of words) can help you remember exactly which words are coordinating conjunctions: *FANBOYS* (for, and, nor, but, or, yet, so). Table 6.1 lists the coordinating conjunctions, the meaning relationship that each one signals, and the kinds of sentence parts each can combine.

Table 6.1. The Coordinating Conjunctions

Conjunction		Meaning	Types of Sentence Parts Combined
F	*for*	reason, evidence	clauses only
A	*and*	addition, time sequence	words, phrases, clauses
N	*nor*	neither one of two choices	clauses
B	*but*	contrast	words, phrases, clauses
O	*or*	choice	words, phrases, clauses
Y	*yet*	contrast	words, phrases, clauses
S	*so*	result	clauses

Though the acronym *FANBOYS* helps us to remember the conjunctions, it does not tell us which conjunctions are the most important or frequent. In fact, the most common coordinating conjunctions are *and, but, or,* and *so,* and much less common are *for, yet,* and *nor.*

And

And is the most frequent conjunction. It can combine two or more words, phrases, or clauses, so long as the parts it connects are of the same type—a word with a word, a phrase with a phrase, or a clause with a clause. In Sentence (1), from Barbara Kingsolver's novel *Pigs in Heaven, and* joins together two clauses that potentially could stand alone as separate sentences. The conjunction *and* is italicized, and the clauses it connects are underlined. Notice that a comma separates the first clause from the conjunction:

1. Each table has three different kinds of honey in a cloverleaf-shaped container, *and* the busy-bee waitresses wear antennae headbands with bobbling yellow balls on long springs.

Sentence (2) shows that *and* can tie together three potentially independent clauses that could stand as separate sentences. Notice that a comma separates the first clause from the second, another comma follows the second clause, and the word *and* appears only between the second and third clauses:

2. Dellon's long hair is loose, his T-shirt looks like what grasshoppers do to crops, *and* his beefy shoulders seem slumped this morning with the weight of fatherhood. [from *Pigs in Heaven*]

And can also join two or more words or phrases of the same kind. Sentence (3) provides an example of *and* connecting two words that are nouns, *wife* and *husband;* no comma is used when only two words are connected. Notice that the article *a* equally introduces either noun:

3. At a table nearby, a wife *and* husband are having a fight. [from *Pigs in Heaven*]

Finally, *and* may connect two or more phrases, always of the same type. In Sentence (4), the combined noun phrases together serve as the object of the preposition *in*. As with words, no comma separates the first phrase from the conjunction:

4. A big woman in Lycra shorts *and* a tight yellow T-shirt appears, arms open, to envelop Lucky like a starfish. [from *Pigs in Heaven*]

In Sentence (5), *and* connects two predicate phrases that share the single subject *she:*

5. She leaves the bed quietly *and* switches on the lamp in the living room. [from *Pigs in Heaven*]

When three words, phrases, or clauses are connected with *and*, a comma follows each of the first two. In Sentence (6), from James Finn Garner's satire *Politically Correct Bedtime Stories*, two free-standing nouns and a noun phrase are connected, and in Sentence (7), from Bill Cosby's memoir *Childhood*, three predicate phrases are joined; notice that a comma follows each of the first two elements in each sentence:

6. After this ordeal, Red Riding Hood, Grandma, *and* the wolf felt a certain commonality of purpose.

7. I grabbed a piece of bread, soaked it in the spinach, *and* took a delightful bite.

Sentence (8), from Iris Murdoch's novel *A Word Child*, has three clauses connected with *and*. Notice the comma following each of the first two clauses:

8. Again and again <u>the trick failed to work</u>, <u>the briskness turned to severity</u>, *and* <u>the jollity ended in tears</u>.

But

The conjunction *but*, like *and*, may also connect words, phrases, or clauses, but instead of adding ideas together, it signals a contrast between the two sentence parts it joins. In Sentence (9), from Edgar Maass's novel *The Queen's Physician*, *but* connects two adjectives. The use of *but* in (9) suggests that although one would not expect a minor accident to be important, it nonetheless was; it was *fateful:*

9. The Count had returned to his wife and child in Holstein, on the way suffering a <u>minor</u> *but* <u>fateful</u> accident.

But may connect two phrases, and when it does, no comma is necessary. For example, no comma follows the first of two coordinated predicate phrases in Sentence (10), from *Pigs in Heaven:*

10. She <u>heaves the watering can</u> *but* <u>can't tell where it's gone</u>.

However, as with *and*, a comma follows the first of the two independent clauses joined with *but* in Sentence (11):

11. <u>The air isn't any cooler outside the house</u>, *but* <u>being outdoors in her sheer nightgown arouses Alice with the possibility of freedom</u>. [from *Pigs in Heaven*]

Yet

The conjunction *yet* is similar to *but* in expressing a contrast between words, phrases, and clauses, though *yet* is much less common than *but*, both in speaking and in writing. In addition, the conjunction *and* may precede *yet*, though it may never precede *but*. In Sentence (12), from Edgar Allan Poe's short novel *The Fall of the House of Usher*, the words *tempestuous* and *beautiful*—adjectives modifying *night*—are connected:

12. It was, indeed, a <u>tempestuous</u> *yet* <u>beautiful</u> night.

In Sentence (13), from *Zelda*, a biography by Nancy Mitford, two predicate phrases are connected, and no comma is used. In this sentence, two conjunctions together, *and yet*, do the work of connecting, but it is *yet* that expresses the contrast:

13. Suddenly Zelda was crying because things <u>were the same</u> *and yet* <u>were not the same</u>.

Clauses, too, may be connected with *yet*, as in Sentence (14) from *Usher*. As with the other conjunctions you have studied so far, a comma separates the first clause from the conjunction:

14. <u>No torch or other artificial source of light was discernible</u>, *yet* <u>a flood of intense rays rolled throughout</u>.

Just as with phrases, *and* may precede *yet* when it connects two clauses, as it does in Sentence (15) from *Usher:*

15. <u>I regarded her with an utter astonishment not unmingled with dread</u>, *and yet* <u>I found it impossible to account for such feelings</u>.

Or

Or can connect words, phrases, or clauses, providing a choice typically between two alternatives. Sentence (16), from Bill Cosby's book *Fatherhood*, shows *or* connecting two words:

16. Sometimes, at <u>three</u> *or* <u>four</u> in the morning, I open the door to one of the children's bedrooms and watch the light softly fall across their little faces.

Sentence (17), from *Pigs in Heaven*, provides an example of two prepositional phrases connected with *or:*

17. The coyote's belly hangs low <u>with incipient pups</u> *or* <u>with milk</u>.

In Sentence (18), from *A Word Child*, two noun phrases are connected with *or:*

18. Here and there <u>a gaping window</u> *or* <u>a doorless doorway</u>
     proclaimed the abandonment of hope.

Sentence (19), from Poe's *Usher*, shows *or* connecting two clauses.
In this case, just as with clauses connected with *and* or *but*, a comma
follows the first clause:

19. <u>We painted and read together,</u> *or* <u>I listened as if in a dream
     to the wild improvisations of his speaking guitar.</u>

Nor

Nor may only connect two clauses (but see the discussion of *neither
. . . nor* below). When it does, the second clause continues a negative
idea from the first clause, and two important changes occur. The second
clause will omit words that are identical to words in the first clause, and
the second clause has the auxiliary verb first, followed by the subject.
Sentence (20), adapted from *Zelda*, shows all these features. The first
clause has a negative contraction (*didn't*), and the second clause has the
auxiliary before the subject (*did she*) and does not express the word
advice, which is implied:

20. <u>She didn't ask for advice,</u> *nor* <u>did she give any.</u>

That *nor* does not connect words or phrases arises from writers'
preference to use *or* with phrases when the second element serves to
continue a negative idea from the first element, so long as the negative
idea is not expressed by *neither* (see the discussion of *neither . . . nor*
below). In the following examples, though you might expect *nor* to do
the connecting, *or* is used.

21. By the time they arrived, I had met **no** spirit, <u>blithe</u> *or* <u>vile</u>.
     [Tom Sullivan, *If You Could See What I Feel*]

22. His clothes were worn in combinations **never** before <u>seen</u> *or*
     <u>imagined</u>. [James Finn Garner, *Politically Correct Bedtime
     Stories*]

23. He was **not** <u>fussing</u> *or* <u>crying</u> but really screaming, writhing
     in Rachel's arms. [Stephen King, *Pet Sematary*]

So

So typically connects two clauses together. *So* indicates that the event of the second clause is the result of the event of the first clause. Notice that a comma appears after the first clause of Sentence (24) from *Pigs in Heaven:*

24. <u>Harland ordered the Cornucopia Of Bowls from the shopping channel for their wedding anniversary,</u> *so* <u>now their home has a bowl for every purpose.</u>

For

The conjunction *for* has a distinctly literary flavor; we almost never hear it in casual conversation, whereas the conjunctions *and, or, but,* and *so* (but not *yet*) are commonplace. The conjunction *for* should not be confused with the preposition *for.* Though the words are identical, they do not perform the same work. The conjunction *for* connects only entire clauses; the information given in the second clause typically provides the reason or the evidence for the statement in the first. Sentence (25) from *Zelda* provides an example of a clause beginning with *for.* It supplies the reason that the Sayres "usually rented homes":

25. <u>They usually rented homes,</u> *for* <u>Mr. Sayre refused to be in debt, even to the extent of taking on a mortgage.</u>

Exercise 6.1

Circle the conjunction in each of the following sentences from *Zelda.* Then underline what the conjunction connects. Remember that the sentence parts connected by conjunctions must be equal. In the space below, note the kind of sentence parts that are connected. Be as specific as possible (for example, *predicate phrases*).

1. She had a small clear soprano voice, and she played the piano nicely.

2. Madchen learned of his daughter's adventure and was outraged.

3. Minnie returned to Kentucky immediately, but she had suffered a disappointment she never forgot.

4. He worried constantly over their finances, for there were now nine members in his household.

5. He worked relentlessly and well, becoming in his thirties a member of the Alabama House of Representatives.

6. Mrs. Sayre indulged Zelda completely and was charmed by her.

7. World War I would do a little to change the social rigidity, but for the time being it persisted.

8. Her skirts, which were rolled at the waist to shorten them, were uneven, and her slip usually showed.

9. That lack of style must have been something she shared with her mother, for Mrs. Sayre rather than a seamstress made all her clothes.

10. There were chaperones at the dances, but Zelda completely ignored them.

11. Francis Scott Key Fitzgerald was Irish, a Roman Catholic, and a Midwesterner.

12. The Fitzgeralds lived always on the edge of the best neighborhood in St. Paul but never at its center.

13. They settled finally and firmly at the end of the finest street in the area, Summit Avenue.

14. She was absent frequently, and her conduct report sank to "unsatisfactory" in the marking period before graduation.

15. Zelda's release from that world was suddenly within reach, for with the United States' entry into World War I in the summer of 1917 Montgomery altered profoundly.

16. In September, 1917, Zelda began her senior year in a flurry of dances and parties.

17. There was to be no more stopping or talking in the halls.

18. During the summer he wrote and produced a Civil War melodrama called *The Coward.*

19. All of the dances on Zelda's card were taken, but Scott's name was not on it.

20. Her trip had disconcerted him, for while he was trying to break into journalism in New York, his girl was not exactly cooling her heels at home.

21. Zelda was delighted with the ring and told Scott it was beautiful.

22. Whether the timing of their marriage date was Zelda's or Scott's idea is unknown.

23. I haven't the remotest idea of what it's like, so I am afraid to make any suggestions.

24. The first sale to the *Post* was important to Scott, for he intended to make money, a lot of it.

25. He knew that the smaller magazines or the more literary ones couldn't be expected to pay as the *Post* would.

Exercise 6.2

The following sentences come from *Devil in a Blue Dress*, a novel by Walter Mosley. Examine the conjunction used in each sentence; then insert commas where they are needed (I have removed all the commas that may be required by coordination). If a sentence is correct as it is, write *correct* under the sentence.

1. Joppy was still at the bar, leaning over his big stomach and buffing the marble.

2. The sky was still light at that time of year but I could see a crescent moon peeking over the inner roof.

3. The grinner tried to put his hand against my chest but I grabbed him by the wrist.

4. I turned back at the door to salute him goodbye but DeWitt Albright had filled his glass and shifted his gaze to the far wall.

5. The Japanese farmers grew artichokes lettuce and strawberries along the sides of the road.

6. That night the fields were dark under the slight moon and the air was chill but not cold.

7. It felt good and familiar to be back there.

8. He was hovering over me and I could feel the violence come off of him in waves.

9. He took a seat behind the desk kicked his foot up on it and lit a cigarette.

10. He leaned farther back in his chair and hunched his large shoulders.

11. DeWitt Albright had his bottle and his gun right out there in plain view.

12. He needed all his children to kneel down and let him be the boss.

13. I need a house to live in and a place to raise children.

14. The street was empty and the neighborhood was quiet.

15. One was tall and skinny and he was wearing a dark blue suit.

16. The men strode quickly in my direction but I just turned slowly and walked toward my door.

17. They were holding me by my arms and I was sagging with my head down.

18. I had recovered from the punch but I didn't want them to know it.

19. I sat down in the chair and looked up at the leaves coming in through the windows.

20. Mason moved again but this time I turned.

CORRELATIVE CONJUNCTIONS

The **correlative conjunctions** are linked pairs of function words that tie together two words or phrases, and sometimes two clauses. The first half of the pair precedes the first word or phrase, and the second precedes the second word or phrase. The common correlative conjunctions are listed in Table 6.2.

Both . . . And

The correlative pair *both . . . and* shows that the two connected elements operate together or equally. It may connect only two words or phrases of equal status; it never connects two independent clauses. In Sentence (26), from *Zelda*, two nouns, *planter* and *lawyer*, are presented as equally descriptive of the subject, *he*:

26. As *both* <u>planter</u> *and* <u>lawyer</u> he belonged to the ruling class.

In Sentence (27) from *Zelda*, a noun phrase (*her family*) is connected to a freestanding proper noun (*Montgomery*):

Table 6.2. Common Correlative Conjunctions

Correlative Pair	Meaning	Types of Sentence Parts Combined
both . . . and	two together or equally	words, phrases
either . . . or	only one of two, not both	words, phrases, clauses
neither . . . nor	not the first or second of two	words, phrases
not . . . but	not the first of two but the second instead	words, phrases
not only . . . but (also)	both of two, and especially the second	words, phrases, clauses

27. She felt herself being suffocated in the small arena that *both* <u>her family</u> *and* <u>Montgomery</u> offered her.

In Sentence (28), *both . . . and* connects two infinitive phrases.

28. Scott always managed *both* <u>to give Zelda her cigarette</u> *and* <u>to straighten out the Renault</u> along the narrow turn. [from *Zelda*]

Neither . . . Nor

The correlative pair *neither . . . nor* is exactly opposite in meaning to *both . . . and*; it excludes both of the alternatives. It connects words or phrases of similar kinds, as in Sentence (29), where the pair connects two freestanding nouns, and Sentence (30), where it connects two predicate phrases:

29. *Neither* <u>Zelda</u> *nor* <u>Hadley</u> was included in their literary discussions. [from *Zelda*]

30. She *neither* <u>asked for advice</u> *nor* <u>gave it</u>. [from *Zelda*]

Neither . . . nor may not connect clauses; *nor* functions alone in such cases (see discussion on *nor* above).

Either . . . Or

Either . . . or emphasizes the choice between two alternatives, and it can join words, phrases, and clauses. Sentence (31), from *A Word Child*, shows the connection of two adjectives:

31. Laura, no longer *either* <u>young</u> *or* <u>slim,</u> was a good-looking woman.

Sentence (32) has two prepositional phrases connected:

32. *Either* <u>as a result of the favorable reaction to her review of</u> <u>*The Beautiful and Damned*</u> *or* <u>through Rascoe's efforts,</u> Zelda was asked by *McCall's* magazine for a 2,500-word article on the modern flapper. [from *Zelda*]

Sentence (33) shows the connection of two clauses. Note the comma after the first clause:

33. *Either* <u>she has gotten caught in traffic,</u> *or* <u>she has decided</u> <u>not to come.</u>

Not Only . . . But Also

Words, clauses, or phrases may be connected by *not only . . . but* (*also*) to indicate that both elements are included (like *both . . . and*), and the second especially so. In Sentence (34), two nouns (*talent* and *effort*) are connected to show that talent and effort are necessary, but effort is especially important:

34. As they quarreled about Lois Moran, he told Zelda that at least the girl did something with herself, something that required *not only* <u>talent</u> *but* <u>effort.</u> [from *Zelda*]

In Sentence (35), two noun phrases are connected:

35. Edward Fitzgerald instilled in his son *not only* <u>beautiful</u> <u>manners</u> *but* <u>a sense of honor.</u> [from *Zelda*]

Two clauses may also be combined, as in Sentence (36), but similar to the rules for *nor*, the auxiliary or a form of *be* is moved in front of the subject following the negative part of the correlative (*not only*), and any repeated material is omitted from the second clause:

36.   *Not only* <u>is talent necessary,</u> *but* <u>effort is too.</u>

Not . . . But

Not . . . but connects only words or phrases to assert that the second of two elements is true or accurate, whereas the first is inaccurate, as in Sentence (37), where two noun phrases are connected:

37.   Her husband was also connected with the air force, although he was *not* <u>a pilot</u> *but* <u>an inspector of all sorts of transportation matters.</u> [Amy Tan, *The Kitchen God's Wife*]

Exercise 6.3

Find the correlative conjunction pair in each of the following sentences from *Zelda*, put a circle around each half of the pair, and then underline the two connected words, phrases, or clauses. (Other conjunctions also appear; for this exercise, focus only on correlative conjunctions.) In the space below, describe as accurately as possible the kinds of elements that are connected (for example, nouns).

1.   What had compelled her toward Jozan, he neither understood nor sought to understand.

2.   It was neither his mother nor his prosperous Irish relatives whom Scott Fitzgerald admired.

3.   The passion of her letter, the wild and intense description of her love for Scott, was an indication not only of her need for him but also of her uncertainly about herself.

4.   He has an amazing grasp of the superficialities of the men and women about him, but he has not yet a profound understanding of their motives, either intellectual or passionate.

5. There was not a hint of discord between Scott and Zelda apparent to either Seldes or his wife during their entire visit.

6. Neither the Judge nor Mrs. Sayre went with Zelda to New York.

7. Xandra Kalman not only found the Fitzgeralds a summer house on White Bear Lake but also purchased all of the baby things the Fitzgeralds would soon require.

8. He was not only a successful sports writer but also the author of satirical sketches and stories, poems, and comic burlesques.

9. The watch was the one he had given her during their courtship in Alabama, and it was the first object of value, both sentimental and actual, that she received from him.

10. Playfully Scott told her that according to both Browning and Keats he should marry her.

CONNECTED CLAUSES WITH NO CONJUNCTION

Sometimes two clauses are connected in some way, even though no conjunction appears. In such cases, the clauses can be combined into a single sentence, but they *must* be separated by a semicolon (;). Sentences (38) and (39) from *Zelda* have independent clauses connected with a semicolon:

38. There were very definite lines of social distinction; one was not invited to parties on The Hill if one was in trade, or Catholic, or Italian, or Shanty Irish.

39. But Scott was not the only man who courted her; a mustached aviator amused her for a while, until he proposed and she flatly turned him down.

If a comma is mistakenly used instead of the semicolon, the result is a writing error called the **comma-splice**.

Conjunctive Adverbs and Adverbials

Sometimes, when ideas are connected across sentences, specific words and phrases do the work of making the connection absolutely clear. These connecting words and phrases, called **conjunctive adverbs** (or *adverbials*, in the case of prepositional phrases that do this work), cannot be used to tie together anything but entire clauses or sentences. Table 6.3 provides a list of some common adverbial connectives and the relationships they signal.

As a rule, a conjunctive adverb appears in the second of the two clauses or sentences that it connects. In Example (40), from Tom Wolfe's nonfiction book *The Right Stuff, instead* begins the second sentence; it is separated from the rest of the sentence by a comma:

40.   A young man might go into military flight training believing that he was entering some sort of technical school in which he was simply going to acquire a certain set of skills.
Instead, he found himself all at once enclosed in a fraternity.

A conjunctive adverb may appear anywhere within the second sentence, so long as it does not break up a noun phrase. In (41), *however* appears at the end of the second sentence:

41.   Herein the world was divided into those who had it and those who did not. This quality, this *it,* was never named, *however.*

Table 6.3. Common Conjunctive Adverbs

Meaning	Conjunctive Adverbs/Adverbials			
Addition	*furthermore*	*in addition*	*likewise*	*moreover*
Contrast	*however*	*instead*	*nevertheless nonetheless*	*on the other hand*
Result	*thus*	*therefore*		
Emphasis	*in fact*	*indeed*		

In Example (42), *however* appears in the middle of a sentence that begins a paragraph. This sentence is understood as a contrast to points made in the preceding paragraph. Notice that the conjunctive adverb is set off from the rest of the sentence by commas:

42. What really made Conrad feel that something *eccentric* was going on here, *however,* was the business of the electrode in the thumb muscle.

Sometimes, instead of a period separating the two sentences, a semicolon is used, as in (43). A comma follows the conjunctive adverb:

43. They believed that the gods determined the outcome of single combat; *therefore,* it was useless for the losing side to engage in a full-scale battle.

A comma used in place of the semicolon in (43) would result in a comma-splice. This means that unlike conjunctions, conjunctive adverbs alone cannot join clauses into a single sentence. Therefore, a semicolon must do the work, as it does when clauses have some connection to each other, but no conjunction.

Exercise 6.4

Circle the conjunctive adverb or adverbial in each of the following passages from *The Right Stuff.* In the space below the sentence, write the meaning relationship it indicates.

1. Beano—Al Bean—wasn't quite so brilliant; on the other hand, he was still here.

2. A man either had it or he didn't! There was no such thing as having *most* of it. Moreover, it could blow at any seam.

3. To be grounded for a medical reason was no humiliation, looked at objectively. But it was a humiliation, nonetheless!—for it meant you no longer had that indefinable, unutterable, integral stuff.

4. Likewise, "hassling"—mock dogfighting—was strictly forbidden, and so naturally young fighter jocks could hardly wait to go up in, say, a pair of F-100s and start the duel.

5. It was no longer the fashion for serious writers to describe the glories of war. Instead, they dwelt upon its horrors, often with cynicism or disgust.

6. [Yeager] amazed his instructors with his ability at stunt-team flying, not to mention the unofficial business of hassling. This plus his up-hollow drawl had everybody saying, "He's a natural-born stick 'n' rudder man." Nevertheless, there was something extraordinary about it when a man so young, with so little experience in flight test, was selected to go to Muroc field in California for the XS-1 project.

7. Conrad broke into his full cackle of mirth, much the way Wally might have. No one was swept up in the joke, however.

8. These things were never pleasant; in fact, they were a bit humiliating.

9. Word of all this circulated quickly, too, and everyone was quite delighted. There was no indication, however, then or later, that Dr. Gladys Loring was amused in the slightest.

10. In other cases, however, the single combat settled the affair, and there was no full-scale battle.

Exercise 6.5

The following sentences appeared in Exercise 6.1. Rewrite each sentence so that you convert the conjunctions into conjunctive adverbs or adverbials wherever possible and change the punctuation to make it appropriate. Be sure to pick an adverb or adverbial that conveys a meaning similar to that of the original conjunction. If no conjunctive adverb is similar enough in meaning to the conjunction, use a semicolon.

1. She had a small clear soprano voice, and she played the piano nicely.

2. Minnie returned to Kentucky immediately, but she had suffered a disappointment she never forgot.

3. He worried constantly over their finances, for there were now nine members in his household.

4. World War I would do a little to change the social rigidity, but for the time being it persisted.

5. Her skirts, which were rolled at the waist to shorten them, were uneven, and her slip usually showed.

6. There were chaperones at the dances, but Zelda completely ignored them.

7. She was absent frequently, and her conduct report sank to "unsatisfactory" in the marking period before graduation.

8. Zelda's release from that world was suddenly within reach, for with the United States' entry into World War I in the summer of 1917 Montgomery altered profoundly.

9. All of the dances on Zelda's card were taken, but Scott's name was not on it.

10.   Her trip had disconcerted him, for while he was trying to break into journalism in New York, his girl was not exactly cooling her heels at home.

11.   I haven't the remotest idea of what it's like, so I am afraid to make any suggestions.

12.   The first sale to the *Post* was important to Scott, for he intended to make money, a lot of it.

SUMMARY

Two or more words, phrases, or clauses of the same kind may be combined into a single but larger phrase or sentence. This process may occur through the use of coordinating conjunctions, correlative conjunctions, or conjunctive adverbs. Special rules of punctuation apply, involving the comma and the semicolon.

Projects for Chapter Six

1.   Write a brief report detailing the difference between coordinating conjunctions and adverbial connectives. Make up sentences to illustrate your answer. Be sure to discuss punctuation.

2.   Choose several articles from your local newspaper or from a magazine such as *Time* or *Newsweek*. Find the sentences that use coordinating conjunctions, and make a list of which conjunctions occur and what sorts of sentence elements they connect (words, phrases, clauses). Which are the most common conjunctions? Do all of the coordinating conjunctions appear? If not, which are

missing? Write a report detailing your findings. Be sure to include examples in your discussion.

3. Choose several articles from a newspaper or magazine. Look for sentences that use the semicolon as the connecting device. Make a list of these sentences, and try to determine what meaning relationship ties the two clauses together. Write a report detailing your findings.

4. The following terms appeared in this chapter. Be sure you are familiar with all of them. Use the index and/or the glossary in the back of this book to help you.

comma-splice
conjunctive adverb
coordinating conjunction

coordination
correlative conjunction

CHAPTER SEVEN

Agreement

Now that you have learned about the major elements of English grammar, you are ready to explore **agreement**—the process by which a specific part of a sentence indicates its relationship to some other word or phrase. In particular, a verb phrase must **agree** with its subject, and a pronoun must agree with its antecedent, even if the antecedent appears in another sentence. In this chapter, you will learn how these general rules of agreement operate with different types of subjects and antecedents.

SUBJECT-VERB AGREEMENT

Subjects and verbs of English sentences have a special relationship. A verb must agree with its subject in person and number. This means that if the subject is plural, the verb must be a plural form; if the subject is singular, the verb must be a singular form; and if the subject is third person *and* singular, the verb must reflect this feature as well. When the subject is a pronoun, the number and person of the subject are indicated in the pronoun (see Chapter 1 for a review). Nouns and noun phrases are always third person, but they may be singular or plural. For example, in Sentences (1) through (3) from *Moon Passage*, a novel by Jane LeCompte, each subject (underlined) is a noun or noun phrase. In brackets next to each subject is the pronoun that can replace the noun phrase. In the parentheses following the sentence is the number and person of the pronoun. *All* the pronouns are third person:

1. <u>Ellen</u> [she] has stopped eating. (third-person singular, feminine)

2. <u>Ellen's voice</u> [it] cracks. (third-person singular, neuter)

3. <u>Her fists</u> [they] lie on either side of her Burger King bag. (third-person plural)

Present-Tense Verbs

In Chapter 2, you learned that the present tense is expressed by the base form of a verb with the *-s* suffix attached if the subject is a third-person singular pronoun (*he, she, it, this, that*, and so on) or a singular noun or noun phrase. All other subjects require the present tense to be expressed by the base form of the verb with no suffix at all. (The exceptions to this rule are the verbs *have*, which has the third-person singular form *has; do*, which has the third-person singular form *does*; and *be*, which is discussed below.) Sentences (4) through (8) from *Moon Passage* illustrate this rule. The subject of each sentence is underlined once. The verb is underlined twice:

4. <u>The sun</u> <u>burns</u> off the last of the fog and <u>heats</u> the air. [singular noun phrase is subject; there are two verbs because of coordination; the verbs have the *-s* suffix]

5. <u>Only the gulls</u> <u>break</u> the silence. [plural noun phrase is subject; the verb has no suffix]

6. <u>Ellen</u> <u>looks</u> at me. [singular noun is subject; the verb has the *-s* suffix]

7. <u>He</u> <u>craves</u> laughter, the noise of conversation, knots of people holding wineglasses and arguing. [third-person singular pronoun is subject; the verb has the *-s* suffix]

8. I <u>drive</u> to town and <u>buy</u> red snapper and the other things on my list. [first-person singular pronoun is subject; the verb has no suffix]

Past-Tense Verbs

In the past tense, except for *be*, the verb does not change to reflect the person and number of the subject at all. In each of Sentences (9) through (12), from Margaret Atwood's novel *The Handmaid's Tale*, a past-tense verb, underlined twice, appears. In the brackets following each sentence are the number and the person of the subject. Though the number and the person of the four subjects differ, all the past-tense verbs are formed in the same way. Each is the base form of the verb plus the *-ed* suffix. The form of a regular past-tense verb does not change, regardless of the number and person of the subject:

9. I <u>looked</u> at the cigarette with longing. [first-person singular subject; verb is *look + -ed*]

10. <u>We</u> <u>yearned</u> for the future. [first-person plural subject; verb is *yearn + -ed*]

11. <u>The woman</u> <u>handed</u> me one of the magazines. [third-person singular subject; verb is *hand + -ed*]

12. <u>Aunt Sara and Aunt Elizabeth</u> <u>patrolled</u>. [third-person plural subject; verb is *patrol + -ed*]

Even when the verb is irregular, there is only one past form, regardless of person and number. Therefore, in Sentences (13) and (14), where irregular past-tense verbs appear, there is no change in verb form if we change the number or person of the subject:

13. <u>The Guardian</u> <u>rang</u> the doorbell for me. [third-person singular subject]
    (*Compare:* I <u>rang</u> the doorbell, <u>we</u> <u>rang</u> the doorbell, <u>they</u> <u>rang</u> the doorbell.)

14. <u>We</u> <u>stole</u> extra paper packets of sugar for her, from the cafeteria at mealtimes. [first-person plural subject]

(*Compare:* I <u>stole</u> extra paper packets, <u>you</u> <u>stole</u> extra paper packets, <u>they</u> <u>stole</u> extra paper packets.)

Exercise 7.1

The verb of each of the following sentences from *Moon Passage* has been omitted. In the space provided, write the correct form of the verb given in brackets.

1. He _____ there in his jeans and scuffed work boots, shirtless in the August heat. [past tense of *stand*]

2. Savory steam _____ in the cool evening air like a cloud of incense. [present tense of *billow*]

3. The sun _____ atop a rock column out to sea. [present tense of *hang*]

4. Pollen _____ the tiny hairs of her skin. [past tense of *gild*]

5. She _____ , her eyes on my steaming bowl. [present tense of *come*]

6. She _____ at the tabletop. [present tense of *gaze*]

7. I _____ her stiff, slender figure, Egyptian in its stubborn angularity. [present tense of *consider*]

8. They _____ in front of us. [past tense of *meet*]

9. I _____ at her across the chasm between our frames of reference. [present tense of *stare*]

10. Adrenaline _____ in my ears and veins. [present tense of *buzz*]

11. Ellen _____ down the towel. [present tense of *put*]

12. Ellen _____ her arms around her knees. [present tense of *wrap*]

13. She _____ away from me. [present tense of *turn*]

14. Toby _____ his hand into mine. [past tense of *slip*]

15. Her attention _____ like a toddler's. [past tense of *wander*]

16. Her impregnable happiness _____ him more and more miserable. [past tense of *make*]

17. A car _____ by on the highway across the field, loud in the quiet night. [past tense of *go*]

18. You _____ struck an important blow in the fight to deconstruct the destructive fantasy of romantic love. [present tense of *have*]

19. The Bellamys _____ him home. [past tense of *take*]

20. My lungs _____ to ache. [present tense of *begin*]

The Verb *Be*

When the verb *be* appears in a sentence, either as a main verb or as the first auxiliary in the verb phrase, the rules of subject-verb agreement apply, and they are more complicated than they are for other verbs. In the past tense of *be*, there are two forms, one singular (*was*), and one plural (*were*). In the present tense, the plural form is *are*, but there are two different forms for the singular. The first-person singular is *am*, and the third-person singular is *is*. The second person is special; there is only one pronoun for both singular and plural (*you*), and it always takes *are* when the present tense of *be* is required and *were* when the past is required. These facts are presented in Table 7.1.

Because *be* is the most common linking verb, and because it serves as the auxiliary for the progressive aspect and for the passive voice, it appears very frequently, and so subject-verb agreement often must take account of more facts than you might assume, given how the process works for other verbs.

A present-tense form of *be* appears in Sentence (15), from Gary Soto's *Small Faces*. The *be* verb is underlined twice; its subject is underlined once. Notice that the plural noun phrase *my wife and I* requires the plural form, *are*:

15. <u>My wife and I</u> <u>are</u> devoted to Masterpiece Theatre.

Sentence (16), from *Knock Wood*, has the singular past-tense form, *was*, with a singular noun phrase subject, *my father*:

16. <u>My father</u> <u>was</u> a life-long Swedish loyalist, and the Swedish pancakes arrived in the hands of Simon, the Swedish houseman, hot off the griddle of Aina, the Swedish cook.

Sentence (17), from *The Kitchen God's Wife*, illustrates the use of *were* with a plural subject, *the drawers*:

17. <u>The drawers</u> <u>were</u> lined with cedar, so that the moment you opened them, a good scent flew out.

Table 7.1. Forms of Be

	Present Tense		Past Tense	
Person	**Singular**	**Plural**	**Singular**	**Plural**
First	*I am*	*we are*	*I was*	*we were*
Second	*you are*		*you were*	
Third	*he/she/it is*	*they are*	*he/she/it was*	*they were*

Sentence (18), from *Devil in a Blue Dress*, has *am* with a first person singular subject:

18. I am calling you about a problem with a friend of yours.

Exercise 7.2

Each of the following sentences from *The Kitchen God's Wife* contains a form of the verb *be*. Underline it, describe it as an auxiliary or a main verb, and give its tense (present or past), its number (singular or plural), and, if it is present-tense singular, its person.

1. I was the one who gave Beautiful Betty the sewing machine.

2. She was wearing a strange smile, one I had never seen before.

3. His skin was smooth and light-colored, not like the face of someone who worked outdoors all day long.

4. This student was a man named Lu, a Marxist, just the kind of person Gung-gung would have hated.

5. At the time, I was living in the house on Tsungming Island, my home for almost twelve years.

6. And after he abandoned it, the greenhouse was used only as a strange storage place.

7. It was a romance story called Chin Ping Mei, a forbidden book.

8. If she was blushing under her white powder, I could not tell.

9. After more money was exchanged, the woman wrote Peanut's name on a piece of red paper, along with her birthdate and the date of the fortune.

10. I was ladling out bowls of boiled dumplings when Wen Fu approached me.

11. And when the dogs died, he bought rifles and shot pigeons, real pigeons because the clay ones were too expensive.

12. Above the casket, a white banner made out of ten feet of butcher paper is stuck to the wall with masking tape.

13. I only put that down because my sister-in-law is absentminded.

14. Inside are a few tangerines, a roll of toilet paper, a canister of Grand Auntie's tea, and the picture of my father that I accidentally knocked over last month.

15. After I wrote my telegram, the operator girl said to me, "Do you really think we are soon *taonan* [forced to flee]?"

Agreement with Inverted Subjects

Sometimes, the subject of a declarative sentence is not at the beginning of the sentence and in front of the verb as you have come to expect. Instead, the order of the subject and the verb is inverted. That is, the subject follows the verb, even though the sentence is not a question but a statement. Such inversion is likely to occur when the subject is very lengthy, as in Sentence (19), which you first encountered in the last exercise. The first word in the sentence is an adverb that locates the subject, the verb is the linking verb *are*, and the subject is the entire coordinated phrase that follows *are* (it is underlined):

19. Inside are <u>a few tangerines, a roll of toilet paper, a canister of Grand Auntie's tea, and the picture of my father that I accidentally knocked over last month.</u>

The verb in Sentence (19) is plural, not only because *a few tangerines* is a plural noun phrase, but also because that noun phrase is coordinated with the noun phrases that follow it. In this example, coordination combines four noun phrases into a single—but plural—subject.

A similar inversion occurs when a sentence begins with *there*. In *there + be* constructions, the subject follows the verb. If the subject is singular, the verb takes a singular form, such as *was* in Sentence (20):

20. There <u>was a newspaper</u> on the desk.

However, a plural verb is used if the noun phrase following the verb is plural, as in Sentence (21):

21. I was trying to move quietly, but there <u>were</u> <u>crunching</u> <u>leaves and twigs</u> everywhere I stepped. [from *The Kitchen God's Wife*]

Agreement in Relative Clauses

As with any subordinate clause, a relative clause has its own subject and verb, and that subject and verb must agree. However, because there are no separate singular and plural forms for relative pronouns, a relative pronoun that is the subject of its clause cannot tell you whether the verb should be singular or plural. Therefore, when a relative pronoun is the subject of the relative clause, you must find its antecedent and make the subordinate verb agree in number with that antecedent. In Sentence (22), for instance, the verb of the relative clause, *were*, is plural because the relative pronoun *that* finds its antecedent in the plural noun phrase *the ones:*

22. Because I did not know my father's house that well, I did not notice any other changes, **the ones** <u>that</u> <u>were</u> later pointed out to me. [from *The Kitchen God's Wife*]

In Sentence (23), on the other hand, the verb of the relative clause is the singular *is*, because *which*, the subject of the clause, finds its antecedent in the singular noun phrase *a baby-pink sateen Chinese dress:*

23. For this special occasion, she has on **a baby-pink sateen Chinese dress**, <u>which</u> <u>is</u> too tight for her plump body and already creased at her lap and above her round stomach. [from *The Kitchen God's Wife*]

Agreement with Coordinated Subjects

When a subject is a noun phrase with nouns or noun phrases coordinated by *and*, it is plural, even if each of the nouns is singular. The subjects of Sentences (24) and (25), from *Pigs in Heaven*, are coordinations of two singular nouns, so their verbs are plural:

24. At a table nearby, <u>a wife *and* husband</u> <u>are</u> having a fight.

25. <u>Turtle *and* Taylor</u> <u>take</u> one last stroll across Mr. Hoover's concrete dream.

However, if two singular nouns are connected with *either . . . or* or *neither . . . nor*, the verb is not always plural; it agrees with the second of the two nouns, as in Sentence (26a), from *Zelda:*

26a. <u>*Neither* Zelda *nor* Hadley</u> <u>was</u> included in their literary discussions.

If the second noun of the correlative construction in Sentence (26a) were plural, the verb would be plural, as in Sentence (26b):

26b. <u>*Neither* Zelda *nor* her friends</u> <u>were</u> included in their literary discussions.

Agreement with Subjects That Are Content Clauses or Verbals

If the subject of a sentence is a content clause or a verbal, the verb is always singular, regardless of whether the subject is moved to the end of the sentence. In Sentence (27), from *Pet Sematary*, a content clause is the subject, and it appears in the ordinary subject position, just before the verb. The present tense verb *goes* is third-person singular:

27. <u>That such events have their own Rube Goldberg absurdity</u> <u>goes</u> almost without saying.

The verb of a sentence with a content clause subject is singular even when the clause is moved to the end of the sentence. Recall that the pronoun *it* holds the place of the moved subject and is a third-person singular form. Sentence (28) has a moved subject and a singular verb, *was:*

28. It <u>was</u> pretty clear <u>that he had backed her into a corner</u>. [from *Pet Sematary*]

Exactly the same pattern is found for subjects that are verbals. Singular verbs appear in Sentences (29) and (30), which have infinitive phrases as subjects:

29. <u>To have your father marry your mortal enemy's older sister</u> <u>is</u> a bit too coincidental for my taste. [from *Heartburn*]

30. But it <u>was</u> hopeless <u>to resist those eyes</u>. [from *Pet Sematary*]

The verb is also singular when a participle phrase is the subject, as Sentence (31), from *Pet Sematary*, demonstrates:

31. <u>Shoving his sheets down the laundry chute</u> <u>was</u> absolutely the best thing he could have done.

Agreement with Modified Subjects

Possibly the most difficult kind of agreement is that between a verb or verb phrase and a subject that includes a modifier. Agreement is especially tricky when the chief noun of the subject noun phrase and an object in the phrase or clause that modifies it do not have the same number. Because the object in the modifying clause or phrase immediately precedes the verb, we tend to make the verb agree with it. However, the rule is that the verb must agree with the chief noun of the subject noun phrase, as you can see in Sentences (32) and (33), from *Pigs in Heaven*, where the subjects are underlined once and the chief noun is boldfaced:

32. <u>A big **woman** in Lycra shorts and a tight yellow T-shirt</u> <u>appears</u>, arms open, to envelop Lucky like a starfish.

33. <u>A **herd** of paper cups and soda straws</u> <u>rolls</u> eastward in unison.

Agreement with Indefinite Subjects

Chapter 1 introduced indefinite pronouns, which point to antecedents that are not specific and that may be implied rather than expressed. Many indefinite pronouns are singular, even though they seem to point to more than one individual, for example *everyone, everything*, all the other pronouns that end in *-one, -thing*, or *-body*, and *each* and *either*. Some other indefinite pronouns are plural, such as *both, few*, and *many*, and still others are sometimes singular and sometimes plural, such as *all* or *some*. Table 7.2 provides a list.

Table 7.2. Number of Indefinite Pronouns

Always Singular	Always Plural	Singular or Plural
anyone, anybody, anything	*both*	*all*
each, either	*few*	*both*
everyone, everybody, everything	*many*	*none*
no one, nobody, nothing someone, somebody, something		*some*

An indefinite pronoun that is always singular takes a singular verb, even when the pronoun is followed by a modifying phrase that includes a plural noun:

34. <u>Everything</u> <u>is</u> fine.

35. <u>Everybody</u> <u>loves</u> a clown.

36. When a subject is a noun phrase with nouns or noun phrases coordinated by *and*, it is plural, even if **<u>each of the nouns</u> <u>is</u>** singular. [from this chapter]

The plural indefinite pronouns take plural verbs:

37. <u>Many</u> <u>are</u> called, but <u>few</u> <u>are</u> chosen.

The indefinite pronouns *all, any, none,* and *some* are sometimes singular and sometimes plural, depending on whether they refer to something that is singular or something that is plural. Sometimes this information is provided in a modifying phrase. In a certain sense, indefinite pronouns of this type seem to violate the rules for subject-verb agreement because the modifying phrase helps to decide the form of the verb. Notice, however, that the pronouns in this category are used to describe a part of something. If that something is made up of many elements, like a bag full of apples, then it is sensible to talk about a part of that "something" as having at least several elements. If the "something" is a substance without parts of its own, then a part of that substance is simply one thing as well:

38. <u>Some (of the apples)</u> <u>were</u> rotten.

39. <u>Some (of the oil)</u> <u>was</u> scented.

Exercise 7.3

Underline the correct verb form in the parentheses for each of the following. The first two sentences are taken from *Pet Sematary;* the remainder come from *The Kitchen God's Wife.*

1. Perhaps it (was, were) ultimately for the better that he had changed.

2. Goldman knew he (was, were) pretending.

3. As we (get, gets) closer to her house, she (point, points) to a place on Clement Street, Happy Super, where she always (do, does) her grocery shopping.

4. She (was, were) plump, but not in that classical way of a peach whose pink skin (is, are) nearly bursting with sweetness.

5. Almost everyone else who lived there (was, were) poor.

6. The matchmaker he found (was, were) an old lady we called Auntie Miao.

7. Auntie Du looked at the guard, whose eyes (was, were) rolling toward sleep.

8. All the women in the monastery noticed one another, because there (was, were) only six of us.

9. Hulan's hands (was, were) shaking as she held my shoulders.

10. And the front of each drawer (was, were) inlaid with mahogany, oak, and mother-of-pearl in a pattern that burst open like a fan.

11. And suddenly everything—the flower arrangements on the plastic-topped tables, my mother's memories of my childhood, the whole family—everything (feel, feels) like a sham.

12. It reminds me of a time when I (was, were) five years old, that age when anything (was, were) possible if you could just imagine it.

13. Nothing (is, are) wrong.

14. Something (has, have) been bothering her.

15. So it was Old Aunt who said that my half brother Kun (was, were) a big revolutionary hero!

PRONOUN-ANTECEDENT AGREEMENT

A pronoun must agree with its antecedent in person, number, and gender. Since first- and second-person pronouns typically have either no antecedents or other first- and second-person pronouns as antecedents, and since they do not express gender, the agreement rule poses little difficulty. Third-person pronouns, on the other hand, present some confusion because the singular forms come in three genders—masculine, feminine, and neuter.

The gender of the third-person pronoun is never at issue when the antecedent is plural; the third-person plural pronouns *they, them,* and *their* do not express gender, so it makes no difference whether the antecedent indicates male or female individuals or even lifeless things. Pronoun agreement treats as plural those noun phrases that are considered plural for subject-verb agreement.

The situation becomes more troublesome, however, for third-person singular pronouns whose antecedents are either male or female. Antecedents such as *student, teacher, spouse, child, engineer,* and *governor,* when used in a singular but general sense (for instance, *The student is expected to complete all work*) and all the singular indefinite pronouns force us to choose a singular pronoun. The problem is that all third-person singular pronouns have gender, and when you choose one of them, you must also make a choice about gender.

Whenever the antecedent is singular but unambiguously masculine, feminine, or neuter, the pronoun choice is straightforward, as in Sentence (40), where the antecedent (boldfaced) is clearly female, and Sentence (41), where the antecedent is clearly male:

40. **Jane** was tall and slender and had rich brown hair and high cheekbones and wide brown eyes. <u>She</u> looked a little like the actress Jean Simmons. <u>Her</u> father was a rancher in southwestern Texas. [from *The Right Stuff*]

41. Occasionally **a man** would look coldly at the binary problem <u>he</u> was now confronting every day—Right Stuff/Death—and decide it wasn't worth it. [from *The Right Stuff*]

Even noun phrases that may refer to either a male or female person under particular circumstances pose no difficulty if the discussion involves only one gender. For example, *The Right Stuff* documents a period in American aviation history when only men were *fighter pilots;* thus author Tom Wolfe chooses the masculine pronoun to replace this noun phrase in Sentence (42):

42. **A fighter pilot** soon found <u>he</u> wanted to associate only with other fighter pilots.

Until recently, generic nouns were treated as masculine for purposes of agreement. In Sentence (43), from Jacob Bronowski's history of science, *The Ascent of Man*, we find *Homo sapiens*, the scientific label for human beings, treated as masculine for purposes of agreement:

43. Fire is the symbol of the hearth, and from the time ***Homo sapiens*** began to leave the mark of <u>his</u> hand thirty thousand years ago, the hearth was the cave.

Because many people now consider such treatment biased, authors have been combining masculine and feminine pronouns with a slash mark, as Edward Hall does in Sentence (44), from *The Silent Language:*

44. **The American** asks, "What percentage of the asking price shall I give as my first offer?" What <u>he/she</u> doesn't know is that there are several asking prices.

Still others cast all generic nouns in the plural, thus avoiding the question of gender altogether. This solution is found in (45), from Marvin Harris' history of culture, *Our Kind:*

45. To achieve maximum genealogical depth, **genealogists** resort to a questionable strategy. <u>They</u> trace descent from only one direct lineal ancestor—usually a male—thereby neglecting hundreds if not thousands of other equally direct lineal ancestors.

Exercise 7.4

The following passage from *Idols of the Tribe*, a collection of essays by Harold R. Isaacs, uses the masculine pronoun to replace the generic noun phrase *a child*. First, underline every pronoun you find and circle its antecedent. Then rewrite the passage so that it no longer uses the masculine pronoun for generic reference. (Hint: Try making the noun phrase plural. Remember to make verbs agree with their subjects.)

The cadences of the mother tongue are among the earliest sounds a child hears. He begins to hear what the psychoanalyst Paul Schilder has called "the melody of speech" long before he can distinguish any of its words. It conveys to him some of the first sensations, emotions, and meaning that he begins to experience, that is, to learn. Long before he can speak words, he comes to understand them; and not long thereafter, with speech, he makes the words his own. Thus he begins to acquire a language, the most distinctive of all human attributes. The language he learns becomes one of the means—some would say the single most decisive means—by which he discovers himself, his family, his kind, his culture, his view of the world.

SUMMARY

In this chapter, you learned about the process of agreement that ties a verb to its subject and a pronoun to its antecedent. In some ways, the processes are related; what counts as a singular or a plural noun phrase for purposes of subject-verb agreement also counts in pronoun-antecedent agreement. In other ways, the processes are somewhat dissimilar; pronoun agreement can take place across sentences, whereas subject-verb agreement is internal to a particular sentence. You also learned that agreement processes can be tricky. For example, a modifier intervening between noun and verb can mislead you as to the noun or pronoun with which the verb must agree, and generic nouns can cause problems for pronoun agreement when gender cannot be matched.

Projects for Chapter Seven

1. Write a brief report explaining the changes you had to make in the passage in Exercise 7.4. Be sure to talk about subject-verb agreement as well as pronoun agreement.

2. Write a description of the room you are in, including the people who may be in it, using the present tense only (of course, the verb phrase may also be progressive or passive). When you are done, put two lines under every verb that shows tense and one line under its subject. Make certain that the verb agrees with its subject. If you find you have made an error, list that error and its correction on a separate piece of paper. Make the correction, and explain briefly why a correction is necessary.

3. Get a copy of today's newspaper or a current news magazine. Find an article that uses generic nouns (for example, *an American, a citizen*) and/or indefinite pronouns. Discuss how the author handles problems of agreement. (Hint: Are all generic nouns plural? Does the author use the *he/she* strategy? Is there another strategy you may have noticed that is not discussed in this chapter?)

Punctuation

This final chapter deals directly with punctuation, but little new information is introduced. You have already learned about punctuation throughout this book in the discussions of specific parts of the grammar. In this chapter, you will find in a single place the rules you have already learned, as well as a few others you will need in everyday writing tasks.

SENTENCE-FINAL PUNCTUATION

Three kinds of punctuation marks are used at the ends of sentences: the period, the question mark, and the exclamation point. In general, the period belongs at the end of the declarative sentence, the question mark ends a question, and the exclamation point finishes an exclamation.

The Period (.)

Declarative sentences end with periods. Sentences (1) through (3), from Josephine Tey's mystery *A Shilling for Candles*, are declarative sentences, so each ends with a period. Recall that a sentence has a subject and a predicate phrase and that the predicate phrase includes the verb and any objects, complements, and modifiers (Sentence 1). It may also include coordinated elements (Sentence 2) and one or more subordinate clauses (Sentence 3):

1. Williams was not in the mood for butter.

2. Grant rolled the honey on his tongue and swallowed it.

3. As Jammy made his way to a seat, he observed that it was filled with the most fashionable audience that he had seen at any gathering since the Beaushire-Curzon wedding.

The Question Mark (?)

Several different types of questions require the question mark. Sentences beginning with the question words *who, what, where, when,* and so on, such as Sentences (4) and (5) from *A Shilling for Candles,* end with a question mark:

4. *Who* had piloted that plane?

5. *Where* was Marta when Christine was drowned?

The yes/no question, which has subject-auxiliary inversion but no question word, also requires the question mark. Sentence (6) from *Shilling* is such a sentence:

6. Was she interested in him herself?

In addition, a question mark ends the tag question, which is a statement followed by a comma, an auxiliary, and a subject-form pronoun that has the subject as its antecedent. The material that follows the statement is called a "tag." If the statement is negative, the tag is not, as in Sentence (7) from *Shilling:*

7. You don't mean Keats, do you?

If the statement portion of a tag question is affirmative, however, then the tag includes the negative *contraction* of the auxiliary, as in Sentence (8) from *Shilling.* A question mark is required:

8. That made Christine a double rival of hers, didn't it?

Sometimes, a declarative sentence contains a subordinate clause that is, at least in meaning, a question. In this case, because the sentence is declarative, it requires a period. In Sentence (9) from *Shilling*, a question is the direct object of the participle *wondering;* in Sentence (10), a question is the direct object of the verb phrase *didn't know:*

> **9.** He found himself wondering <u>if Marta was a good swimmer</u>.
> (Compare: Is Marta a good swimmer?)

> **10.** He didn't know <u>what he had expected</u>.
> (Compare: What had he expected?)

The Exclamation Point (!)

The exclamation point is used with free-standing phrases to show strong emotion, as shown in Sentences (11) and (12) from *Shilling:*

> **11.** The silly fools!

> **12.** An utterly disgusting exhibition!

Full-blown exclamatory sentences also require the exclamation point. Sentence (13), a famous exclamatory sentence, comes from Bram Stoker's horror classic, *Dracula:*

> **13.** The children of the night, what music they make!

In formal writing assignments such as essays and term papers, because logical argument is expected, the exclamation point is used infrequently.

Exercise 8.1

 Each of the following sentences from *A Shilling for Candles* lacks a sentence-final punctuation mark. Put a period, a question mark, or an exclamation point at the end of each sentence.

1. Are you Mr. Rickett

2. I wanted to know whether you knew a Mr. Herbert Gotobed

3. I want you to let me stay in your shop until Mr. Gotobed comes to claim his letter

4. What time do you close

5. A row of first story windows looked down upon the alley

6. Grant asked to see the principal

7. I have to ask that you will let me find him

8. In the dimness of the moment, when all his faculties were trying to summon his stunned body to its duty, he wondered detachedly how the man would kill him

9. Darling, how wonderful of you

10. I have a right to know, haven't I

PUNCTUATION INSIDE THE SENTENCE

In addition to ending sentences, punctuation is needed within sentences. In the following sections, you will review the uses of the comma and the semicolon and learn to use the colon.

The Comma (,)

When I was a schoolgirl, one of my teachers taught my class a valuable rule about comma placement: "When in doubt, leave it out!" That happens to be a pretty good rule, because far more problems arise from commas appearing where they don't belong than from commas being omitted. Nevertheless, since most commas result from specific grammatical processes, like the movement of adverbials, the connection brought about by coordination, and the requirements of nonrestrictive modifiers, you should be left with little doubt about where a comma is needed. The following sections review the facts you have learned about comma use.

The Comma with Introductory Adverbials

In Chapter 3, you learned that since adverbs and adverbials typically express background details of time, location, manner, and the like, they often appear first in the sentence as a guidepost to the main event. When such introductory adverbials appear, they are typically set off from the main part of the sentence by a comma, such as the adverbial prepositional phrase of Sentence (14) and the adverbial subordinate clause of Sentence (15):

> **14.** <u>On the exposed rocks out of water</u>, the barnacles bubble behind their closed doors. [from *Gift from the Sea*]

> **15.** <u>As we left the city</u>, we passed Sorrowfree Lake. [from *The Kitchen God's Wife*]

The Comma with Nonrestrictive Modifiers

You have studied nonrestrictive modifiers of several types in the preceding chapters. You learned about appositives, nonrestrictive adjective phrases, nonrestrictive participle phrases, and nonrestrictive relative clauses. All of these nonrestrictive modifiers are set off from the rest of the sentence by commas. Sentence (16) provides an example of a nonrestrictive appositive:

> **16.** I considered my fiancee, <u>Carolyn</u>, and she didn't look poor. [from *Small Faces*]

Sentence (17) has a nonrestrictive adjective phrase:

> **17.** He was a bright and brassy kid, <u>confident, cocksure</u>. [from *Knock Wood*]

Sentence (18) provides a nonrestrictive participle phrase:

> **18.** <u>Drawn back to the cabin by the yellow glow of a reading lamp in the living room</u>, I stood outside the window for a long time and looked in at my wife. [from *Uh-Oh*]

Sentence (19) has a nonrestrictive relative clause:

19. Edgar passed him every day and then made sketches, <u>which he gave to a barkeeper called Mack</u>. [from *Knock Wood*]

The Comma with Coordinated Clauses and Phrases

Several rules of comma placement apply when a coordinating conjunction connects two equal sentence elements. If the conjoined elements are two independent clauses, a comma separates the first clause from the conjunction. Sentences (20) through (22), from *Pigs in Heaven*, show a comma following the first of two clauses coordinated with *and*, *but*, and *so:*

20. <u>Each table has three different kinds of honey in a cloverleaf-shaped container,</u> *and* <u>the busy-bee waitresses wear antennae headbands with bobbling yellow balls on long springs.</u>

21. <u>The air isn't any cooler outside the house,</u> *but* <u>being outdoors in her sheer nightgown arouses Alice with the possibility of freedom.</u>

22. <u>Harland ordered the Cornucopia Of Bowls from the shopping channel for their wedding anniversary,</u> *so* <u>now their home has a bowl for every purpose.</u>

If three clauses are connected with *and*, a comma separates the first clause from the second, another comma follows the second clause, and the word *and* appears only between the second and third clauses:

23. <u>Dellon's long hair is loose, his T-shirt looks like what grasshoppers do to crops,</u> *and* <u>his beefy shoulders seem slumped this morning with the weight of fatherhood</u>. [from *Pigs*]

When two phrases are connected with any coordinating conjunction, no comma is used:

24. A big woman in <u>Lycra shorts</u> *and* <u>a tight yellow T-shirt</u> appears. [from *Pigs*]

25. She <u>heaves the watering can</u> *but* <u>can't tell where it's gone</u>. [from *Pigs*]

When three or more phrases are connected with *and*, a comma follows each of the conjoined phrases preceding the conjunction:

26. I grabbed a piece of bread, soaked it in the spinach, *and* took a delightful bite. [from *Childhood*]

The Comma with Items in a List

A comma also is used to separate items in a list. For example, in Sentence (27), from the introduction by M. S. Handler to *The Autobiography of Malcolm X* as told to Alex Haley, commas separate the adjectives modifying *Negroes*. Notice that a comma does *not* separate the last adjective from the noun it modifies:

27. I was the only white person in the restaurant, an immaculate establishment tended by somber, handsome, uncommunicative Negroes.

The Comma with Conjunctive Adverbs

Conjunctive adverbs such as *however, moreover, instead,* and *therefore* and adverbial phrases such as *on the other hand* are separated from the rest of the sentence by a comma:

28. Herein the world was divided into those who had it and those who did not. This quality, this *it*, was never named, however. [from *The Right Stuff*]

29. Jason Harmer, on the other hand, had not moved a muscle. [from *A Shilling for Candles*]

The Colon (:)

The colon is used to introduce information that elaborates on a particular element in a sentence. For example, the colon in Sentence (30) from the introduction to *Malcolm X* introduces a list of particular "ills" mentioned in the main part of the sentence. Notice, too, that commas separate the items in the list:

30. Malcolm had purged himself of all the ills that afflict the depressed Negro mass: drugs, alcohol, tobacco, not to speak of criminal pursuits.

If, however, a list of items is *not* an elaboration of something in another part of the sentence but is a coordination of phrases serving as the direct object, as in Sentence (31), or the subject, as in Sentence (32), *no* colon is used:

31. He craves laughter, the noise of conversation, knots of people holding wineglasses and arguing. [from *Moon Passage*]

32. Inside are a few tangerines, a roll of toilet paper, a canister of Grand Auntie's tea, and the picture of my father that I accidentally knocked over last month. [from *The Kitchen God's Wife*]

In addition to its use in introducing lists, a colon is sometimes used to introduce a direct quotation in a formal essay. Such a use is found in the following passage from the introduction to *Malcolm X:*

33. A group of these artists gathered one Sunday in my home, and we talked about Malcolm. Their devotion to him as a man was moving. One said: "Malcolm will never betray us. We have suffered too much from betrayals in the past."

The Semicolon (;)

A semicolon is used to connect independent clauses without a coordinating conjunction and to set off items in a list when one or more of the items is a phrase that contains commas.

When two independent clauses are connected in some unspecified way without a conjunction, a semicolon appears between them and not a comma:

34. There were very definite lines of social distinction; one was not invited to parties on The Hill if one was in trade, or Catholic, or Italian, or Shanty Irish. [from *Zelda*]

Because it does not coordinate, a conjunctive adverb that begins the second of two connected clauses within a sentence *must* be separated from the previous clause by a semicolon to avoid the punctuation error known as a "comma-splice." Thus, although a comma follows the conjunctive adverb, the semicolon must precede it when it comes at the beginning of the second clause:

35.   They believed that the gods determined the outcome of single combat; <u>therefore,</u> it was useless for the losing side to engage in a full-scale battle. [from *The Right Stuff*]

In a previous section of this chapter, you learned that items in a list must be separated by a comma. Sometimes, however, individual items in the list have commas inside them for other reasons. For example, in Sentence (36) from *Pigs in Heaven*, the second item in the list, *two tall, skinny white girls in braces who could be sisters,* includes a comma to separate the adjectives *tall* and *skinny*. If a comma were used elsewhere in the list, the result would be confusing to the reader. Therefore, the author uses a semicolon to separate the items in the list of "kids":

36.   There are four kids: a show-off boy in a scout uniform who keeps patting the hand of his huge father; two tall, skinny white girls in braces who could be sisters; and the Indian girl in overalls.

Exercise 8.2

 Some of these sentences from *Pigs in Heaven* are correct as is; some have missing punctuation. Add punctuation where it is needed; write *correct* under the sentences that need no changes.

1.   Her husband Harland is sleeping like a brick and snoring.

2.   To all appearances they're a satisfied couple sliding home free into their golden years but Alice knows that's not how it's going to go.

3.   She leaves the bed quietly and switches on the lamp in the living room.

4.   Cash Stillwater looks up from his work and sees a splash of white birds like water thrown at the sky.

5. They make their circle again and again flaunting their animal joy

6. He counts the birds without knowing it sorting the shifting group into rows of odd and even.

7. Old people might marry gracefully once in a while but their houses rarely do.

8. She raised a daughter in this house and planted all the flowers in the yard but that's nothing to hold her here.

9. Cash glances at Rose who is peevishly brushing ash off her blouse.

10. She picks up another one and gives it a fling.

11. Cash knows these women they come into the store and go crazy over anything herbal.

12. After he bought it he decided he had to get it cleaned.

13. Lou Ann Ruiz who is like a second mother to Turtle tends toward an obsession with health and safety.

14. The cluster of tin bells over the door jingles behind Cash but it's a customer a tall thin man wearing sandals and gray-speckled socks.

15. He nods at Rose who is at the register.

16. He made me speak English and he pushed me to do well in school.

17. She picks up her fork and idly begins poking things with it her plate the tablecloth her hair.

18. The old man walks five or six careful steps toward the east and takes a place at the edge of the clearing.

19. The song sounds a little different but the dance is still the same gentle stomping in a circle.

20. Annawake folds and unfolds the cotton square on her lap.

THE APOSTROPHE (')

Unlike the period, the comma, and the other punctuation marks you have studied so far, which operate at the level of the sentence, the apostrophe operates at the level of the word. It has two main uses: It is used to indicate the possessive relationship in noun phrases, and it is used to show that letters have been omitted in contractions.

The Apostrophe in the Possessive

In Chapter 1, you learned that for many noun phrases, the possessive relationship is expressed through the addition of -'s on the first of two nouns. For example, you studied Sentence (37) from *It Was on Fire When I Lay Down on It*, which has such a noun phrase, *Molly's bag*. In this noun phrase, *Molly's* has an -'s suffix, which shows possession:

37. I tore open <u>Molly's bag</u> and shook out the contents.

To form the possessive of a singular noun, add -'s, as in Sentence (38):

38. <u>Owasso's</u> greatest claim to fame is that it is the home town of Thomas E. Dewey. [from *Malcolm X*]

Though the addition of this suffix seems straightforward, a difficulty arises when the first noun—the "possessing" noun—is a plural formed by the addition of -*s* or otherwise ends with *s*. In this case, the apostrophe follows the -*s* or -*es* that indicates the plural, and no additional -*s* is added. For example, Sentence (39) from *Malcolm X* tells about the *Gohannas family*, whose family name ends in -*s*. When Malcolm talks about the family as a group, he makes the family name plural (a plural that is not possessive has no apostrophe):

39. The state people, we found out, had interviewed the <u>Gohannas</u> family, and the <u>Gohannases</u> had said that they would take me into their home.

When this plural proper noun appears in Sentence (40), it is a possessive noun. Notice that the apostrophe follows the plural -*es*, and no other -*s* follows:

40. When finally I was sent to the <u>Gohannases'</u> home, at least in a surface way I was glad.

Even a singular noun ending in -*s*, such as *James* or the family name *Williams*, typically has only the apostrophe to show possession. Sentence (41) from *Malcolm X* has such a possessive form:

41. It made me feel great to visit him and Wesley over at <u>Mrs. Williams'</u> house.

Because they do not end in -*s*, irregular plural nouns, such as *children* and *men*, form the possessive like singular nouns. Sentence (42) provides an example:

42. I couldn't get over marveling at how their hair was straight and shiny like white <u>men's</u> hair. [from *Malcolm X*]

Though pronouns have possessive forms, only the indefinite pronouns form the possessive like nouns, by adding -'*s*. Personal pronouns have special possessive forms, and these forms *never* use the apostrophe. As you will see in the next section, an -'*s* attached to a personal pronoun makes the word a contraction, not a possessive form.

The Apostrophe in Contractions

In informal or personal writing, contractions are commonly used. A contraction is a shortened form of a word combination that omits letters and uses an apostrophe to show where the omission has occurred, such as *can't* (for *cannot*) or *she's* (for *she is*). Contractions occur in Sentences (43) through (48). The full form is given in brackets next to each contraction:

43. You <u>don't</u> [do not] mean Keats, do you? [from *Shilling*]

44. He <u>didn't</u> [did not] know what he had expected. [from *Shilling*]

45. I have a right to know, <u>haven't</u> [have not] I? [from *Shilling*]

46. The air <u>isn't</u> [is not] any cooler outside the house. [from *Pigs in Heaven*]

47. To all appearances <u>they're</u> [they are] a satisfied couple sliding home free into their golden years, but Alice knows <u>that's</u> [that is] not how <u>it's</u> [it is] going to go. [from *Pigs*]

48. I <u>couldn't</u> [could not] get over marveling at how their hair was straight and shiny like white men's hair. [from *Malcolm X*]

Table 8.1 on page 180 lists the types of words that are likely to be contracted and their contracted forms. Notice that the contracted forms for *had* and *would* are identical. Thus the meaning must be determined from the context.

Table 8.1. Common Contractions

Present Tense Forms of *Be*	*Will* and *Would*	Present and Past Tense Forms of *Have*	*Not*
I'm = I am	I'll = I will	I've = I have	isn't = is not
we're = we are	we'll = we will	we've = we have	aren't = are not
you're = you are	you'll = you will	you've = you have	wasn't = was not
he's = he is	he'll = he will	he's = he has	weren't = were not
she's = she is	she'll = she will	she's = she has	haven't = have not
it's = it is	it'll = it will	it's = it has	hadn't = had not
they're = they are	they'll = they will	they've = they have	don't = do not
	I'd = I would	I'd = I had	doesn't = does not
	you'd = you would	you'd = you had	didn't = did not
	he'd = he would	he'd = he had	can't = cannot
	she'd = she would	she'd = she had	couldn't = could not
	we'd = we would	we'd = we had	won't = will not
	they'd = they would	they'd = they had	wouldn't = would not
			shouldn't = should not
			mustn't = must not

Exercise 8.3

Each of the following sentences from *The Autobiography of Malcolm X* has at least one word that requires an apostrophe. Underline that word, and rewrite it in the space below, inserting the apostrophe where it is needed. Be careful not to mistake ordinary plurals for possessive forms.

1. Especially, I liked to drop in and visit at the Gohannases home.

2. I didnt want to leave Hilda, who was like my second mother.

3. I had my fathers .22 caliber rifle.

4. A lot of times in these later years since I became a Muslim, Ive thought back to that fight and reflected that it was Allahs work to stop me.

5. Her husbands name was Duane Lathrop.

6. I began to sweep and mop and dust around in the Swerlins house.

7. The Lyonses and I, as it happened, were the towns only Negroes.

8. Whenever our team walked into another schools gym for the dance, with me among them, I could feel the freeze.

9. I think the major impact of Ellas arrival, at least upon me, was that she was the first really proud black woman I had ever seen in my life.

10. From my seat in the back of the bus, I gawked out of the window at white mans America rolling past for what seemed a month.

11. Its funny how I seemed to think of Mary as Ellas sister, instead of her being, just as Ella is, my own half-sister.

12. Those tough Negroes heyday had been before the big 1931 Seabury Investigation that started Dutch Schultz on the way out, until his career ended with his 1934 assassination.

13. I was one of his top students, one of the schools top students.

14. Malcolm, one of lifes first needs is for us to be realistic.

15. Youre good with your hands.

16.   You havent had any experience shining shoes.

17.   I thought Id have to catch her.

18.   Many of the New Haven Lines cooks and waiters still in railroad
      service today will remember old Pappy Cousins.

19.   Only my oldest brother, Wilfred, wasnt there.

20.   This was my best early lesson in how most white mens hearts
      and guts will turn over inside of them, whatever they may have
      you believe, whenever they see a Negro man on close terms
      with a white woman.

PUNCTUATION IN DIRECT QUOTATION

Special rules for punctuation apply in directly quoted speech.
The following passage from Alan Dershowitz's memoir *The Best
Defense* provides several examples:

49a.   On the first day of my clerkship with Justice Arthur
           Goldberg of the United States Supreme Court during the
           summer of 1963, the Justice called me into his office and
           asked, "Have you given much thought to capital
           punishment?"
               "I certainly have," came my enthusiastic reply.
               "Well, I have an idea that I think will interest you," the
           Justice said.

Notice that a quoted sentence is separated from the sentence that contains it by a comma (though as you have seen in the discussion on the
colon, a colon may be used in more formal circumstances). The comma
is followed by a space and then the opening quotation mark; there is no
space between the quotation mark and the first word of the quotation,
which begins with a capital letter, as in Sentence (49b):

49b. [T]he Justice called me into his office and asked, "Have you given much thought to capital punishment?"

If the quoted sentence is a question, as in Sentence (49b), it will end in a question mark that appears *inside* the quotation mark. Notice that a period does *not* follow the closing quotation mark, in spite of the fact that the containing sentence is a statement. The same rule applies to exclamations and the exclamation point: If the quoted sentence is an exclamation, the exclamation point goes inside the quotation marks, and no period follows.

However, let's imagine that Sentence (49b) were worded as Sentence (49c), with the quoted question preceding the containing sentence. As with Sentence (49b), the question mark appears inside the quotation marks, and no comma is used at all; the first word in the containing sentence begins with a lowercase letter:

49c. "Have you given much thought to capital punishment?" he asked.

If, on the other hand, the quoted sentence is a statement and precedes the containing sentence, as it does in Sentence (49d), a comma and not a period is used, and it is placed *inside* the quotation mark:

49d. "Well, I have an idea that I think will interest you," the Justice said.

If the quotation in Sentence (49d) followed rather than preceded the containing sentence, as in Sentence (49e), a period would appear *inside* the ending quotation; no other sentence-final punctuation would appear:

49e. The Justice said, "Well, I have an idea that I think will interest you."

When quoted material is longer than a single sentence, part of it appears in a sentence of its own, but surrounded by quotation marks, as happens in Sentence (49f). Notice that the final period appears inside the quotation mark:

49f. "Well, I have an idea that I think will interest you," the Justice said. "I would like you to work up a memorandum

for me on the constitutional issues surrounding the
imposition of the death penalty."

Table 8.2 will help you sort out some of the rules about punctuation in direct quotation.

Table 8.2. Placement of Final Punctuation for Sentences Ending in Direct Quotation

If Containing Sentence Is:	And Quoted Sentence Is:		
	Statement	Question	Exclamation
Statement	End with a period inside quotation marks: *She said, "I am leaving tomorrow."*	End with a question mark inside quotation marks: *She asked, "Where are you going?"*	End with an exclamation point inside quotation marks: *She shouted, "How extraordinary!"*
Question	End with a question mark outside quotation marks: *Did she say, "I am leaving tomorrow"?*	End with *one* question mark outside quotation marks: *Did she ask, "Where are you going"?*	End with a question mark outside quotation marks: *Did she shout, "How extraordinary"?*
Exclamation	End with an exclamation point outside quotation marks: *I can't believe she said, "I am leaving tomorrow"!*	End with an exclamation point outside quotation marks: *I can't believe she asked, "Where are you going"!*	End with *one* exclamation point outside quotation marks: *I can't believe she shouted, "How extraordinary"!*

Exercise 8.4

The following passage from *Childhood*, by Bill Cosby, involves direct quotation. I have left off some of the punctuation, including the quotation marks. Add punctuation where it is necessary.

There's a *frog* in my milk he noted one morning. Bill, *you* know how a frog got into my milk?

They can really get around I replied

And I wonder how *you'll* be getting around he said meaningfully

SUMMARY

Punctuation is not arbitrary, nor does it depend on where one might pause in speaking. It is based on the grammatical structure of the sentence. In particular, a sentence must end with a period, a question mark, or an exclamation point, and nonrestrictive modifiers must be set off by commas, as must introductory adverbial modifiers; coordinated elements also need commas under specific circumstances. A semicolon is necessary when two independent clauses have an implied connection but no conjunction to bind them together, and a colon frequently is used before a list of items that elaborates on some element in the main part of the sentence. Finally, quotation marks require special attention to the placement and choice of all other punctuation marks. In some circumstances, punctuation goes inside the quotation marks; in other circumstances, it goes outside. In no circumstance, however, do two sentence-final punctuation marks appear at the end of any quotation.

Projects for Chapter Eight

1. From your daily newspaper, select an article and choose a section of about 250 words. Note all uses of commas and explain why each one occurs. Write a brief report detailing your findings.

2. Tape record a conversation between two of your friends or two members of your family. Be sure to let them know what you are doing and to get their permission. Transcribe the tape and edit the transcript so that it conforms to written standards. Be especially careful to use appropriate punctuation and quotation marks where necessary.

3. As you read your daily newspaper, look for examples of possessive nouns formed with the apostrophe. Make a list of these nouns and write a brief report detailing why each noun takes the form it does. Features such as singular and plural for regular nouns are important, as is the form of singular nouns ending in *'s*. Did you find any irregular plurals? How was the possessive formed?

abstract noun: a noun that designates a quality, action, or idea, such as *warmth, exercise,* or *music:*

<u>Warmth</u> is a wonderful quality in a friend.

active voice: the form of the verb phrase of a sentence whose subject acts upon the direct object:

My mother's uncle Blaine <u>had married</u> my father's aunt, Ruby. [Staples]

adjective: a modifier that describes and ordinarily precedes a noun:

Behind the house lies a vast <u>wild</u> <u>tangled</u> <u>garden</u>. [Nin]

adverb: a word that modifies a verb, adjective, or another adverb:

Iole had <u>always</u> scolded our family for our disdain for physical comforts. [S. Cheever]

adverbial: a prepositional phrase, noun phrase, or adverb phrase that modifies the verb or verb phrase of a sentence by providing details of time, location, direction, purpose, cause, extent, condition, and concession:

My mother had given me choices <u>all my life.</u> [Simpson]

agree: a verb is said to *agree* with its subject, and a pronoun is said to *agree* with its antecedent; these statements mean that the forms of verbs and subjects and of pronouns and antecedents match in an important way.

agreement: the process by which a specific part of a sentence indicates its relationship to some other word or phrase; in particular, a verb phrase must agree with its subject, and a pronoun must agree with its antecedent, even if the antecedent appears in another sentence:

<u>Ellen</u> <u>looks</u> at me. (singular subject, singular verb) [LeCompte]

Occasionally <u>a man</u> would look coldly at the binary problem <u>he</u> was now confronting every day—Right Stuff/Death—and decide it wasn't worth it.

(third-person singular, masculine noun, third-person singular, masculine pronoun) [Wolfe]

antecedent: the noun or noun phrase for which a pronoun substitutes:

<u>Jane</u> was tall and slender and had rich brown hair and high cheekbones and wide brown eyes. She looked a little like the actress Jean Simmons. [Wolfe]

appositive: a noun or noun phrase that modifies another noun or noun phrase:

For my childhood friend <u>Jackie</u> and me, there was no recognition of animal life, other than cats and dogs and an occasional squirrel that from a distance looked like a baseball mitt nailed to a tree. [Soto]

article: one of the function words *the* and *a (an)* that often begin noun phrases:

<u>The</u> fountain emerges like <u>the</u> headstone of <u>a</u> tomb.

aspect: a change in form in the main verb that indicates whether an event is continuing or completed:

We <u>were dragging</u> Dupree from the car to her door. (progressive aspect) [Mosley]

auxiliary verb: a helping verb that has little meaning but that indicates certain shadings of action or time (see Table 2.3).

comma splice: a writing error in which a comma is mistakenly used instead of a semicolon:

They believed that the gods determined the outcome of single <u>combat, therefore,</u> it was useless for the losing side to engage in a full-scale battle. [Wolfe]

common noun: a noun that indicates any member of a class of individuals:

Last <u>night</u> he asked me to serve <u>dinner</u> on a <u>tray</u> in front of "Star Trek." [O'Reilly]

complement: a noun, noun phrase, or adjective that follows a linking verb and describes or identifies the subject or that follows a direct object and describes or identifies the object:

Miss Emma looked <u>tired</u>. [Gaines]

The jury of twelve white men found Jefferson <u>guilty</u>. [Gaines]

compound noun: a noun made up of two or more nouns, such as *police dog, church bell,* and *prison gate:*

The clearest indication of the complexity of modern relationships is that
<u>greeting card companies</u> are forced to put out cards that are blank on the
inside. [Seinfeld]

conjunctive adverb: a specific word or phrase that connects ideas across
sentences or clauses. (See Table 6.3):

They believed that the gods determined the outcome of single combat;
<u>therefore,</u> it was useless for the losing side to engage in a full-scale battle.
[Wolfe]

content clause: an entire subordinate clause that serves as subject, object,
or complement in another sentence:

As a doctor, he knew <u>that death was, except perhaps for childbirth, the
most natural thing in the world</u>. [King]

contractions: shortened forms of word combinations that use apostrophes, such as *can't* (for *cannot*) or *she's* (for *she is*):

<u>I'm</u> looking for somebody, for a friend. [Mosley]

coordinating conjunction: one of a very small set of function words that
combines two or more words, phrases, or clauses into a single, but larger
phrase or sentence (see Table 6.1).

coordination: the connection of two or more of any sentence elements of
the same status through the use of coordinating conjunctions:

At a table nearby, a <u>wife</u> *and* <u>husband</u> are having a fight. [Kingsolver]

correlative conjunctions: linked pairs of function words that tie together
two words or phrases; the first half of the pair precedes the first word or
phrase, and the second precedes the second (see Table 6.2).

count noun: a word designating any one individual of a class of living
creatures or inanimate objects, such as *dog, boy, house, restaurant,* and
elephant:

The big <u>garden</u> is in the <u>back</u> of the <u>house</u>. [Nin]

declarative sentence: a sentence that makes a statement:

I don't have any pets. [Fulghum]

definite article: the word *the,* which is used to introduce a noun phrase
with specific reference:

Then I slipped down into the seat and went to sleep. [Nin]

demonstrative pronouns: the demonstratives *this* and *that* and their plural forms *these* and *those* when they appear by themselves, without any accompanying nouns:

The refrain "<u>this</u> is not your country" echoed for a lifetime. [Rodriguez]

determiner: a noun modifier that always precedes any adjectives modifying the same noun; unlike an adjective, a determiner does not provide a characteristic of the noun but determines whether the noun phrase is definite or indefinite, near or far, and so on. (See Table 1.1.)

direct object: a noun, noun phrase, or pronoun that follows the verb and is acted upon by the subject:

He locked <u>the cell door</u>. [Gaines]

fragment: a partial sentence; a group of words that doesn't form a sentence but is punctuated as one:

At the Feather River Inn near the town of Blairsden in the Sierra Nevada Mountains of northern California. [Fulghum]

gender: an indication in a word that points to a male being, a female being, or something that is taken to be neither male nor female:

A couple of mornings ago, the lady who lives in the houseboat across the way from me was really getting down with Aretha Franklin as the stereo pounded out "R-E-S-P-E-C-T." (feminine gender) [Fulghum]

indefinite article: either *a* or *an*, which precedes a singular noun when the speaker/writer does not have a specific item in mind:

For my childhood friend Jackie and me, there was no recognition of animal life, other than cats and dogs and <u>an</u> occasional squirrel that from a distance looked like a baseball mitt nailed to a tree. [Soto]

indefinite pronoun: a pronoun whose antecedent is not specific and may even be implied rather than expressed; words such as *someone, somebody,* and *something,* as well as many quantifying words, are indefinite pronouns. (See Table 1.5.)

indirect object: one of two objects of some transitive verbs whose subject transfers something (the direct object) to someone (the indirect object):

Claude handed <u>him</u> the safety razor. [Gaines]

infinitive: a verb form that has no suffix to indicate tense or anything else, such as *walk, jump,* or *eat:*

From the window, she could <u>see</u> the tall white buildings of downtown Kobe and the mountains to the north. [Mori]

infinitive phrase: a phrase that usually begins with the function word *to*, followed by a verb in the infinitive form and any objects and adverbials that complete the verb:

I attempted <u>to follow the budget debate</u>. [Ephron]

intransitive verb: a verb or verb phrase in the predicate phrase that does not take a direct object and that appears alone or with an adverb or adverbial:

The parade <u>stopped</u>.

irregular verb: a verb that expresses past tense in one of several ways, but not by adding *-d* or *-ed*. (See Table 2.2.)

linking verb: a verb that connects the element that follows it—usually a noun or noun phrase or an adjective or adjective phrase—to the subject:

The store <u>was</u> empty.

main clause: a clause that can stand by itself as a sentence; often has a subordinate clause as a subject, object, complement, or modifier:

<u>Larry was a college friend</u> who lived under a tree. [Soto]

main verb: the verb that is the most important element in the verb phrase of a sentence:

We were <u>dragging</u> Dupree from the car to her door. [Mosley]

mass noun: a noun that typically indicates a formless substance, such as *water, flour,* and *sand;* mass nouns generally do not have plural forms.

modal auxiliary: a function word that expresses the "mood" of the speaker or writer (thus the word *modal*) about the necessity, possibility, or the intention of doing the action expressed in the main verb. (See Table 2.7.)

modifier: a word or phrase that limits or describes another word or phrase:

We folded our clothes <u>neatly</u> and laid them on the stools <u>at the ends of the beds</u>. [Atwood]

nonrestrictive adjective phrase: an adjective phrase similar in function to the nonrestrictive appositive, but it has no noun; it typically follows the noun or noun phrase it modifies and provides additional but nonessential information about the noun or noun phrase:

They are filming my father, <u>splendid and somber in top hat and overcoat,</u> who holds the Northeastern telephone directory, from which he pretends to read the eulogy. [Bergen]

nonrestrictive appositive: a noun or noun phrase that typically follows the noun or noun phrase it modifies and provides additional but nonessential information about the noun or noun phrase:

I considered my fiancee, <u>Carolyn,</u> and she didn't look poor. [Soto]

nonrestrictive modifier: a modifier that adds detail to but does not limit the noun it modifies; it provides details that could appear in a separate sentence:

My mother had used the money donated by the First Chinese Baptist Church, <u>where my father had served as an assistant pastor.</u> [Tan]

noun: a word for a living being or lifeless thing, such as *Jane, woman, city,* and *handkerchief.*

noun phrase: a group of words that has a noun and any elements that modify the noun in some way:

Behind <u>the house</u> lies <u>a vast wild tangled garden.</u> [Nin]

number: a suffix or form (as with pronouns) that points to one individual (singular) or to more than one (plural).

object of the preposition: the noun, noun phrase, or pronoun that follows a preposition in a prepositional phrase:

Most nights we stayed in <u>those motels.</u> [Simpson]

participle phrase: a group of words that consists of a participle verb form along with any objects or adverbials:

A trumpet <u>made from a ram's horn</u> is blown, <u>summoning the people for judgment and self-improvement.</u> [Fulghum]

passive voice: the form of the verb phrase in a sentence whose subject is not the instigator of the action but is acted upon; the auxiliary *be* occurs in the verb phrase with the past participle of the main verb:

Without effort, confusion, or much thought, four round stones <u>were rolled</u> together on the little beach. [Steinbeck]

past participle: the principle part of a verb that usually ends in *-ed* or *-en,* and is accompanied by an auxiliary in the verb phrase:

Though probably no more than twelve, he had already <u>developed</u> a degree of compassion. [Sullivan]

perfect aspect: a verb phrase made up of *have* and the past participle of the main verb; typically it expresses a completed event:

> Though probably no more than twelve, he <u>had already developed</u> a degree of compassion. [Sullivan]

perfect progressive aspect: the aspect that expresses continuing activity begun at an earlier point by combining the perfect and progressive aspects:

> He <u>had been standing</u> to the side of the door, where Junior couldn't see, but then he stood out in plain sight. [Mosley]

person: an indication in a verb or pronoun as to whether the subject of the verb or the antecedent of the pronoun is the speaker (first person), the addressee (second person), or what is spoken about (third person).

personal pronoun: a pronoun form that expresses person (that is, first person, second person, or third person). (See Table 1.3.)

possessive pronoun: a pronoun that indicates possession or other association between the pronoun and a noun that follows it. (See Table 1.4.)

predicate phrase: the part of a sentence that comprises the verb or verb phrase together with other elements that may complete the verb, such as a noun or noun phrase, an adverb or adverb phrase, or an adverbial:

> He <u>locked the cell door</u>. [Gaines]

preposition: a function word that indicates a relationship of time, location, direction, or association between the word or phrase that follows it (its object) and another element in a sentence, usually a noun or a verb. (See Table 3.1.)

prepositional phrase: a group of words beginning with a preposition:

> They were looking <u>at the fire</u>. [Gaines]

present participle: a verb form ending in *-ing:*

> He was <u>wearing</u> a woolly brown suit and bright blue shoes. [Mosley]

principal parts: the infinitive, the past tense, the past participle, and the present participle of any verb. (See Table 2.1 and Table 2.2.)

progressive aspect: a form of the verb phrase formed from *be* plus the present participle of the main verb; expresses a continuing event:

> He <u>was holding</u> a few damp bills in his hand. [Mosley]

pronoun: a word that replaces a freestanding noun or a noun phrase:

<u>My</u> son is addicted. Last night <u>he</u> asked <u>me</u> to serve dinner on a tray in front of "Star Trek." Last night <u>I</u> unplugged <u>him</u>. <u>He</u> has been the fourth Stooge long enough. [O'Reilly]

proper noun: a noun that names a particular or unique entity, either living or inanimate, such as *Marilyn, Mr. Peabody,* and *Illinois;* it always begins with a capital letter.

reflexive pronoun: a pronoun that ends in the suffix *-self* (singular) or *-selves* (plural); a reflexive pronoun never serves as the subject. (See Table 3.2.)

regular verb: a verb that forms the past tense by adding *-d* or *-ed* to its base form. (See Table 2.1.)

relative clause: a modifier that has all the characteristics of a sentence but cannot stand alone and that provides information about the noun phrase it modifies:

Larry was a college friend <u>who lived under a tree</u>. [Soto]

relative pronoun: a pronoun that begins a relative clause and points back to a noun or noun phrase in the main clause:

Larry was a college friend <u>who</u> lived under a tree. [Soto]

restrictive modifier: a modifier that narrows the reference of a very general noun (such as *person, child, book*) so that it can indicate a particular individual or a specific case:

There are few people <u>whom I really love</u>. [Austen]

subject: the part of the sentence, usually a noun, noun phrase, or pronoun, that performs the activity expressed in the verb:

Over the course of years <u>everyone in Cannery Row</u> owed him money. [Steinbeck]

subordinate clause: a sentence-like construction that serves as a part of another sentence:

As a doctor, he knew <u>that death was, except perhaps for childbirth, the most natural thing in the world</u>. [King]

subordinating conjunction: a function word that introduces a subordinate clause—*because* is a good example (see Table 4.2).

tense: the time reference of a verb, either past (often indicated with *-ed*) or present (indicated with *-s* for third person singular):

I frown<u>ed</u> up at her, sticky with apple juice and dizzy with heat. [LeCompte]

transitive verb: a verb or verb phrase that takes a direct object:

The rogue biologist <u>had been watching</u> the cottage for some time. [Garner]

verb: a word that expresses action, being, or condition and that changes form to show time, such as *run, be,* and *sit.*

verbal particle: a word selected from the set of prepositions that alters the meaning of a verb in a particular way; it can "hop" over the noun phrase that follows it:

Miss Emma dished <u>up</u> the food. (Miss Emma dished the food <u>up</u>.) [Gaines]

verbals: participle phrases and infinitive phrases taken as a group:

Julie Siegel and I managed <u>to wangle the recipe from the proprietor of a restaurant in Rome</u>. [Ephron]

I couldn't stop <u>shaking my head</u>. [Ephron]

verb phrase: a group of words containing a main verb and any auxiliaries or particles:

The rogue biologist <u>had been watching</u> the cottage for some time. [Garner]

Exercise 1.1

1. *The* street runs down unevenly towards *the* Seine.
2. By *the* Seine there is *a* tavern and *a* restaurant.
3. *The* dogs bark at night.
4. *The* fountain emerges like *the* headstone of *a* tomb.
5. *The* day begins always with *the* sound of gravel crushed by *the* car.
6. *The* shutters are pushed open by Emilia, and *the* day admitted.
7. Below *the* rug, I felt, was *the* earth.
8. *The* fountain was gay and sprightly.
9. He would have passed anonymously through *a* crowd.
10. Then I slipped down into *the* seat and went to sleep.

Exercise 1.2

1. When [the bell] rings, the *Spanish* maid swings open the *large* gate and the cars drive up the *gravel* path, making a *crackling* sound.
2. There are eleven windows showing between the *wooden* trellis covered with ivy.
3. Every room is painted a *different* color.
4. I seek only the *high* moments.
5. The *big* garden is in the back of the house.

Exercise 1.3

1. *No* adrenaline was left in *her* body.
2. On *the* tenth anniversary of *this* disastrous affair, *a* party was held.
3. I don't have *any* pets.
4. Yes, I know, there is *an* old lady up in *that* tree over there.
5. At *some* point *your* genetic code presses *a* switch in *your* head.
6. *Your* life becomes like *your* old car—just as long as it runs and gets you there, who cares how it looks?
7. Sometimes *the* old geek asks *another* lady to dance.

8. After _the_ dishes are washed and _the_ sink rinsed out, there remains in _the_ strainer at _the_ bottom of _the_ sink what I will call, momentarily, _some_ "stuff."
9. _A_ willingness to do _your_ share of cleaning up the mess is _a_ test.
10. _The_ sons leave, kick away and burn _all_ bridges, never to be seen again.
11. But sometimes they come back in _their_ own way and in _their_ own time and take _their_ own fathers in _their_ arms.
12. _The_ ultimate source of _this_ information was _the_ snake in _the_ Garden of Eden.
13. There is _no_ water.
14. She was anchored to _her_ seat by _her_ own dignity.
15. _A_ new religion could be founded on _this_ one sacrament.

Exercise 1.4

1. What is a date really, but a job interview that lasts all night?
2. Don't get me wrong, the wedding ceremony is a beautiful thing.
3. For men, the transplant is the hair procedure of choice.
4. The hair plug is an interesting process.
5. One of the most popular procedures today is the nose job.
6. I was in the drug store the other day trying to get a cold medication.
7. The other day I was watching women in a department store looking at clothes.
8. To me nothing matches the phone machine as a modern technological accomplishment.
9. Somebody just gave me a shower radio.
10. I also love the gift certificate.
11. Wouldn't it be nice if you could have a car alarm that was a little more subtle?
12. I don't know why people always have the same reaction when they hear about a plane crash.
13. You go up to the ticket agent.
14. I hate the waiting room because it's called the waiting room so there's no chance of no waiting.
15. Do the security guards in the art museums ever stop anybody from taking the paintings?
16. Little Jimmy here needs an organ transplant.
17. I'd like once for a sweepstakes company to have some guts, come out with the truth, just be honest with people one time.
18. A person suffering from fear of success is scraping the bottom of the fear barrel.
19. Whenever you ask for the doggie bag at a restaurant, there's a certain sense of failure there, isn't there?
20. I've never really understood the importance of the orchestra conductor.
21. The thing about L.A. that kind of threw me was the smog alerts.
22. But the health clubs are a little too strict.
23. I don't even know where the wall outlets are anymore.
24. When I was a kid, my favorite ride was the bumper cars.
25. I always preferred a machine ride to anything live, like a pony ride.

Exercise 1.5

Chaos Science has led <u>researchers</u> back to the most fundamental everyday matters—the formation of <u>clouds</u>, the mixing of <u>paint</u>, the flow of <u>traffic</u>, the spread of <u>disease</u>, and the freezing of <u>water</u> in <u>pipes</u>. The cycles of <u>earthquakes</u> and the eruption of <u>volcanoes</u> fits into <u>Chaos Science</u>, too, which is pretty important these days if you live in <u>California</u> or in the Cascade Mountains.

Chaos Science is an abstract noun and, as used by Fulghum here, a proper noun as well. *Researchers, clouds, pipes, earthquakes* are indefinite plural nouns. *Paint* and *water* are indefinite mass nouns. *California* is a proper noun.

Exercise 1.6

1. <u>We</u> folded <u>our</u> clothes neatly and laid <u>them</u> on the stools at the ends of the beds.
   (1) first, plural, subject form; (2) first, plural, possessive; (3) third, plural, object form
2. The Guardian from the previous posting brought <u>me</u> to the front door.
   first, singular, object form
3. The Guardian set down the bag and saluted <u>her</u>.
   third, singular, object form, feminine
4. <u>She</u> waited until the car started up and pulled away.
   third, singular, subject form, feminine
5. <u>I</u> looked at the cigarette with longing.
   first, singular, subject form
6. <u>We</u> stole extra paper packets of sugar for <u>her</u>, from the cafeteria at mealtimes.
   (1) first, plural, subject form; (2) third, singular, object form, feminine
7. <u>He</u> pulls a chair out for <u>me</u>, sets <u>it</u> in front of <u>his</u> desk.
   (1) third, singular, subject form, masculine; (2) first, singular, object form; (3) third, singular, neuter; (4) third, singular, possessive, masculine
8. <u>I</u> simply look at <u>him</u>.
   (1) first, singular, subject form; (2) third, singular, object form, masculine
9. The Commander and <u>I</u> have an arrangement.
   first, singular, subject form
10. <u>They</u> get sick a lot, these Wives of the Commanders.
    third, plural, subject form
11. <u>It</u> adds interest to <u>their</u> lives.
    (1) third, singular, neuter; (2) third, plural, possessive
12. As for <u>us</u>, the Handmaids and even the Marthas, <u>we</u> avoid illness.
    (1) first, plural, object form; (2) first, plural, subject form

13.   Deftly <u>he</u> adds up <u>our</u> final scores on <u>his</u> pocket computer.
       (1) third, singular, subject form, masculine; (2) first, plural, possessive; (3) third,
       singular, possessive, masculine
14.   "<u>You</u> ran away with <u>it</u>," <u>he</u> says.
       (1) second; (2) third, singular, neuter; (3) third, singular, subject form, masculine
15.   <u>She</u> plunges <u>her</u> big hand down, selects a match, hands <u>it</u> over to <u>me</u>.
       (1) third, singular, subject form, feminine; (2) third, singular, possessive, femi-
       nine; (3) third, singular, neuter; (4) first, singular, object form

Exercise 1.7

1.   Suddenly <u>everything</u> around <u>me</u> exploded.
      (1) indefinite; (2) personal
2.   <u>She</u> didn't say <u>anything</u>, just turned around and left.
      (1) personal; (2) indefinite
3.   The driver of the DeSoto tried to pull out, but <u>somebody</u> threw a brick at <u>his</u>
      head.
      (1) indefinite; (2) possessive
4.   But <u>he</u> also knew <u>it</u> might involve crossing Puppet, and <u>he</u> wanted to avoid <u>this</u>
      more than <u>anything</u>.
      (1) personal; (2) personal; (3) personal; (4) demonstrative; (5) indefinite
5.   Puppet looked intently at <u>everyone</u>, especially Toots in a corner with Lourdes.
      indefinite
6.   In fact, Puppet didn't care about <u>anybody</u>.
      indefinite
7.   <u>I</u> felt edgy, <u>my</u> muscles straining, <u>my</u> leg striking a beat against the back of the
      seat.
      (1) personal; (2) possessive; (3) possessive
8.   <u>Everybody</u> got out safely, but the back of the house went up in flames and the
      rest of <u>it</u> sustained irreparable water damage from the fire hoses.
      (1) indefinite; (2) personal
9.   <u>Everything</u> lost <u>its</u> value for <u>me</u>: Love, Life and Women.
      (1) indefinite; (2) possessive; (3) personal
10.   <u>We</u> yelled: *<u>You</u> can't touch <u>this</u>!*, but *Come kill <u>me</u>!* was the inner cry.
      (1) personal; (2) personal; (3) demonstrative; (4) personal
11.   One day at lunch time, <u>I</u> passed a number of hefty dudes in lettered jackets.
      personal
12.   <u>One</u> of them said <u>something</u>.
      (1) indefinite; (2) indefinite
13.   Maybe <u>it</u> had <u>nothing</u> to do with <u>me</u>.
      (1) personal; (2) indefinite; (3) personal
14.   "<u>I</u> don't know about <u>any</u> of <u>this</u>, <u>all</u> <u>I</u> know is you did wrong. <u>You</u> stole from me.
      <u>You</u> have to pay <u>something</u> for <u>it</u>."
      (1) personal; (2) indefinite; (3) demonstrative; (4) indefinite; (5) personal; (6)
      personal; (7) indefinite

Exercise 2.1

1. I <u>avoid</u> her for a day.
   present
2. She <u>gazes</u> at the tabletop.
   present
3. Ellen <u>looks</u> at me.
   present
4. I <u>followed</u> her, five steps behind, to the orchard.
   past
5. Yellow apples <u>glowed</u> among the leaves.
   past
6. I <u>frowned</u> up at her, sticky with apple juice and dizzy with heat.
   past
7. I <u>stare</u> at her across the chasm between our frames of reference.
   present
8. Adrenaline <u>buzzes</u> in my ears and veins.
   present
9. You <u>startled</u> me.
   past
10. Only the gulls <u>break</u> the silence.
    present
11. She <u>turns</u> away from me.
    present
12. My voice <u>surprised</u> me.
    past
13. I <u>gazed</u> at him.
    past
14. Jay <u>shifted</u> uneasily.
    past
15. We <u>groped</u> slowly and painfully back to equilibrium.
    past
16. Ellen <u>wants</u> something from me.
    present
17. She <u>stands</u> still and silent.
    present
18. Ellen's eyes <u>widen</u>.
    present
19. Jay's shoulders <u>twitched</u>.
    past
20. Her smile <u>offends</u> me.
    present

Exercise 2.2

1. We <u>watched</u> until the boats <u>became</u> a row of tiny white gulls on the horizon.
    (1) watch; (2) become
2. Mama <u>shook</u> her head.
    shake
3. And, in the case of my older brothers and sisters, we <u>went</u> with a certain amount of relief.
    go
4. The bus <u>felt</u> very secure to me.
    feel
5. We <u>rode</u> all day.
    ride
6. No one <u>waved</u> or <u>spoke</u>.
    (1) wave; (2) speak
7. They just <u>stared</u> out the windows, ominously silent.
    stare
8. I <u>slept</u> with her every night after that until Papa <u>came</u> back.
    (1) sleep; (2) come
9. An old seamstress <u>took</u> a peacoat of mine, <u>tore</u> the lining out, <u>opened</u> and <u>flat-tened</u> the sleeves, <u>added</u> a collar, <u>put</u> arm holes in and <u>handed</u> me back a beauti-ful cape.
    (1) take; (2) tear; (3) open; (4) flatten; (5) add; (6) put; (7) hand
10. When she <u>stood</u>, only her head <u>showed</u> over the top.
    (1) stand; (2) show
11. We <u>ate</u> in shifts, and I <u>yearned</u> all the more for our huge round table in Ocean Park.
    (1) eat; (2) yearn
12. He <u>kept</u> that cane for years, and it <u>served</u> him well.
    (1) keep; (2) serve
13. He <u>reached</u> Honolulu in 1904, with a letter of introduction to a cousin who <u>taught</u> school on Oahu.
    (1) reach; (2) teach
14. She <u>met</u> Papa early one summer morning at a wholesale market where her fam-ily <u>sold</u> produce.
    (1) meet; (2) sell
15. The next morning I <u>awoke</u> long after sunup.
    awake
16. Woody, Chizu, and Mama <u>knew</u> the tune, so they <u>hummed</u> along while Papa and the other woman <u>sang</u> the words.
    (1) know; (2) hum; (3) sing
17. In Japan, before the turn of the century, outside my father's house there <u>stood</u> one of those stone lanterns, with four stubby legs and a small pagoda-like roof.
    stand

18. He <u>hauled</u> stones in off the desert and <u>built</u> a small rock garden outside our doorway, with succulents and a patch of moss.
    (1) haul; (2) build
19. Because they <u>came</u> from wealthy families and <u>spoke</u> and understood both English and Japanese, they <u>had</u> high opinions of themselves.
    (1) come; (2) speak; (3) understand; (4) have
20. One night the local PTA <u>held</u> an awards dinner for all the students in the scholarship society.
    hold

Exercise 2.3

1. His eyes *were* <u>boring</u> a hole in the opposite wall.
2. She *was* <u>smoothing</u> down the skirt of her dress.
3. The matron *was* <u>standing</u> to the left of the door, almost in front of the men's room.
4. You *can* <u>take</u> care of that tomorrow.
5. Aunt Sarah *had* <u>continued</u> her turkey-smoking instructions even while Blanche and one of the bag boys *were* <u>hoisting</u> her to her feet.
6. As for worry, Miz Cora *has* <u>handled</u> a whole lot worse than this!
7. The door *was* <u>moving</u> slowly inward.
8. Blanche *was* <u>staring</u> up at the cupids painted on the ceiling.
9. He *was* <u>pushing</u> a wheelchair.
10. A long black limousine *was* <u>waiting</u> for them at the bottom of the wide front stairs.
11. Aunt *will* <u>want</u> her dinner around five.
12. She *could* <u>feel</u> it in the house, too, a kind of dour restlessness.
13. Grace *was* <u>breathing</u> through her mouth in short, quick bursts.
14. She *could* <u>see</u> their round, plump faces, replicas of their daddy's sloe-eyed Geechee good looks.
15. She *was* <u>carrying</u> Mumsfield's automobile tools under her left arm.
16. She *could* <u>hear</u> three different birds' songs, none of which she could identify.
17. Somehow she *would* <u>convince</u> her mother to give up the children.
18. Rosalie *had* <u>loved</u> her children dearly.
19. Dr. Haley *is* <u>expecting</u> you.
20. Either Emmeline or that husband of hers *is* <u>driving</u> this girl's blood pressure right on up there!

Exercise 2.4

1. A small boy <u>climbed</u> over the seat. He <u>was wearing</u> soiled briefs and dirty white socks.
   (1) past tense; (2) past tense, progressive aspect

2. He <u>was holding</u> a few damp bills in his hand.
    past tense, progressive aspect

3. "I <u>am calling</u> you about a problem with a friend of yours."
    present tense, progressive aspect

4. "Yeah," Curtis Cross <u>said</u>. He <u>was sitting</u> in front of a plate of rice at the dining table.
    (1) past tense; (2) past tense, progressive aspect

5. The short woman and two big-bellied Mexican men <u>were coming</u> our way. One of the men <u>was swinging</u> a nightstick. They <u>stopped</u> a foot from me.
    (1) past tense, progressive aspect; (2) past tense, progressive aspect; (3) past tense

6. A grizzled old man in overalls and a tee-shirt <u>was sitting</u> in an aluminum chair at the foot of the stairs.
    past tense, progressive aspect

7. I'<u>m looking</u> for somebody, for a friend.
    present tense, progressive aspect

8. He <u>was smiling</u> at me.
    past tense, progressive aspect

9. He <u>was staring</u> into someplace far from that dirty basement.
    past tense, progressive aspect

10. He <u>was wearing</u> a woolly brown suit and bright blue shoes.
    past tense, progressive aspect

Exercise 2.5

1. Pammy <u>drove</u> and I <u>was bellowing</u> at the top of my lungs the entire way.
    (1) past tense; (2) past tense, progressive aspect

2. Even the oldest black people at my church <u>had been laughing</u> when they <u>saw</u> me the week before.
    (1) past tense, perfect progressive aspect; (2) past tense

3. He <u>sounds</u> like a baby dolphin.
    present tense

4. Big Sam <u>was drawing</u> a picture of dolphins and whales and an octopus for baby Sam.
    past tense, progressive aspect

5. My friend Armistead <u>called</u> the other day.
    past tense

6. The baby <u>is sleeping</u>.
    present tense, progressive aspect

7. This <u>has become</u> my specialty.
    present tense, perfect aspect

8. The kitty <u>is lying</u> beside me asleep.
    present tense, progressive aspect

9. My mother <u>lives</u> about twenty minutes up the highway.
   present tense

10. Yesterday we <u>took</u> a fabulous Polaroid of Pammy and Sam.
    past tense

11. The sun <u>was pouring</u> in through the tops of the redwoods.
    past tense, progressive aspect

12. People <u>have been inviting</u> me and Sam to their parties lately.
    present tense, perfect progressive aspect

13. They <u>have lived</u> in the same home for forty years.
    present tense, perfect aspect

14. Pammy <u>is coming</u> for a pool party this afternoon.
    present tense, progressive aspect

15. Emmy and Bill <u>came</u> by with some groceries.
    past tense

16. He <u>inches</u> around the living room like a spy.
    present tense

17. All of the birds <u>were singing</u>, and Sam <u>fell</u> asleep in my arms.
    (1) past tense, progressive aspect; (2) past tense

18. Pammy <u>has gone</u> to Morocco for a month.
    present tense, perfect aspect

19. "Hey, babe, you'<u>ve been working</u> too hard."
    present tense, perfect progressive aspect

20. Alice <u>had been cooking</u> a roast all afternoon.
    past tense, perfect progressive aspect

Exercise 2.6

1. She <u>would be</u> so unhappy.
2. Your things <u>should arrive</u> on the truck next week.
3. You <u>must understand</u> how awkward it <u>would be</u> otherwise.
4. Through the open gate, in the background, she <u>could imagine</u> the green leaves of the trees in the temple garden.
5. Maybe we <u>should leave</u> them.
6. "Somebody <u>will notice</u> them," her mother said.
7. Maybe we <u>can meet</u> in Uzumoridai Park.
8. He <u>must go</u> to the boys' high school in eastern Kobe.
9. "You <u>must give</u> me back my clothes."
10. Besides, she <u>can get</u> to the woods and back faster than any of us.
11. Nobody <u>could see</u> the frogs under the bushes.
12. Soon, a door slammed. Her stepmother <u>must have walked</u> out.
13. Soon, her own room <u>would look</u> the same.
14. If we leave them outside, the neighbors' children <u>might pull</u> things out, and then their parents <u>might talk</u>.
15. I <u>should have seen</u> him more often.

Exercise 2.7

1. Beyond the hedge a truck <u>was rumbling</u> down the road.
   past tense, progressive aspect
2. She <u>has grown</u> an inch or two.
   present tense, perfect aspect
3. I <u>can hear</u> the squeak of her crayons across a sheet of paper.
   present tense
4. Porky Sullivan <u>had waited</u> fourteen years for a son.
   past tense, perfect aspect
5. Dad <u>did not coo</u>.
   past tense
6. She <u>could not understand</u> my whining reluctance.
   past tense
7. I <u>had not held</u> a pane of glass before.
   past tense, perfect aspect
8. Dad and a friend <u>had bought</u> a pony.
   past tense, perfect aspect
9. We <u>continued</u> our walk and <u>were crossing</u> a parking lot.
   (1) past tense; (2) past tense, progressive aspect
10. I <u>may have learned</u> the rudiments of the art and the Queensberry rules from Tussey Russell.
    present tense, perfect aspect
11. Sheila <u>didn't reject</u> his friends.
    past tense
12. Our new neighbors <u>did not speak</u> in Boston Irish but in the accents of blue-blooded New England Yankees.
    past tense
13. He <u>did not answer</u> immediately, and for a while we <u>listened</u> to the crickets and the frogs.
    (1) past tense; (2) past tense
14. Cynicism and love <u>cannot be</u> companions in one human heart, for they <u>are</u> mortal and eternal enemies.
    (1) present tense; (2) present tense
15. The face <u>can be</u> a mask.
    present tense

Exercise 2.8

1. The late nineteenth century in Boston <u>was</u> a fertile time for dreams.
   past tense
2. The city <u>had named</u> itself the "Athens of America."
   past tense, perfect aspect
3. Longfellow <u>was teaching</u> at Harvard.
   past tense, progressive aspect

4. Electric trolleys and trains <u>provided</u> fast, clean transportation.
   past tense

5. Elias Howe <u>had just invented</u> the sewing machine.
   past tense, perfect aspect

6. Anything <u>seemed</u> possible.
   past tense

7. He <u>had done</u> definitive work on war gases as a captain in World War I.
   past tense, perfect aspect

8. My mother <u>doesn't talk</u> very much about her mother.
   present tense

9. They <u>didn't like</u> her high society manner.
   past tense

10. Buff's story <u>is not</u> part of our family myth.
    present tense

11. Buff <u>could match</u> her father's insincerity.
    past tense

12. She <u>had never worked</u> for money.
    past tense, perfect aspect

13. [Polly] <u>had always favored</u> my mother.
    past tense, perfect aspect

14. He <u>was wearing</u> his overalls and those high-top sneakers.
    past tense, progressive aspect

15. Every family <u>has</u> its own cast of characters—the pretty and the plain, the weak and the strong, the bright and the dull, the cop and the rebel.
    present tense

16. He <u>lives</u> in a house at the edge of a thick pine grove on a lake in the Alabama woods.
    present tense

17. Tom <u>could never get</u> anything quite right.
    past tense

18. The researchers at Bell Labs <u>can't tell</u> me much.
    present tense

19. Tom <u>has been working</u> in top secret military communications all these years.
    present tense, perfect progressive aspect

20. My father <u>was just telling</u> stories.
    past tense, progressive aspect

21. He <u>writes</u> for readers.
    present tense

22. Of course he <u>couldn't take</u> care of himself.
    past tense

23. My brother Ben and I <u>are sitting</u> on a wooden bench in a windowless room in the federal courthouse of the Southern District Court in White Plains.
    present tense, progressive aspect

24. Judge Goettel <u>interrupts</u> the questioning of my mother.
    present tense

25.   Iole <u>had always scolded</u> our family for our disdain for physical comforts.
      past tense, perfect aspect

Exercise 3.1

1.   <u>Red Riding Hood</u> walked on along the main path.
     Did <u>Red Riding Hood</u> walk on along the main path?
2.   <u>The parade</u> began with great hoopla.
     Did <u>the parade</u> begin with great hoopla?
3.   <u>The emperor</u> is naked.
     Is <u>the emperor</u> naked?
4.   <u>The parade</u> stopped.
     Did <u>the parade</u> stop?
5.   <u>The emperor</u> paused.
     Did <u>the emperor</u> pause?
6.   <u>The emperor</u> is merely endorsing a clothing-optional lifestyle!
     Is <u>the emperor</u> merely endorsing a clothing-optional lifestyle?
7.   <u>The frightened pigs</u> ran to the house of sticks, with the wolf in hot pursuit.
     Did <u>the frightened pigs</u> run to the house of sticks, with the wolf in hot pursuit?
8.   <u>The tinker and his wife</u> lived in a little hovel next to the modest estate of a local
     witch.
     Did <u>the tinker and his wife</u> live in a little hovel next to the modest estate of a
     local witch?
9.   <u>The wife of the tinker</u> was pregnant.
     Was <u>the wife of the tinker</u> pregnant?
10. <u>They</u> named the baby Rapunzel, after a type of lettuce.
     Did <u>they</u> name the baby Rapunzel, after a type of lettuce?
11. <u>The witch</u> was Rapunzel's only companion.
     Was <u>the witch</u> Rapunzel's only companion?
12. <u>Papa Bear</u> had prepared big bowls of all-natural porridge for them to eat.
     Had <u>Papa Bear</u> prepared big bowls of all-natural porridge for them to eat?
13. <u>The rogue biologist</u> had been watching the cottage for some time.
     Had <u>the rogue biologist</u> been watching the cottage for some time?
14. <u>They</u> moved into the bedroom with growing alarm.
     Did <u>they</u> move into the bedroom with growing alarm?
15. <u>Baby Bear</u> watched with astonishment.
     Did <u>Baby Bear</u> watch with astonishment?

Exercise 3.2

1.   The big black iron pots still hung <u>against the wall</u>.
2.   A black patent-leather purse hung <u>from her right shoulder</u>.
3.   He was waiting <u>for his drink</u>.

4. We danced <u>for a while</u>.
5. He fidgeted <u>with his hat</u>.
6. The four white men split <u>into pairs</u>.
7. The thin, brown-skinned man nodded <u>at me</u>.
8. The program began <u>at seven o'clock</u>.
9. They were looking <u>at the fire</u>.
10. We had stopped <u>for a moment</u>.

Exercise 3.3

1. <u>That summer</u>, Ben and I sat in the fields outside.
2. [The perfume] would last me <u>five years</u> probably.
3. She bought things <u>all the time</u>.
4. <u>A lot of times</u>, I've thought about it.
5. I've heard my mother say that <u>fifty times</u>.
6. She only had me <u>six more years</u>.
7. You said it <u>this afternoon</u>.
8. <u>All day</u> the air conditioners in the arena hummed like the inside of a refrigerator.
9. <u>A minute later</u>, I was in trouble in the kitchen.
10. Tim drew <u>all the time</u>, on everything.
11. <u>A few seconds later</u>, she called from the back of the house.
12. <u>A week later</u>, my mother ran to my room.
13. <u>All of a sudden</u>, I was starving.
14. <u>Every mile or so</u> he would lazily turn back and circle around to us.
15. Then, <u>a few squares of sidewalk later</u>, he looked back and stood there.
16. They never went to bed <u>that night</u>.
17. They had been married <u>three years</u> but they never had any furniture.
18. <u>The next morning</u> my mother came in and sat on the edge of my bed.
19. <u>The first week in June</u> the weather turned.
20. We were going over the bridge; the steel underneath roared <u>every ten feet</u>.

Exercise 3.4

1. The two old men <u>had continued</u> [their conversation].
2. The fat man <u>shrugged</u> [his shoulders].
3. He <u>did not answer</u> [her].
4. Miss Emma <u>dished up</u> [the food].
5. He <u>would not open</u> [his mouth].
6. The audience <u>appreciated</u> [the singing].
7. Vivian <u>put on</u> [her galoshes].
8. I <u>put down</u> [my fork].
9. An old automobile tire <u>surrounded</u> [each flower].
10. A white sharecropper <u>must have been plowing</u> [the ground].

11. Paul <u>stuck out</u> [his hand].
12. He <u>wore</u> [a black pin-striped suit].
13. Vivian <u>lowered</u> [her head].
14. Dr. Joseph <u>acknowledged</u> [their greeting].
15. The old man <u>nodded</u> [his head] emphatically.

Exercise 3.5

1. The woman in the gray dress <u>had offered</u> (them) [tea].
    The woman in the gray dress had offered tea to them.
2. She <u>gave</u> (me) [a five-dollar bill].
    She gave a five-dollar bill to me.
3. She <u>put down</u> [her spoon].
4. I <u>passed</u> (her) [the salad].
    I passed the salad to her.
5. She also <u>gave</u> (us each) [a plate-sized salad].
    She also gave a plate-sized salad to us each.
6. She <u>served</u> (us) [protein snacks].
    She served protein snacks to us.
7. She <u>made</u> (us) [steak tartare] for breakfast.
    She made steak tartare for us for breakfast.
8. We <u>told</u> (her) [little bits].
    We told little bits to her.
9. She <u>gave</u> (me) [her old Sears jacket].
    She gave her old Sears jacket to me.
10. I <u>lifted up</u> [the chrome door handle].
11. Benny <u>kicked</u> [me] with a wet foot.
12. She <u>made</u> (me) [cinnamon toast].
    She made cinnamon toast for me.
13. My mother <u>handed</u> (him) [the receiver].
    My mother handed the receiver to him.
14. I <u>gave</u> (her) [the marbles].
    I gave the marbles to her.
15. The men <u>wore</u> [V-necked T-shirts].

Exercise 3.6

1. I'<u>d have just left</u> [it] {dirty}.
    It was dirty.
2. I <u>crossed</u> [my arms] over my chest.
3. She <u>must have found</u> [me] {terribly plain}.
    I was terribly plain.
4. The waiter <u>left</u> [us] {alone}.
    We were alone.

5. That <u>made</u> [me] {exhausted}.
   I was exhausted.
6. Her bright voice <u>made</u> [me] {angry}.
   I was angry.
7. We <u>painted</u> [my bedroom floor] {white}.
   My bedroom floor was white.
8. My mother <u>rested</u> [her chin] on her hands.
9. My mother <u>loved</u> [that car].
10. Milton <u>shook</u> [me] {awake}.
    I was awake.

Exercise 3.7

1. I <u>like</u> [my work].
2. She <u>flings</u> [her baggage] in all directions.
3. The waitress <u>gave</u> (me) [a kiss].
4. I <u>left</u> (her) [a two-dollar tip].
5. I <u>gave</u> (her) [the clock].
6. I <u>told</u> (her) [the story].
7. They <u>bought</u> (themselves) [an 18-speed mountain bicycle].
8. Elias Schwartz <u>repairs</u> [shoes].
9. With regret in his voice he <u>pronounced</u> [them] {unworthy}.
10. I <u>accepted</u> [the unwelcome judgment].

Exercise 3.8

1. The deputy <u>was looking</u> {very mean}.
2. The three of them <u>were</u> (in the kitchen).
3. Miss Emma <u>looked</u> {tired}.
4. She <u>was</u> {tired}.
5. His breakfast <u>was</u> {two homemade biscuit sandwiches}.
6. His godmother <u>became</u> {immobile}.
7. The store <u>was</u> {empty}.
8. Jefferson <u>became</u> {frightened}.
9. The prosecutor's story <u>was</u> {different}.
10. The Rainbow Club <u>was</u> {quiet}.

Exercise 3.9

1. (That afternoon) <u>he</u> had come into the grocery.
2. (In fine weather) <u>they</u> lived in the shadow of the black cypress tree at the top of the lot.
3. (During the depression) <u>she</u> was hardest hit.

4. (After a while) <u>William</u> went disconsolately back to the Bear Flag.
5. (In the evening just at dusk), <u>a curious thing</u> happened on Cannery Row.
6. (In his hand) <u>he</u> carried a covered wicker basket.
7. (To the left) <u>the office</u> opens into a library.
8. (Over a period of years) <u>Doc</u> dug himself into Cannery Row.
9. (In the laboratory) <u>the girls from Dora's</u> heard the Plain Songs and Gregorian music for the first time.
10. (On the reef) <u>the whistling buoy</u> bellows like a sad and patient bull.
11. (Quite often) <u>he</u> went collecting with Doc.
12. (On a good night) <u>Eddie</u> got three-quarters of a gallon.
13. (In April 1932) <u>the boiler at the Hediondo Cannery</u> blew a tube for the third time in two weeks.
14. (In a few minutes) <u>Hazel</u> came damply up the chicken walk to the Palace.
15. (For a week or so) <u>he</u> just stood outside the basement door and looked in.
16. (Then one day) <u>he</u> stood inside the door.
17. (Ten days later) <u>he</u> was in the basement.
18. (Finally) <u>Frankie</u> got to the work bench.
19. (One afternoon) <u>he</u> did a desperate thing.
20. (For a moment) <u>Frankie</u> stood still.
21. (One morning) <u>elderly Mr. Carriaga</u> was walking from his house on the hill down toward Alvarado Street.
22. (In those days) <u>little boys</u> were courteous.
23. (Some time before dawn) <u>Eddie</u> came back.
24. (Over the hill) <u>a fox</u> was barking sharply.

Exercise 3.10

1. The deceased, twenty-two-year-old Negro male, <u>was allegedly shot</u> by another person on the premises of a night club.
    passive
2. No weapon <u>was found</u> on or near his body.
    passive
3. The jury <u>turned back</u> the prosecution's request for a conviction of murder in the first degree.
    active
4. Mark <u>was found</u> guilty of second-degree murder.
    passive
5. The coroner <u>describes</u> the wounds in detail.
    active
6. The surgical incision and its grisly clamps <u>are dismissed</u> in a single sentence.
    passive
7. The six bullet holes <u>receive</u> one full paragraph each.
    active
8. Blake and I <u>were making</u> small talk.
    active

9. For him, everything about the killing <u>had been said</u>.
   passive
10. In bed, I <u>was shocked</u> awake by groaning timbers or voices.
    passive
11. Downtown, near the police station or the courthouse, he <u>could have been stopped</u> at any time.
    passive
12. The ceremony <u>was performed</u> in the log house.
    passive
13. The way for this marriage <u>was smoothed</u> by a previous union between the Pattersons of Hollins and the Staples of Troutville.
    passive
14. My mother's uncle Blaine <u>had married</u> my father's aunt, Ruby.
    active
15. I <u>visited</u> the log house in Hollins as a small boy in the 1950s.
    active
16. I <u>remember</u> Hollins as a place of women.
    active
17. My father <u>was not included</u> in these trips.
    passive
18. Enormous tins of lard <u>were lined up</u> around the smokehouse walls.
    passive
19. My father <u>missed</u> the luck of the draw.
    active
20. He <u>was raised</u> in the home of Ada's father, Tom Perdue, a brown-skinned version of Simon Legree.
    passive

Exercise 4.1

1. <u>These mixtures (of blood)</u> had made them a highly spirited pack.
2. She was <u>the daughter (of sainted Amelia)</u>.
3. Sears then remembered <u>a scene (with Estelle)</u>.
4. <u>His feeling (for Renee)</u> was confused and profound.
5. <u>The loveliness (of the landscape)</u> had been restored.
6. Maybelle was <u>the name (of the checkout clerk)</u>.
7. His doctor had given him <u>a list (of psychiatrists)</u>.
8. <u>The politics (in this profession)</u> are absolutely indescribable.
9. <u>This turn (of thought)</u> troubled Chisholm.
10. <u>The tape (of an operatic soprano's voice)</u> led them on.

Exercise 4.2

1. <u>The driver</u>, <u>a rancher from Oxnard</u>, bought him burgers and Cokes.
   nonrestrictive
2. <u>My sister</u>, <u>a fight fan from the year one</u>, pounded a fist into her palm and wished Chacon all the luck.
   nonrestrictive
3. We drove to <u>the Ivy Room in Albany</u>, <u>a bar with cable television</u>.
   nonrestrictive
4. <u>Tony Perez</u>, <u>the referee</u>, stepped between them to stop the fight.
   nonrestrictive
5. One summer I heard <u>our three-year-old daughter</u> <u>Mariko</u> say, "The days are filled with air."
   restrictive

Exercise 4.3

1. <u>An only child</u>, <u>she</u> had a less strong bond with her mother, Lillie Mae.
2. In Los Angeles, Lillie Mae met and married <u>Parry Boyd</u>, <u>a handsome devil from a fine family</u>.
3. I moved in with <u>my Dutch governess</u>, <u>Dena</u>.
4. <u>Mrs. Grimaldi</u>—<u>round, blond, and fluffy, much like her poodles</u>—spoke in strange cooing sounds.
5. <u>Bobby</u>, <u>the Western Union delivery man</u>, lived down the road over the Barrymore garage.
6. And so, one Sunday, off I went to a burro ranch with <u>my governess</u>, <u>Dee</u>, and <u>her boyfriend</u>, <u>Don</u>.
7. <u>Not a particularly patient man</u>, <u>he</u> was intolerant and short-tempered with slowness or stupidity.
8. One of my playmates was <u>Carla Kirkeby</u>, <u>the daughter of a hotel magnate</u>.
9. <u>Relentlessly cheerful, infallibly good-hearted</u>, <u>Dee</u> was the constant in my life.
10. The two of us became <u>a team of sorts</u>, <u>a prep school Laurel and Hardy</u>.
11. These were all <u>decent people</u>, <u>kind and hard-working</u>.
12. <u>Young and self-absorbed</u>, <u>I</u> scarcely suffered from an excess of sensitivity.
13. <u>My old Montesano roommate</u>, <u>Veronica</u>, had written inviting me to visit her in Rhodesia that summer.
14. <u>His most recent film</u>, *<u>A Man and a Woman</u>*, had been an enormous success.
15. <u>Yves Montand</u> was an idol in France: <u>charming, talented, debonair</u>.
16. The Beach Boys had bought <u>Edgar Rice Burroughs' house</u>, <u>a gracious Mediterranean villa</u>.
17. <u>His seven-hour documentary</u>, *<u>Phantom India</u>*, had been unanimously acclaimed everywhere but in that country.

18. That first meeting was <u>an edgy encounter</u>, <u>awkward and uncomfortable</u>.
19. <u>He</u> entered, <u>breathless from the cold</u>.
20. <u>David Lazer</u>, <u>a family friend</u>, flew in from London.

Exercise 4.4

1. <u>Elgar's *Pomp and Circumstance* march</u>, <u>named out of a speech of farewell in Othello</u>, spills its solemn dignity over this scene of passage.
    nonrestrictive
2. <u>Not wanting any kind of heart trouble</u>, <u>I</u> took the cook's advice.
    nonrestrictive
3. <u>I</u> had taken a cable car from Union Square to the foot of Columbus Street, <u>intending to walk back through the old Italian quarter of North Beach</u>.
    nonrestrictive
4. <u>Leaning against a tree</u>, <u>I</u> cut the end off the cigar with my pocketknife and carefully lit up.
    nonrestrictive
5. <u>Placing the lit cigar carefully on the wide brick window ledge of the coffeehouse</u>, <u>I</u> went inside to order.
    nonrestrictive
6. <u>Tossing my briefcase in the closet</u>, <u>I</u> headed for the door without any baggage.
    nonrestrictive
7. <u>Riding home in a thunderstorm</u>, <u>Sarah</u> fell asleep in her car seat beside me.
    nonrestrictive
8. <u>Talking to her father the next day</u>, <u>I</u> inquired of Sarah's report on our excursion.
    nonrestrictive
9. <u>Facing east</u>, <u>they</u> would greet the rising sun with hymns and prayers.
    nonrestrictive
10. In <u>a gesture</u> <u>combining dismissal and blessing</u>, he waved me off to bed.
    restrictive
11. <u>She</u> chases after him, <u>urgently honking her horn</u>.
    nonrestrictive
12. <u>The coffin</u> was brought up from the hearse, <u>carried by sons and grandsons</u>.
    nonrestrictive
13. <u>The superintendent of schools</u> <u>sitting beside me</u> knows.
    restrictive
14. <u>He</u> is sitting very quiet and very still, <u>looking into the mirror that the moving line of seniors is for him</u>.
    nonrestrictive
15. The bowl was painted with <u>a simple curving design</u> <u>representing the four winds</u>.
    restrictive

Exercise 4.5

1. And then there's <u>my cousin Bao-bao</u>, <u>whose real name is Roger</u>.
   nonrestrictive
2. At the front of the shop, <u>the only place</u> <u>that gets filtered daylight for a few hours</u>
   <u>a day</u>, are her "long-lasting bargains."
   restrictive
3. My mother is groping for <u>the piece of string</u> <u>that snaps on the light</u>.
   restrictive
4. Phil offers my mother <u>a good-night kiss</u>, <u>which she cautiously accepts with a stiff</u>
   <u>upturned cheek</u>.
   nonrestrictive
5. I ran down Columbus, toward the bay, ignoring <u>the tourists</u> <u>who stared at my</u>
   <u>angry, tear-streaked face</u>.
   restrictive
6. And now I remember <u>the care package</u> <u>my mother gave us</u>.
   restrictive
7. And we have <u>a kind of loyalty</u> <u>that has no word in this country</u>.
   restrictive
8. In my mind, I can still see <u>that steep tunnel of stairs</u> <u>that wound down one floor</u>
   <u>after another</u>.
   restrictive
9. <u>The servant</u> <u>who brought me my food</u> said nothing.
   restrictive
10. I walked up to <u>Old Aunt</u>, <u>who had arrived that day</u>, and she said, "Don't talk
    about this anymore."
    nonrestrictive
11. You should have seen Peanut! She huffed like this—hnh! hnh! hnh!—looking as
    mad as <u>a queen</u> <u>whose servants had run off with her sedan</u>.
    restrictive
12. And <u>Wen Fu's mother</u>, <u>who never liked this servant in the first place</u>, soon came
    to an angry conclusion.
    nonrestrictive

Exercise 4.6

1. And then we went to <u>Little East Gate</u>, <u>where all the best seafood vendors put</u>
   <u>up their stands</u>.
   nonrestrictive
2. Lu had been born in Shandong, <u>that place up north of Shanghai</u> <u>where all the</u>
   <u>good seafood swim</u>.
   restrictive. Notice that the modified noun phrase, together with its
   relative clause, serves as a nonrestrictive appositive to the proper noun
   Shandong.

3. <u>One day</u>, <u>when I was nine or ten</u>, I found a painting of a pretty woman, wearing a plain blue dress, her hair pulled back, looking straight ahead.
   nonrestrictive

4. And later I found <u>a secret place in the green house</u> where Peanut could put on her makeup.
   restrictive

5. She lived in <u>the Japanese section</u>, <u>where buildings curved around corners just like the long body of a dragon.</u>
   nonrestrictive

Exercise 4.7

1. All the women in the monastery noticed one another, <u>because there were only six of us</u>.
   cause

2. <u>After Gan told me this story</u>, he was trembling hard.
   time

3. <u>When she opened her mouth and cried</u>, I cried too.
   time

4. <u>After the nurse left</u>, I thought about this question she had asked.
   time

5. I turned down an alley, <u>because that was faster</u>.
   cause

6. <u>When my senses came together</u>, I was lying with my face to the ground.
   time

7. <u>Just as we reached the place where the bombs fell</u>, the rain started.
   time [*just* is an adverb modifying *as*. The relative clause *where the bombs fell* is inside the adverbial clause.]

8. <u>After we ate</u>, we exchanged addresses.
   time

9. <u>Before we left</u>, Hulan and I held hands.
   time

10. She looked more like someone who cleaned things <u>when no one was looking</u>.
    time

11. <u>When the servant opened the door</u>, she screamed then fainted.
    time

12. <u>Before I married</u>, I had come from a poor family.
    time

13. <u>Because he was Wen Fu's boss, the vice-captain</u>, he was certainly more powerful.
    cause [*The vice-captain* is an appositive to *Wen Fu's boss*.]

14. Little Yu's mother was still cooking <u>when we went downstairs</u>.
    time

15. The airplane noise became louder, <u>until they were over our backs, roaring like</u>
    <u>elephants</u>.
    time [*Roaring like elephants* modifies *they*.]
16. Hulan's hands were shaking <u>as she held my shoulders</u>.
    time
17. <u>After more money was exchanged</u>, the woman wrote Peanut's name on a piece
    of red paper, along with her birthdate and the date of the fortune.
    time
18. She knew people in Tientsin, good people who could hide me <u>until I got my</u>
    <u>divorce</u>.
    time [The adverbial clause is inside a relative clause.]
19. Old Aunt had kicked them out of the sitting room, <u>because they had been</u>
    <u>smoking cigars</u>.
    cause
20. And Yau grew more and more dazed with love for this girl, <u>even though she was</u>
    <u>already his wife</u>.
    concession

Exercise 4.8

1. Two days later, the tobacco lobby rented the grand ballroom of the Washington
   Hilton <u>to celebrate his ouster</u>.
2. A week later, she checked out of the hospital, filed for divorce, and went to New
   Mexico <u>to find God</u>.
3. We all have stories like that, stories we rely on <u>to establish our charm in the</u>
   <u>beginning of relationships</u>.
4. Every so often I would fly to New York for one thing or another, and would go
   by <u>to see Vera</u>.
5. I turned <u>to look behind me</u>.
6. A few days after Mr. Abbey's body was discovered, Homicide Detective
   Hartman came back <u>to take another crack at my subconscious</u>.
7. Mark deserted me the minute we got to the terminal at La Guardia and went off
   <u>to buy magazines and newspapers</u>.
8. He and Mrs. Welland and May drove out to old Mrs. Manson Mingott's <u>to</u>
   <u>receive that venerable ancestress's blessing</u>.
9. She had returned the previous year from a long sojourn in Europe <u>to lay siege to</u>
   <u>the tight little citadel of New York</u>.
10. She always gave her ball on an Opera night <u>in order to emphasize her complete</u>
    <u>superiority to household care</u>.

Exercise 4.9

This is my neighbor, <u>a nice lady coming out her front door, on her way</u>
<u>to work and in her "looking good" mode</u>. She's locking the door now

and picking up her daily luggage: purse, lunch bag, gym bag for aerobics, and the garbage bucket to take out. She turns, sees me, gives me the big, smiling hello, takes three steps across her front porch. <u>At</u> about the level of a fire engine at full cry, <u>she</u> goes "AAAAAAAAAGGGGGGGGGHHHH-HHHHH!!!" *(That's a direct quote.)* She has walked full force into a spider web.

Exercise 5.1

1. In the dim light Louis <u>thought</u> <u>the old man looked a hundred and twenty</u>.
2. Louis <u>guessed</u> <u>that the writing on these [gravemarkers] might have been done with chalk or crayon</u>.
3. I'<u>d guess</u> <u>that most men tell their wives a smart of lies</u>.
4. For one moment Louis <u>thought</u> <u>[Jud] had been struck by a sudden pain</u>.
5. Ellie cast a strange, vulnerable glance back over her shoulder, as if to <u>ask</u> them <u>if there might not yet be time to abort this inevitable process</u>.
6. He <u>supposed</u> <u>that even if none of those terrible things had happened, he would have remembered the day forever</u>.
7. After a winter in Maine, most of it in Ludlow, he <u>thought</u> <u>that she needed all the getting out she could lay her hands on</u>.
8. Louis <u>saw</u> <u>that there were no tears in his father-in-law's eyes</u>.
9. Now, as Louis passed the East Room on his way out, he <u>saw</u> <u>that the room was almost empty</u>.
10. By the time Louis had finished three beers, he <u>felt</u> <u>that he had some sort of equilibrium</u> for the first time that day.
11. I <u>don't believe</u> <u>that there's anything new under the sun</u>.
12. And he <u>felt</u> <u>that in truth he was walking along a narrow beam over a gulf of insanity</u>.
13. Suddenly the mist lost its light and Louis <u>realized</u> <u>that a face was hanging in the air ahead of him, leering and gibbering</u>.
14. And in these dreams he <u>would sense</u> <u>that something huge had shrugged by him</u>.
15. He <u>wondered</u> <u>if he had always been within touching distance of such mad irrationalities</u>.

Exercise 5.2

1. When I sat down in the car, I said that we had paid seven dollars for that.
2. My mother said that she was just going to cancel.
3. Her hand on my arm, the taller girl asked me what my father did for a living.
4. Looking down hard, she whispered that I was cuter than Buff.
5. I asked my mother if I should give Peter her coat.

Exercise 5.3

1. Later, Louis would reflect <u>that horses must feel much the same free-floating anxiety when they smell the first smoke of a prairie fire</u>.
   object
2. Tomorrow he would mention casually <u>that he hadn't seen Church around</u>.
   object
3. The day after he would suggest <u>that perhaps Church had wandered off</u>.
   object
4. He felt <u>that he was in his place</u>.
   object
5. It occurred to him <u>that *this* was very much like a dream</u>.
   subject
6. His first guess was <u>that this had not been a grave seizure</u>.
   complement
7. It had also occurred to him <u>that the whole adventure had been dangerous</u>.
   complement
8. It might be <u>that there was less than a month of really good [days] in any natural man's life in the best of circumstances</u>.
   subject
9. Steve saw <u>that Louis had gone insane</u>.
   object
10. I don't think <u>children ever forget the lies their parents tell them</u>.
    object

Exercise 5.4

1. I <u>kept</u> <u>coming back to that</u>.
   participle phrase
2. I <u>never wanted</u> <u>to see him again</u>.
   infinitive phrase
3. Everyone <u>managed</u> <u>to say nice things to me</u> except Diana.
   infinitive phrase
4. I <u>had always meant</u> <u>to write down some of the words</u>.
   infinitive phrase
5. The Secretary of Health, Education and Welfare <u>was preparing</u> <u>to go on the lecture circuit</u>.
   infinitive phrase
6. He <u>said</u> he would stop <u>seeing Thelma</u>.
   participle phrase
7. Then she <u>began</u> <u>pasting [plaid stamps] into stamp books</u>.
   participle phrase
8. Sam <u>began</u> <u>methodically removing the books from the bookshelves</u>.
   participle phrase

9. Mark <u>finished</u> <u>reading to Sam</u>.
    participle phrase
10. Maybe you <u>remember</u> <u>reading about it</u>.
    participle phrase

Exercise 5.5

1. He was a young man, age approximately twenty, and it took Louis less than three seconds <u>to make the only diagnosis that mattered</u>.
    subject of *took*
2. But it was hopeless <u>to resist those eyes</u>.
    subject of *was*
3. He tried desperately <u>to hold on to the dream idea</u>.
    direct object of *tried*
4. Gage began <u>to yell indignantly</u>.
    direct object of *began*
5. It took a good deal longer than seven minutes <u>to shut the machine down that night</u>.
    subject of *took*
6. The nasty death of Victor Pascow on the first day of the fall semester began <u>to fade in the memory of the student body and in Louis's own</u>.
    direct object of *began*
7. <u>Looking at her</u> made his heart ache.
    subject of *made*
8. Goldman told him <u>to get out</u>.
    direct object of *told*
9. I started <u>to scream</u> because I knew she was dead.
    direct object of *started*
10. He did not want <u>to be seen at all</u>.
    direct object of *did not want*
11. It took another ten minutes <u>to pile up the rocks Jud handed him one by one</u>.
    subject of *took*
12. <u>Having a baby</u> had changed our lives together.
    subject of *had changed*
13. (1) <u>Accepting that answer</u> meant (2) <u>accepting that I would never really know what had happened</u>.
    (1) subject of *meant*, (2) direct object of *meant*
14. I might consider <u>coming back under certain circumstances</u>.
    direct object of *might consider*
15. I remember <u>thinking that no one had ever told me how much I would love my child</u>.
    direct object of *remember*

Exercise 5.6

1. There's a real problem <u>in</u> <u>dragging a group into a book</u>.
2. He's known <u>for</u> <u>being chronically perverse about politics</u>.
3. Sometimes the idea <u>of</u> <u>being single</u> interests me.
4. Perhaps this is Mark's way <u>of</u> <u>being understated</u>.
5. I accused Mark <u>of</u> <u>looking at houses</u>.
6. He accused me <u>of</u> <u>snooping in places I didn't belong</u>.
7. It was always a little mystifying to me how we had gone <u>from</u> <u>having so much money</u> <u>to</u> <u>having so little</u>.
8. She responds <u>by</u> <u>having all the feelings I'm refusing to have</u>.
9. I hated her <u>for</u> <u>turning Mark from the man I had fallen in love with into a cold, cruel stranger</u>.
10. It was hard enough putting a marriage back together <u>without</u> <u>becoming known publicly as a marriage-in-trouble</u>.

Exercise 6.1

1. <u>She had a small clear soprano voice</u>, *and* <u>she played the piano nicely</u>.
    clauses
2. Madchen <u>learned of his daughter's adventure</u> *and* <u>was outraged</u>.
    predicate phrases
3. <u>Minnie returned to Kentucky immediately</u>, *but* <u>she had suffered a disappointment she never forgot</u>.
    clauses
4. <u>He worried constantly over their finances</u>, *for* <u>there were now nine members in his household</u>.
    clauses
5. He worked <u>relentlessly</u> *and* <u>well</u>, becoming in his thirties a member of the Alabama House of Representatives.
    adverbs
6. Mrs. Sayre <u>indulged Zelda completely</u> *and* <u>was charmed by her</u>.
    predicate phrases
7. <u>World War I would do a little to change the social rigidity</u>, *but* <u>for the time being it persisted</u>.
    predicate phrases
8. <u>Her skirts, which were rolled at the waist to shorten them, were uneven</u>, *and* <u>her slip usually showed</u>.
    clauses
9. <u>That lack of style must have been something she shared with her mother</u>, *for* <u>Mrs. Sayre rather than a seamstress made all her clothes</u>.
    clauses
10. <u>There were chaperones at the dances</u>, *but* <u>Zelda completely ignored them</u>.
    clauses

11. Francis Scott Key Fitzgerald was <u>Irish</u>, <u>a Roman Catholic</u>, *and* <u>a Midwesterner</u>.
    complements of *was* (an adjective is connected to two noun phrases)
12. The Fitzgeralds lived <u>always on the edge of the best neighborhood in St. Paul</u> *but* <u>never at its center</u>.
    prepositional phrases
13. They settled <u>finally</u> *and* <u>firmly</u> at the end of the finest street in the area, Summit Avenue.
    adverbs
14. <u>She was absent frequently</u>, *and* <u>her conduct report sank to "unsatisfactory" in the marking period before graduation</u>.
    clauses
15. <u>Zelda's release from that world was suddenly within reach</u>, *for* <u>with the United States' entry into World War I in the summer of 1917 Montgomery altered profoundly</u>.
    clauses
16. In September, 1917, Zelda began her senior year in a flurry of <u>dances</u> *and* <u>parties</u>.
    nouns
17. There was to be no more <u>stopping</u> *or* <u>talking</u> in the halls.
    participles used as verbal nouns
18. During the summer he <u>wrote</u> *and* <u>produced</u> a Civil War melodrama called *The Coward*.
    verbs
19. <u>All of the dances on Zelda's card were taken</u>, *but* <u>Scott's name was not on it</u>.
    clauses
20. <u>Her trip had disconcerted him</u>, *for* <u>while he was trying to break into journalism in New York, his girl was not exactly cooling her heels at home</u>.
    clauses
21. Zelda <u>was delighted with the ring</u> *and* <u>told Scott it was beautiful</u>.
    predicate phrases
22. Whether the timing of their marriage date was <u>Zelda's</u> *or* <u>Scott's</u> idea is unknown.
    possessive nouns
23. <u>I haven't the remotest idea of what it's like</u>, *so* <u>I am afraid to make any suggestions</u>.
    clauses
24. <u>The first sale to the *Post* was important to Scott</u>, *for* <u>he intended to make money, a lot of it</u>.
    clauses
25. He knew that <u>the smaller magazines</u> *or* <u>the more literary ones</u> couldn't be expected to pay as the *Post* would.
    noun phrases

Exercise 6.2

1. Joppy was still at the bar, leaning over his big stomach and buffing the marble.
   correct
2. The sky was still light at that time of year, but I could see a crescent moon peeking over the inner roof.
3. The grinner tried to put his hand against my chest, but I grabbed him by the wrist.
4. I turned back at the door to salute him goodbye, but DeWitt Albright had filled his glass and shifted his gaze to the far wall.
5. The Japanese farmers grew artichokes, lettuce, and strawberries along the sides of the road.
6. That night the fields were dark under the slight moon, and the air was chill but not cold.
7. It felt good and familiar to be back there.
   correct
8. He was hovering over me, and I could feel the violence come off of him in waves.
9. He took a seat behind the desk, kicked his foot up on it, and lit a cigarette.
10. He leaned farther back in his chair and hunched his large shoulders.
    correct
11. DeWitt Albright had his bottle and his gun right out there in plain view.
    correct
12. He needed all his children to kneel down and let him be the boss.
    correct
13. I need a house to live in and a place to raise children.
    correct
14. The street was empty, and the neighborhood was quiet.
15. One was tall and skinny, and he was wearing a dark blue suit.
16. The men strode quickly in my direction, but I just turned slowly and walked toward my door.
17. They were holding me by my arms, and I was sagging with my head down.
18. I had recovered from the punch, but I didn't want them to know it.
19. I sat down in the chair and looked up at the leaves coming in through the windows.
    correct
20. Mason moved again, but this time I turned.

Exercise 6.3

1. What had compelled her toward Jozan, he *neither* <u>understood</u> *nor* <u>sought to understand</u>.
   verb and verb phrase that each take the *what* clause as direct object

2. It was *neither* <u>his mother</u> *nor* <u>his prosperous Irish relatives</u> whom Scott Fitzgerald admired.
    noun phrases

3. The passion of her letter, the wild and intense description of her love for Scott, was an indication *not only* <u>of her need for him</u> *but also* <u>of her uncertainly about herself</u>.
    prepositional phrases

4. He has an amazing grasp of the superficialities of the men and women about him, but he has not yet a profound understanding of their motives, *either* <u>intellectual</u> *or* <u>passionate</u>.
    adjectives

5. There was not a hint of discord between Scott and Zelda apparent to *either* <u>Seldes</u> *or* <u>his wife</u> during their entire visit.
    freestanding noun and noun phrase

6. *Neither* <u>the Judge</u> *nor* <u>Mrs. Sayre</u> went with Zelda to New York.
    noun phrase and freestanding noun

7. Xandra Kalman *not only* <u>found the Fitzgeralds a summer house on White Bear Lake</u> *but also* <u>purchased all of the baby things the Fitzgeralds would soon require</u>.
    predicate phrases

8. He was *not only* <u>a successful sports writer</u> *but also* <u>the author of satirical sketches and stories, poems, and comic burlesques</u>.
    noun phrases

9. The watch was the one he had given her during their courtship in Alabama, and it was the first object of value, *both* <u>sentimental</u> *and* <u>actual</u>, that she received from him.
    adjectives

10. Playfully Scott told her that according to *both* <u>Browning</u> *and* <u>Keats</u> he should marry her.
    nouns

Exercise 6.4

1. Beano—Al Bean—wasn't quite so brilliant; <u>on the other hand</u>, he was still here.
    contrast

2. A man either had it or he didn't! There was no such thing as having *most* of it. <u>Moreover</u>, it could blow at any seam.
    addition

3. To be grounded for a medical reason was no humiliation, looked at objectively. But it was a humiliation, <u>nonetheless</u>!—for it meant you no longer had that indefinable, unutterable, integral stuff.
    contrast

4. <u>Likewise</u>, "hassling"—mock dogfighting—was strictly forbidden, and so naturally young fighter jocks could hardly wait to go up in, say, a pair of F-100s and start the duel.
    addition

5. It was no longer the fashion for serious writers to describe the glories of war. Instead, they dwelt upon its horrors, often with cynicism or disgust.
   contrast

6. [Yeager] amazed his instructors with his ability at stunt-team flying, not to mention the unofficial business of hassling. This plus his up-hollow drawl had everybody saying, "He's a natural-born stick 'n' rudder man." Nevertheless, there was something extraordinary about it when a man so young, with so little experience in flight test, was selected to go to Muroc field in California for the XS-1 project.
   contrast

7. Conrad broke into his full cackle of mirth, much the way Wally might have. No one was swept up in the joke, however.
   contrast

8. These things were never pleasant; in fact, they were a bit humiliating.
   emphasis

9. Word of all this circulated quickly, too, and everyone was quite delighted. There was no indication, however, then or later, that Dr. Gladys Loring was amused in the slightest.
   contrast

10. In other cases, however, the single combat settled the affair, and there was no full-scale battle.
    contrast

Exercise 6.5

1. She had a small clear soprano voice; in addition, she played the piano nicely.
2. Minnie returned to Kentucky immediately; however, she had suffered a disappointment she never forgot.
3. He worried constantly over their finances; indeed, there were now nine members in his household.
4. World War I would do a little to change the social rigidity; for the time being, however, it persisted.
5. Her skirts, which were rolled at the waist to shorten them, were uneven; furthermore, her slip usually showed.
6. There were chaperones at the dances; nevertheless, Zelda completely ignored them.
7. She was absent frequently; in addition, her conduct report sank to "unsatisfactory" in the marking period before graduation.
8. Zelda's release from that world was suddenly within reach; with the United States' entry into World War I in the summer of 1917 Montgomery altered profoundly.
9. All of the dances on Zelda's card were taken; Scott's name was not on it, however.

10. Her trip had disconcerted him; while he was trying to break into journalism in New York, his girl was not exactly cooling her heels at home.
11. I haven't the remotest idea of what it's like; therefore, I am afraid to make any suggestions.
12. The first sale to the *Post* was important to Scott; he intended to make money, a lot of it.

Exercise 7.1

1. He <u>stood</u> there in his jeans and scuffed work boots, shirtless in the August heat.
2. Savory steam <u>billows</u> in the cool evening air like a cloud of incense.
3. The sun <u>hangs</u> atop a rock column out to sea.
4. Pollen <u>gilded</u> the tiny hairs of her skin.
5. She <u>comes</u>, her eyes on my steaming bowl.
6. She <u>gazes</u> at the tabletop.
7. I <u>consider</u> her stiff, slender figure, Egyptian in its stubborn angularity.
8. They <u>met</u> in front of us.
9. I <u>stare</u> at her across the chasm between our frames of reference.
10. Adrenaline <u>buzzes</u> in my ears and veins.
11. Ellen <u>puts</u> down the towel.
12. Ellen <u>wraps</u> her arms around her knees.
13. She <u>turns</u> away from me.
14. Toby <u>slipped</u> his hand into mine.
15. Her attention <u>wandered</u> like a toddler's.
16. Her impregnable happiness <u>made</u> him more and more miserable.
17. A car <u>went</u> by on the highway across the field, loud in the quiet night.
18. You <u>have</u> struck an important blow in the fight to deconstruct the destructive fantasy of romantic love.
19. The Bellamys <u>took</u> him home.
20. My lungs <u>begin</u> to ache.

Exercise 7.2

1. I <u>was</u> the one who gave Beautiful Betty the sewing machine.
   main verb, past, singular
2. She <u>was</u> wearing a strange smile, one I had never seen before.
   auxiliary, past, singular
3. His skin <u>was</u> smooth and light-colored, not like the face of someone who worked outdoors all day long.
   main verb, past, singular
4. This student <u>was</u> a man named Lu, a Marxist, just the kind of person Gung-gung would have hated.
   main verb, past, singular

5. At the time, I <u>was</u> living in the house on Tsungming Island, my home for almost twelve years.
    auxiliary, past, singular

6. And after he abandoned it, the greenhouse <u>was</u> used only as a strange storage place.
    auxiliary, past, singular

7. It <u>was</u> a romance story called *Chin Ping Mei*, a forbidden book.
    main verb, past, singular

8. If she <u>was</u> blushing under her white powder, I could not tell.
    auxiliary, past, singular

9. After more money <u>was</u> exchanged, the woman wrote Peanut's name on a piece of red paper, along with her birthdate and the date of the fortune.
    auxiliary, past, singular

10. I <u>was</u> ladling out bowls of boiled dumplings when Wen Fu approached me.
    auxiliary, past, singular

11. And when the dogs died, he bought rifles and shot pigeons, real pigeons because the clay ones <u>were</u> too expensive.
    main verb, past, plural

12. Above the casket, a white banner made out of ten feet of butcher paper <u>is</u> stuck to the wall with masking tape.
    main verb, present, singular, third person

13. I only put that down because my sister-in-law <u>is</u> absentminded.
    main verb, present, singular, third person

14. Inside <u>are</u> a few tangerines, a roll of toilet paper, a canister of Grand Auntie's tea, and the picture of my father that I accidentally knocked over last month.
    main verb, present, plural

15. After I wrote my telegram, the operator girl said to me, "Do you really think we <u>are</u> soon *taonan* [forced to flee]?"
    main verb, present, plural

Exercise 7.3

1. Perhaps it (<u>was</u>, were) ultimately for the better that he had changed.
2. Goldman knew he (<u>was</u>, were) pretending.
3. As we (<u>get</u>, gets) closer to her house, she (point, <u>points</u>) to a place on Clement Street, Happy Super, where she always (do, <u>does</u>) her grocery shopping.
4. She (<u>was</u>, were) plump, but not in that classical way of a peach whose pink skin (<u>is</u>, are) nearly bursting with sweetness.
5. Almost everyone else who lived there (<u>was</u>, were) poor.
6. The matchmaker he found (<u>was</u>, were) an old lady we called Auntie Miao.
7. Auntie Du looked at the guard, whose eyes (was, <u>were</u>) rolling toward sleep.
8. All the women in the monastery noticed one another, because there (was, <u>were</u>) only six of us.

9. Hulan's hands (was, <u>were</u>) shaking as she held my shoulders.
10. And the front of each drawer (<u>was</u>, were) inlaid with mahogany, oak, and mother-of-pearl in a pattern that burst open like a fan.
11. And suddenly everything—the flower arrangements on the plastic-topped tables, my mother's memories of my childhood, the whole family—everything (feel, <u>feels</u>) like a sham.
12. It reminds me of a time when I (<u>was</u>, were) five years old, that age when anything (<u>was</u>, were) possible if you could just imagine it.
13. Nothing (<u>is</u>, are) wrong.
14. Something (<u>has</u>, have) been bothering her.
15. So it was Old Aunt who said that my half brother Kun (<u>was</u>, were) a big revolutionary hero!

Exercise 7.4

The cadences of the mother tongue are among the earliest sounds **a child** hears. <u>He</u> begins to hear what the psychoanalyst Paul Schilder has called "the melody of **speech**" long before <u>he</u> can distinguish any of <u>its</u> words. It conveys to <u>him</u> some of the first sensations, emotions, and meaning that <u>he</u> begins to experience, that is, to learn. Long before <u>he</u> can speak words, <u>he</u> comes to understand them; and not long thereafter, with speech, <u>he</u> makes the words <u>his</u> own. Thus <u>he</u> begins to acquire a language, the most distinctive of all human attributes. The language <u>he</u> learns becomes one of the means—some would say the single most decisive means—by which <u>he</u> discovers <u>himself</u>, <u>his</u> family, <u>his</u> kind, <u>his</u> culture, <u>his</u> view of the world.

In the above passage, *a child* is the antecedent of every occurrence of *he, him, his, himself; speech* is the antecedent of *its.*

Revision

The cadences of the mother tongue are among the earliest sounds **children hear**. <u>They</u> *begin* to hear what the psychoanalyst Paul Schilder has called "**the melody of speech**" long before <u>they</u> can distinguish any of <u>its</u> words. It conveys to <u>them</u> some of the first sensations, emotions, and meaning that <u>they</u> begin to experience, that is, to learn. Long before <u>they</u> can speak words, <u>they</u> *come* to understand them; and not long thereafter, with speech, <u>they</u> *make* the words <u>their</u> own. Thus <u>they</u> *begin* to acquire a language, the most distinctive of all human attributes. The language <u>they</u> learn becomes one of the means—some would say the single most decisive means—by which <u>they</u> *discover* <u>themselves</u>, <u>their</u> *families*, <u>their</u> kind, <u>their</u> *cultures*, <u>their</u> *views* of the world.

Note: The words in italics have been changed to match the changes in pronouns.

Exercise 8.1

1. Are you Mr. Rickett?
2. I wanted to know whether you knew a Mr. Herbert Gotobed.
3. I want you to let me stay in your shop until Mr. Gotobed comes to claim his letter.
4. What time do you close?
5. A row of first story windows looked down upon the alley.
6. Grant asked to see the principal.
7. I have to ask that you will let me find him.
8. In the dimness of the moment, when all his faculties were trying to summon his stunned body to its duty, he wondered detachedly how the man would kill him.
9. Darling, how wonderful of you!
10. I have a right to know, haven't I?

Exercise 8.2

1. Her husband, Harland, is sleeping like a brick and snoring.
2. To all appearances, they're a satisfied couple sliding home free into their golden years, but Alice knows that's not how it's going to go.
3. She leaves the bed quietly and switches on the lamp in the living room.
   correct
4. Cash Stillwater looks up from his work and sees a splash of white birds like water thrown at the sky.
   correct
5. They make their circle again and again, flaunting their animal joy.
6. He counts the birds without knowing it, sorting the shifting group into rows of odd and even.
7. Old people might marry gracefully once in a while, but their houses rarely do.
8. She raised a daughter in this house and planted all the flowers in the yard, but that's nothing to hold her here.
9. Cash glances at Rose, who is peevishly brushing ash off her blouse.
10. She picks up another one and gives it a fling.
    correct
11. Cash knows these women; they come into the store and go crazy over anything herbal.
12. After he bought it, he decided he had to get it cleaned.
13. Lou Ann Ruiz, who is like a second mother to Turtle, tends toward an obsession with health and safety.
14. The cluster of tin bells over the door jingles behind Cash, but it's a customer, a tall, thin man wearing sandals and gray-speckled socks.
15. He nods at Rose, who is at the register.

16. He made me speak English, and he pushed me to do well in school.
17. She picks up her fork and idly begins poking things with it: her plate, the tablecloth, her hair.
18. The old man walks five or six careful steps toward the east and takes a place at the edge of the clearing.
    correct
19. The song sounds a little different, but the dance is still the same gentle stomping in a circle.
20. Annawake folds and unfolds the cotton square on her lap.
    correct

Exercise 8.3

1. Especially, I liked to drop in and visit at the <u>Gohannases'</u> home.
2. I <u>didn't</u> want to leave Hilda, who was like my second mother.
3. I had my <u>father's</u> .22 caliber rifle.
4. A lot of times in these later years since I became a Muslim, <u>I've</u> thought back to that fight and reflected that it was <u>Allah's</u> work to stop me.
5. Her <u>husband's</u> name was Duane Lathrop.
6. I began to sweep and mop and dust around in the <u>Swerlins'</u> house.
7. The Lyonses and I, as it happened, were the <u>town's</u> only Negroes.
8. Whenever our team walked into another <u>school's</u> gym for the dance, with me among them, I could feel the freeze.
9. I think the major impact of <u>Ella's</u> arrival, at least upon me, was that she was the first really proud black woman I had ever seen in my life.
10. From my seat in the back of the bus, I gawked out of the window at white <u>man's</u> America rolling past for what seemed a month.
11. <u>It's</u> funny how I seemed to think of Mary as <u>Ella's</u> sister, instead of her being, just as Ella is, my own half-sister.
12. Those tough <u>Negroes'</u> heyday had been before the big 1931 Seabury Investigation that started Dutch Schultz on the way out, until his career ended with his 1934 assassination.
13. I was one of his top students, one of the <u>school's</u> top students.
14. Malcolm, one of <u>life's</u> first needs is for us to be realistic.
15. <u>You're</u> good with your hands.
16. You <u>haven't</u> had any experience shining shoes.
17. I thought <u>I'd</u> have to catch her.
18. Many of the New Haven <u>Line's</u> cooks and waiters still in railroad service today will remember old Pappy Cousins.
19. Only my oldest brother, Wilfred, <u>wasn't</u> there.
20. This was my best early lesson in how most white <u>men's</u> hearts and guts will turn over inside of them, whatever they may have you believe, whenever they see a Negro man on close terms with a white woman.

Exercise 8.4

"There's a *frog* in my milk," he noted one morning. "Bill, *you* know how a frog got into my milk?"

"They can really get around," I replied.

"And I wonder how *you'll* be getting around," he said meaningfully.

Atwood, Margaret. *The Handmaid's Tale.* Boston: Houghton Mifflin, 1986.

Austen, Jane. *Pride and Prejudice.* New York: Century, 1903.

Bergen, Candice. *Knock Wood.* New York: Ballantine Books, 1984.

Bronowski, Jacob. *The Ascent of Man.* Boston: Little, Brown, 1973.

Chang, Jung. *Wild Swans: Three Daughters of China.* New York: Simon & Schuster, 1991.

Cheever, John. *Oh What a Paradise it Seems.* New York: Knopf, 1982.

Cheever, Susan. *Treetops.* New York: Bantam, 1991.

Cosby, Bill. *Childhood.* New York: Putnam, 1991.

---. *Fatherhood.* New York: Berkley Books, 1986.

Dershowitz, Alan. *The Best Defense.* New York: Vintage, 1982.

Ephron, Nora. *Heartburn.* New York: Pocket Books, 1983.

Fulghum, Robert. *All I Really Need to Know I Learned in Kindergarten.* New York: Fawcett Columbine, 1993.

---. *It Was on Fire When I Lay Down on It.* New York: Ivy Books, 1989.

---. *Uh-Oh.* New York: Villard, 1991.

Gaines, Ernest J. *A Lesson Before Dying.* New York: Vintage, 1993.

Garner, James Finn. *Politically Correct Bedtime Stories.* New York: Macmillan, 1994.

Haley, Alex. *The Autobiography of Malcolm X.* New York: Ballantine, 1973.

Hall, Edward. *The Silent Language.* Garden City, NY: Doubleday, 1959.

Harris, Marvin. *Our Kind.* New York: Harper Perennial, 1989.

Houston, Jeanne Wakatsuki, and James D. Houston. *Farewell to Manzanar.* New York: Bantam, 1973.

Isaacs, Harold R. *Idols of the Tribe.* Cambridge, MA: Harvard University Press, 1975.

King, Stephen. *Pet Sematary.* New York: New American Library, 1983.

Kingsolver, Barbara. *Pigs in Heaven.* New York: HarperCollins, 1993.

Kingston, Maxine Hong. *China Men.* New York: Ballantine, 1977, 1978, 1979, 1980.

Lakoff, Robin. *Talking Power.* New York: Basic Books, 1990.

Lamott, Anne. *Operating Instructions: A Journal of My Son's First Year.* New York: Fawcett Columbine, 1993.

LeCompte, Jane. *Moon Passage.* New York: Harper & Row, 1989.

Lindbergh, Anne Morrow. *Gift from the Sea.* New York: Vintage, 1983.

Maass, Edgar. *The Queen's Physician.* New York: Scribner, 1948.

Marshall, Paule. *Praisesong for the Widow.* New York, Plume, 1983.

Mead, Margaret. *Coming of Age in Samoa.* New York: Laurel, 1961.

Mitford, Nancy. *Zelda.* New York: Avon Books, 1970.

Mori, Kyoko. *Shizuko's Daughter.* New York: Holt, 1993.

Mosley, Walter. *Devil in a Blue Dress.* New York: Pocket Books, 1990.

Murdoch, Iris. *A Word Child.* New York: Viking, 1975.

Neely, Barbara. *Blanche on the Lam.* New York: Penguin, 1992.

Nin, Anais. *The Diary of Anais Nin, Volume One, 1931–1934.* (G. Stuhlmann, Ed.). New York: Harvest/HBJ, 1966.

O'Reilly, Jane. *The Girl I Left Behind.* New York: Bantam, 1980.

Poe, Edgar Allan. *The Fall of the House of Usher.* New York: Cheshire House, 1931.

Rodriguez, Luis J. *Always Running—La Vida Loca: Gang Days in L.A.* New York: Touchstone, 1993.

Seinfeld, Jerry. *SeinLanguage.* New York: Bantam, 1993.

Simpson, Mona. *Anywhere But Here.* New York: Vintage, 1986.

Soto, Gary. *Small Faces.* New York: Dell, 1986.

Staples, Brent. *Parallel Time.* New York: Pantheon Books, 1994.

Steinbeck, John. *Cannery Row.* New York: Penguin, 1973.

Sullivan, Tom, and Derek Gill. *If You Could See What I Hear.* New York: New American Library, 1975.

Tan, Amy. *The Kitchen God's Wife.* New York: Vintage, 1993.

Tey, Josephine. *A Shilling for Candles.* New York: Collier Books, 1954.

Wharton, Edith. *The Age of Innocence.* New York: Collier Books, 1948.

Wolfe, Tom. *The Right Stuff.* New York: Bantam Books, 1979.

INSTRUCTOR'S MANUAL

BASIC GRAMMAR IN MANY VOICES

Marilyn N. Silva

California State University, Hayward

NTC *Publishing Group*

a division of NTC/CONTEMPORARY PUBLISHING COMPANY

Lincolnwood, Illinois USA

C O N T E N T S

CHAPTER ONE

Recognizing Nouns and Pronouns

 OBJECTIVES

After completing this chapter, students will be able to

- recognize articles, demonstratives, and other determiners
- recognize nouns and noun phrases by paying attention to grammatical signals appearing in text
- recognize and name the types of pronouns that occur in English
- recognize nouns and pronouns in real text from sources outside the classroom and in their own writing

The purpose of Chapter One is to help students learn to recognize nouns, pronouns, and the constituents in basic noun phrases. Many students have learned the traditional definition of noun as "person, place, or thing," but that definition does little to help them identify nouns reliably. Thus, though the chapter begins with a semantically based definition ("a noun is a word for a living being or lifeless thing"), it quickly moves on to the function words—articles and other determiners—that serve to mark the beginnings of noun phrases. If students learn to recognize these markers, they will not be led into thinking that *walk* in a sentence such as "I'm going for a walk" is a verb.

Probably your students will fall into one of several groups: native speakers of English who speak a more or less standard variety; native speakers who speak a nonstandard variety; and nonnative speakers who may come from many different language backgrounds. Each of these groups may have special needs that you should consider in the English-language classroom.

Students who speak English natively know a great deal about how the language works, even though they are rarely aware of it and may feel intimidated if called upon to give a rule of English. They think they don't know the rules, but they certainly know how to speak, so in some sense they *do* know them. What they may not know, perhaps, is how to talk about the rules they unconsciously use every time they talk.

Nonnative speakers, on the other hand, may know many "rules" of grammar; they may even be able to recite them, but they may not be able to put these rules to use in speaking or writing tasks. Thus, your task with this group differs from your task with the native speakers. For example, native speakers rarely make mistakes in the selection of articles, but nonnative speakers, particularly those from Asian-language backgrounds, have a difficult time using them or using them appropriately. Thus, depending on your class, you may decide to devote more or less time to the study of the article/determiner system.

However, regardless of the audience, I suggest you start your course with the nonsense word exercise I provide on page IM-5. Native speakers will discover that they "know" more about grammar than they thought, and nonnative speakers will discover the importance of function words and other grammatical markers that seem so inconsequential to them and that we penalize them for omitting.

When presenting this exercise, emphasize to your students that there are no right or wrong answers and that they might not be able to do a part of the exercise. They merely need to make an honest attempt. You may wish to have students work in groups of two or three.

Before doing the exercise, many students think that number 2 will be much less difficult than number 1. Number 1 simply has no familiar words, save for relatively meaningless ones like *the* and *and*, whereas number 2 has several ordinary ones they are likely to hear every day. Yet, once they begin the exercise, many students find their expectations to be incorrect, for though they may be at a loss to tell you what the sentence means, they can write a sentence from the "words" in number 1 that *sounds* like English.

Number 2, on the other hand, poses a nearly insurmountable difficulty. Though students recognize many of the words in the list, they find themselves helpless in piecing together from those words a sentence that *sounds like* English. The words in number 1 can form a sentence that has many unfamiliar words, but the sentence is unmistakably English. The words in number 2 *never* form anything remotely similar to an English sentence. At best, the result sounds like a sentence from a foreign language that has borrowed English words.

What can account for these results? Most students find that making a sentence from number 1 is possible because the list includes *the, and, while, up,* and *her* and, in addition, the nonsense words have suffixes such as *-ed* and *-ly*. The second list contains meaningful words (some with suffixes) but none of those little words that turned out to be so crucial in number 1. And even when they try to substitute a nonsense word from number 2 for *the* or *in,* for example, students just can't get the sentence to sound like English.

You can therefore use the nonsense word exercise to show that English words fall into different classes that have been traditionally called the parts of speech. Many grammarians list eight parts of speech: noun, verb, adjective, adverb, pronoun, preposition, conjunction, and interjection, though it is possible to include others, such as articles, demonstratives, complementizers, and so on.

After they discuss their solutions to the exercise and their answers to the questions, have the students look again at the two lists in the exercise. In number 1 they undoubtedly recognized *and, the, up, her,* and *while.* Such high-frequency, low-meaning words are called function words. Because function words occur so frequently, speakers of English recognize them readily and come to rely upon them to provide clues to meaning and interpretation.

Students should also have noticed that certain suffixes provided information that enabled them to construct an English-sounding sentence. They may have known, for example, that *plicked, gerfed,* and *slooned* had something to do with action, though not what the action was. They were able to make this determination because of the suffix *-ed* that occurs at the end of each of these words. In fact, if they already have some knowledge of grammar terms, they probably know that these words have to be verbs because verbs can take the *-ed* suffix, which expresses past tense. Most importantly for Chapter One, many students also may have known that if *the* appears in front of another word, *ballick* for example, the result seems to indicate a thing, a creature, or the like. What they recognize, therefore, is that *the* introduces nouns, and thus *ballick* is a noun because *the* tells them it is. They may not be able to put these notions into words of their own, but they probably understand them intuitively.

Nouns, verbs, and function words are not the only possibilities for the exercise, however. If, for example, students wrote sentences for the first part of the exercise that included a phrase such as *the porfin ballick*, the word *porfin* would be an adjective. An English adjective typically follows a function word like *the* and precedes the noun it modifies. Thus, an adjective occurs as part of a noun phrase, a group of words forming a single chunk of meaning and having a noun as its most important element. In the noun phrase *the big balloon*, for example, *the* indicates that a noun is coming, and *big* is an adjective modifying the noun *balloon*. These are all points you can make to your students to introduce ideas that will come up in Chapter One.

Name ————————————————————

Date ————————————————————

Exercise

Below are two lists of sixteen words each. Look over the words in these lists; some of them may be familiar, whereas others may not be. A dictionary will not help you here, so consulting one will be of no use. Your job is to make two separate sixteen-word sentences that *sound like* English from each of the lists, using all of the words given only once. If a word occurs more than once, you must use it as many times as it occurs. Remember that your goal is to make the sentence *sound like* English.

1. | ballick | her | while | the |
    | and | plicked | gerfed | marfinnet |
    | heldolp | brinnily | up | the |
    | nemmle | the | porfin | slooned |

2. | book | spoke | klune | teacher |
    | wrote | hove | interesting | hove |
    | student | tef | dack | opened |
    | quickly | hove | dulf | thoughts |

3. Now answer the following questions.

    (a) Did you expect one part of the exercise to be easier than the other? If so, which one? Why?

(b) Did you guess correctly? Which part of the exercise turned out to be easier for you? Did either of your sentences sound like English? If so, what made it sound more like English than the other?

Name ——————————————————————————

Date ———————————————————————

Quiz 1.1

All of the sentences on this quiz come from Barbara Neely's mystery novel *Blanche on the Lam*.

Part I: Each of the following sentences includes one or more compound nouns. Underline each compound noun you find.

1. Blanche hung the dish towel on the rack.

2. A dark green lap robe covered her lower body.

3. The country house sat on a rise overlooking a duck pond.

4. A whiff of cigar smoke wrinkled Blanche's nose.

5. The perfect dough floated from the biscuit cutter onto the baking sheet.

Part II: Circle each possessive noun or noun phrase you find in the following sentences; then underline the entire noun phrase that it introduces.

6. The country house is Aunt Emmeline's favorite place.

7. A wry smile lifted the corners of Blanche's mouth.

8. Her mother's words hung in her mind like heavy weather.

9. They'd been fighting for nearly twenty years over Blanche's unstraightened hair.

10. Cousin Murphy's explanation hadn't stopped kids from calling her Ink Spot and Tar Baby.

Part III: In the following sentences, a noun phrase is underlined. On the line below each sentence, write a description of the noun phrase.

> EXAMPLE: <u>A mirthless grin</u> punctuated her words.
> determiner-adjective-noun

11. <u>No buildings</u> could be seen from the road, but the presence of solid old houses with more than one kind of domestic help could be felt in the air.

_____

12. <u>A soft sound</u> came from the back door.

_____

13. He gave Blanche <u>a brief nod</u> and slipped by her into the kitchen.

_____

14. She flashed <u>her eyes</u> at Grace.

_____

15. The man laughed, took <u>her fluttering hands</u>, and held them between his like captured birds.

_____

16. <u>A screened porch</u> extended around three sides of the house.

_____

17. Grace looked at her for <u>a long moment</u>.

_____

18. She fiddled with <u>her fingers</u>.

___

19. She covered her eyes with <u>her right hand</u>.

___

20. Now she gave Mumsfield <u>her full attention</u>.

___

Part IV: Some of the pronouns in the following sentences have been underlined. State whether each pronoun is personal, possessive, demonstrative, or indefinite.

21. <u>We</u> want to leave immediately after lunch.

___

22. The woman turned <u>her</u> head and gave Blanche a smile with more width than warmth in <u>it</u>.

___

23. <u>This</u> was the kind of employer who responded to <u>your</u> need for a surgeon with a bag of dated, cast-off clothes.

___

24. <u>She</u> also called her employers ma'am and sir to <u>their</u> faces.

___

25. <u>Nobody</u> knocked Nate out or threw a lighted cigarette on <u>his</u> old newspapers and roasted <u>him</u> alive.

___

Name _____

Date _____

Quiz 1.2

All of the sentences on this quiz come from Barbara Neely's mystery novel *Blanche on the Lam.*

Part I: Each of the following sentences includes one or more compound nouns. Underline each compound noun you find.

1. Blanche put the bread warmer and other dishes on the sideboard.

2. In the morning, Blanche fiddled with the radio dial until she found a station that promised news.

3. He's never had an accident or even a parking ticket.

4. It happened when an employer was struck by family disaster.

5. A water glass with a small amount of clear liquid in it hung loosely from her right hand.

Part II: Circle each possessive noun or noun phrase you find in the following sentences; then underline the entire noun phrase that it introduces.

6. Emmeline's voice was high and wild.

7. Blanche couldn't make out Grace's reply.

8. Grace's head rested against the back of a large, old-fashioned rattan armchair.

9. Everett leaned forward and whispered something in the old lady's ear.

10.   Grace took Mumsfield's arm and inched him back toward the
       car.

Part III: In the following sentences, a noun phrase is underlined. On
the line below each sentence, write a description of the noun phrase.

> EXAMPLE: <u>A mirthless grin</u> punctuated her words.
>   determiner-adjective-noun

11.   You may use the room up <u>these stairs</u>, first door on the left, to
       freshen up.

       _____

12.   The woman gave Blanche <u>an expectant look</u>.

       _____

13.   Three of <u>its spacious shelves</u> held artfully decorated and
       arranged platters of cold meats and salads, as well as two trays
       of yeast rolls waiting for the oven.

       _____

14.   There was an air of harmlessness about him that was puzzling
       in <u>a white male</u>.

       _____

15.   He closed the door behind him and gave her <u>a shy, gap-toothed
       smile</u>.

       _____

16.   She opened <u>other cabinets</u> but didn't find any plates.

       _____

17.   Mumsfield walked quickly toward <u>the old lady</u>.

_____

18.   She'd meant to call the agency days ago, but it had slipped her mind, until <u>this morning</u>.

_____

19.   <u>His words</u> stumbled over each other.

_____

20.   Blanche began pouring <u>their coffee</u>, but Everett dismissed her with a flip of his wrist.

_____

Part IV: Some of the pronouns in the following sentences have been underlined. State whether each pronoun is personal, possessive, demonstrative, or indefinite.

21.   <u>Nobody</u> burned <u>it</u> down.

_____

22.   Relief made <u>her</u> light-headed.

_____

23.   <u>She</u> was unconsciously humming the usual flat tune of <u>her</u> own composition.

_____

24.   Neither Blanche nor Ardell paid <u>that</u> any mind.

_____

25. <u>He</u> wore a dark blue suit that could have been a uniform.

Name —————————————————————

Date ———————————————————

Quiz 1.3

1. Write a sentence with a freestanding noun. Underline the noun.

————————————————————————

————————————————————————

2. Write a sentence with a determiner-noun combination. Underline the noun phrase.

————————————————————————

————————————————————————

3. Write a sentence with a determiner-adjective-noun combination. Underline the noun phrase.

————————————————————————

————————————————————————

4. Write a sentence with a possessive noun or noun phrase. Circle the possessive noun or noun phrase and underline the entire noun phrase it introduces.

————————————————————————

————————————————————————

5. Write a sentence with a compound noun. Underline the compound noun.

_____

_____

6. Write a sentence with a demonstrative pronoun. Underline the pronoun.

_____

_____

7. Write a sentence with a personal pronoun. Underline the pronoun.

_____

_____

8. Write a sentence with a possessive pronoun. Underline the pronoun.

_____

_____

9. Write a sentence with an indefinite pronoun. Underline the pronoun.

_____

_____

10. Write a sentence of your own choosing. Underline all the nouns/noun phrases and all the pronouns. Give the structure of what you have underlined.

_____

_____

ANSWERS

Quiz 1.1

1. Blanche hung the <u>dish towel</u> on the rack.
2. A dark green <u>lap robe</u> covered her lower body.
3. The <u>country house</u> sat on a rise overlooking a <u>duck pond</u>.
4. A whiff of <u>cigar smoke</u> wrinkled Blanche's nose.
5. The perfect dough floated from the <u>biscuit cutter</u> onto the <u>baking sheet</u>.
6. The country house is <u>*Aunt Emmeline's* favorite place</u>.
7. A wry smile lifted the corners of <u>*Blanche's* mouth</u>.
8. <u>*Her mother's* words</u> hung in her mind like heavy weather.
9. They'd been fighting for nearly twenty years over <u>*Blanche's* unstraightened hair</u>.
10. <u>*Cousin Murphy's* explanation</u> hadn't stopped kids from calling her Ink Spot and Tar Baby.
11. determiner-noun
12. determiner-adjective-noun
13. determiner-adjective-noun
14. determiner-noun
15. determiner-adjective-noun
16. determiner-adjective-noun
17. determiner-adjective-noun
18. determiner-noun
19. determiner-adjective-noun
20. determiner-adjective-noun
21. personal
22. possessive
23. demonstrative, personal
24. personal, possessive
25. indefinite, possessive

Quiz 1.2

1. Blanche put the <u>bread warmer</u> and other dishes on the sideboard.
2. In the morning, Blanche fiddled with the <u>radio dial</u> until she found a station that promised news.
3. He's never had an accident or even a <u>parking ticket</u>.
4. It happened when an employer was struck by <u>family disaster</u>.
5. A <u>water glass</u> with a small amount of clear liquid in it hung loosely from her right hand.
6. <u>*Emmeline's* voice</u> was high and wild.
7. Blanche couldn't make out <u>*Grace's* reply</u>.

8.   <u>*Grace's* head</u> rested against the back of a large, old-fashioned rattan armchair.
9.   Everett leaned forward and whispered something in <u>*the old lady's* ear</u>.
10.   Grace took <u>*Mumsfield's* arm</u> and inched him back toward the car.
11.   determiner-noun
12.   determiner-adjective-noun
13.   determiner-adjective-noun
14.   determiner-adjective-noun
15.   determiner-adjective-adjective-noun
16.   determiner-noun
17.   determiner-adjective-noun
18.   determiner-noun
19.   determiner-noun
20.   determiner-noun
21.   indefinite
22.   personal
23.   personal, possessive
24.   demonstrative
25.   personal

Recognizing Verbs and Verb Phrases

 OBJECTIVES

After completing this chapter, students will be able to

- recognize auxiliary verbs
- distinguish between tense and aspect
- differentiate between nouns and verbs by paying attention to grammatical signals
- differentiate between nouns and verbs in their own writing
- articulate the details of tense and aspect in verbs/verb phrases appearing in authentic text

The major purpose of Chapter Two is to teach students to differentiate between nouns and verbs and thus to recognize verb phrases. Though semantically based definitions of *noun* and *verb* are helpful as a first approximation, most students become quickly lost if these definitions are the only tools they have. In the English language, these categories are quite fluid, and many ordinary words switch classes at the drop of a determiner or a tense suffix. Thus we *man* lifeboats, *salt* our soup, *butter* our toast (and *toast* our bread and *bread* our cutlets). One child of my acquaintance "syrups the pancakes," and computer experts *architect* solutions to software problems. Similarly for exercise, we go on a *hike*, take a *walk*, and do a three mile *run*. To take a *drive* in the country, we *drive* our car. The examples abound. Therefore, encourage students to examine suffixes and other grammatical indicators of verb status, and tie these in to the concepts that were developed in Chapter One.

In Chapter Two, I make a statement that might be considered controversial: "When we find a pronoun in subject form, such as *I, we, he, she, they*, we are typically correct in believing it to be the subject of its sentence." Undoubtedly, you thought of sentences in which subjective case pronouns appear as the complement of a linking verb. However, such sentences are rare, and they are probably nonexistent in the spoken language of our students. In most circumstances, a subjective case pronoun is in fact the subject. My goal is to give students some anchors in the sea of grammar so that they can build some confidence. It is probably not useful at this point in their education to point out all the exceptions to these generalizations.

Some other elements of this chapter may be unfamiliar to you because my approach, though eclectic, is not primarily that of traditional grammar. Rather, it is an approach derived from the linguistic study of English in both the United States and the United Kingdom. Therefore, I describe English as having only two tenses, present and past. Unlike some languages, English indicates as a suffix on the verb only these two tenses. Thus, from this point of view, there is no future *tense* in English, though English certainly has a number of strategies for articulating future time, including the use of the modal auxiliary *will*, the idiomatic expression *be going to*, and the use of the present tense (with or without progressive aspect) with a time adverbial (e.g., We *are taking* final exams *next week*).

A second unfamiliar feature may be the notion of *aspect*, which is an indication of whether an event is complete or incomplete (often, continuing). Separating the time element expressed in English verb phrases into two notions—tense and aspect—is quite helpful to students struggling to understand the time nuances expressed obligatorily in English.

Nonnative speakers may have considerable difficulty with the English verb phrase, particularly speakers of Asian languages that have no tense indications whatsoever. Chinese, for example, expresses only aspect in a sentence, not tense. Speakers of such a language often need to be convinced of the necessity of indicating tense in English. Why does English make us do this, they wonder. The answer is simply

"Because it does!" Appeals to logic will not work. Tense is obligatory in English sentences, and that point needs to be driven home.

Native speakers of English whose home language is a nonstandard dialect may also have difficulties here. In particular, African-American students who speak African-American Vernacular English (AAVE) typically leave out forms of *be* in contexts where it is obligatory in Standard English. Generally speaking, in any context where Standard English contracts the auxiliary *be* or the main verb *be*, AAVE omits it. Because this omission is regular in the dialect, students may be able to supply *be,* but they may continue to have agreement difficulties, though these will not be tackled until Chapter Seven. I suggest that you do not emphasize agreement at this point in the course but wait until students have a clear concept of what constitutes the basic phrasal structures of the language. English speakers have to consider agreement in relative clauses and with coordinated subjects, so it makes sense to withhold discussion of agreement until these issues have been studied.

Name ————————————————————————————

Date ————————————————————————

Quiz 2.1

The sentences on this quiz come from the novels *Pigs in Heaven*, by Barbara Kingsolver, and *Praisesong for the Widow*, by Paule Marshall.

Part I: Underline the verbs or verb phrases in each of the following sentences. In the space under each of the passages, identify the verbs or verb phrases as present tense or past tense. In addition, if aspect is indicated in the verb phrase, write whether the aspect is progressive, perfect, or perfect progressive. Some sentences have more than one verb or verb phrase.

1. Her husband, Harland, is sleeping like a brick.

2. She married him two years ago for love, or so she thought.

3. Sugar is a second cousin and the most famous citizen of Heaven, Oklahoma.

4. A man in a wheelchair rolls toward them.

5. Taylor hands him the camera.

6. Turtle and Taylor take one last stroll across Mr. Hoover's concrete dream.

7. Collie makes an odd noise, a sort of a hiss.

8. Angie arrives again with more food and men.

9. She and Turtle are cruising down the freeway in a long white limousine with smoked-glass windows and baby blue velvet upholstery.

10. He has curly hair and a terrific smile.

11.   The woman had been right.

12.   He turned to her with a polite smile.

13.   She had ignored the woman's outcry.

14.   The airport limousine had deposited her at the door.

15.   The terrifying thought had instantly crossed her mind.

16.   Once in the cabin, she took an antacid.

17.   She was wearing flat-heeled shoes and a pink linen shirtdress.

18.   Now, in a sudden turnabout, he was telling her his family history.

19.   Everything was going along fine.

20.   Outside, the children had abandoned their noisy play and had come up on the beach.

Part II: Circle the modal auxiliary in each of the following sentences. Then underline the entire verb phrase that it begins.

21.   She can barely see the sides of the road.

22.   Jax is a problem in Taylor's life, though she would never say that aloud.

23.   You can't think too much about luck, good or bad.

24.   "Just think," she says, "we could be in Paris, France or Hong Kong. They have McDonald's in every country in the world."

25.   She might be safer out in the sun.

Name ————————————————————————

Date ————————————————————

Quiz 2.2

The sentences on this quiz come from the novels *Pigs in Heaven*, by Barbara Kingsolver, and *Praisesong for the Widow*, by Paule Marshall.

Part I: Underline the verbs or verb phrases in each of the following sentences. In the space under each of the passages, identify the verbs or verb phrases as present tense or past tense. In addition, if aspect is indicated in the verb phrase, write whether the aspect is progressive, perfect, or perfect progressive. Some sentences have more than one verb or verb phrase.

1. Her short, black hair looks wet and oiled, like a sea otter.

2. Her brother and sister-in-law are kneeling on the kitchen floor.

3. She has never seen an ostrich.

4. Taylor doesn't consider Barbie the ideal baby-sitter.

5. The casino robbery seemed adventurous, like piracy or Robin Hood.

6. She has seen so many people show up for court armored in suits and lies.

7. Family has always been our highest value.

8. Lucky and Turtle are asleep in the backseat.

9. He has curly hair and a terrific smile.

10. Turtle is the youngest and has the best story.

11. The man spoke after a long silence.

12. Avey Johnson felt a dangerous confusion.

13. They had reached a final silence.

14. Across the way, Avey Johnson was leaning wearily against the table.

15. Cataracts dimmed her gaze.

16. From the storage space at the bottom, she pulled out another suitcase.

17. Her hands froze on the drawer.

18. Her shoes were in their special caddy.

19. With the church behind them on the walk, they came to the last few houses in the small settlement.

20. The long harangue had taken its toll.

Part II: Circle the modal auxiliary in each of the following sentences. Then underline the entire verb phrase that it begins.

21. People will throw anything in the world on the ground, or even in the water.

22. We might run into rough water.

23. Both sails could stand a good bleaching.

24. The place could serve as a summer camp.

25. The sudden headache would go its way.

Name ————————————————————————————

Date ————————————————————————

Quiz 2.3

1. Write a sentence whose verb is present tense. Underline the verb.

   ————————————————————————————————————

   ————————————————————————————————————

2. Write a sentence whose verb is past tense. Underline the verb.

   ————————————————————————————————————

   ————————————————————————————————————

3. Write a sentence whose verb phrase is present progressive.
   Underline the verb phrase.

   ————————————————————————————————————

   ————————————————————————————————————

4. Write a sentence whose verb phrase is past progressive. Underline
   the verb phrase.

   ————————————————————————————————————

   ————————————————————————————————————

5. Write a sentence whose verb phrase is present perfect. Underline
   the verb phrase.

   ————————————————————————————————————

   ————————————————————————————————————

6. Write a sentence whose verb phrase is past perfect. Underline the verb phrase.

    _____

    _____

7. Write a sentence whose verb phrase expresses perfect progressive aspect. Underline the verb phrase and give its tense.

    _____

    _____

8. Write a sentence that uses *do* as an auxiliary. Underline the verb phrase.

    _____

    _____

9. Write a sentence that uses a modal auxiliary. Underline the verb phrase.

    _____

    _____

10. Write a sentence that includes an adverb in the verb phrase. Underline the verb phrase.

    _____

    _____

ANSWERS

Quiz 2.1

1. Her husband, Harland, <u>is sleeping</u> like a brick.
    present progressive
2. She <u>married</u> him two years ago for love, or so she <u>thought</u>.
    past, past
3. Sugar <u>is</u> a second cousin and the most famous citizen of Heaven, Oklahoma.
    present
4. A man in a wheelchair <u>rolls</u> toward them.
    present
5. Taylor <u>hands</u> him the camera.
    present
6. Turtle and Taylor <u>take</u> one last stroll across Mr. Hoover's concrete dream.
    present
7. Collie <u>makes</u> an odd noise, a sort of a hiss.
    present
8. Angie <u>arrives</u> again with more food and men.
    present
9. She and Turtle <u>are cruising</u> down the freeway in a long white limousine with smoked-glass windows and baby blue velvet upholstery.
    present progressive
10. He <u>has</u> curly hair and a terrific smile.
    present
11. The woman <u>had been</u> right.
    past perfect
12. He <u>turned</u> to her with a polite smile.
    past
13. She <u>had ignored</u> the woman's outcry.
    past perfect
14. The airport limousine <u>had deposited</u> her at the door.
    past perfect
15. The terrifying thought <u>had instantly crossed</u> her mind.
    past perfect
16. Once in the cabin, she <u>took</u> an antacid.
    past
17. She <u>was wearing</u> flat-heeled shoes and a pink linen shirtdress.
    past progressive
18. Now, in a sudden turnabout, he <u>was telling</u> her his family history.
    past progressive
19. Everything <u>was going</u> along fine.
    past progressive

20. Outside, the children <u>had abandoned</u> their noisy play and <u>had come</u> up on the beach.
     past perfect, past perfect
21. She *can barely see* the sides of the road.
22. Jax is a problem in Taylor's life, though she *would* never *say* that aloud.
23. You *can't* <u>think</u> too much about luck, good or bad.
24. "Just think," she says, "we *could be* in Paris, France or Hong Kong. They have McDonald's in every country in the world."
25. She *might* be safer out in the sun.

Quiz 2.2

1. Her short, black hair <u>looks</u> wet and oiled, like a sea otter.
    present
2. Her brother and sister-in-law <u>are kneeling</u> on the kitchen floor.
    present progressive
3. She <u>has never seen</u> an ostrich.
    present perfect
4. Taylor <u>doesn't consider</u> Barbie the ideal baby-sitter.
    present
5. The casino robbery <u>seemed</u> adventurous, like piracy or Robin Hood.
    past
6. She <u>has seen</u> so many people show up for court armored in suits and lies.
    present perfect
7. Family <u>has always been</u> our highest value.
    present perfect
8. Lucky and Turtle <u>are</u> asleep in the backseat.
    present
9. He <u>has</u> curly hair and a terrific smile.
    present
10. Turtle <u>is</u> the youngest and <u>has</u> the best story.
    present, present
11. The man <u>spoke</u> after a long silence.
    past
12. Avey Johnson <u>felt</u> a dangerous confusion.
    past
13. They <u>had reached</u> a final silence.
    past perfect
14. Across the way, Avey Johnson <u>was leaning</u> wearily against the table.
    past progressive
15. Cataracts <u>dimmed</u> her gaze.
    past
16. From the storage space at the bottom, she <u>pulled out</u> another suitcase.
    past

17. Her hands <u>froze</u> on the drawer.
    past
18. Her shoes <u>were</u> in their special caddy.
    past
19. With the church behind them on the walk, they <u>came</u> to the last few houses in the small settlement.
    past
20. The long harangue <u>had taken</u> its toll.
    past perfect
21. People *will* <u>throw</u> anything in the world on the ground, or even in the water.
22. We *might* <u>run</u> into rough water.
23. Both sails *could* <u>stand</u> a good bleaching.
24. The place *could* <u>serve</u> as a summer camp.
25. The sudden headache *would* <u>go</u> its way.

The Basic Sentence

 OBJECTIVES

After completing this chapter, students will be able to

- recognize subjects
- recognize direct objects and indirect objects
- recognize complements and adverbials
- recognize passive voice
- convert active sentences to passive and vice versa

Perhaps the most important objective of this chapter is getting students to recognize subjects reliably, for that skill will help them later when they study subject/verb agreement. Thus, I supplement the traditional notion of subject as "the part of the sentence, usually a noun, noun phrase, or pronoun, that performs the activity expressed in the verb" with a more reliable test for subject status, namely, using the yes/no question equivalent of the declarative sentence. The problem with the meaning-based definition is that it is accurate only for active transitive sentences, whereas it fails for all other types. In passive sentences, the subject is the element acted upon, not the actor. In intransitive sentences, the verb is often not an action at all but some kind of state (e.g., *Mary slept*). Students need more reliable tools.

The section on adverbials can lead to some interesting discussion on the rhetorical consequences of placing an adverbial at the beginning or end of a sentence. Try presenting a sentence such as the following from Edgar Allan Poe: "On one of the staircases, I met the physician of the family" [from *The Fall of the House of Usher*]. Then ask students to imagine what the next sentence in the narrative might be. Typically, they will suggest a sentence that begins with *he* or *the physician*. Then turn the sentence around: "I met the physician of the family on one of the staircases." Ask what the next sentence might be. Students often offer sentences such as "It was dark and winding." In other words, the final part of one sentence leads into the following sentence or sentences. You may want to try the same technique with active and passive sentences.

Name ———————————————————————————

Date ———————————————————————

Quiz 3.1

Part I: All of the following sentences from James Finn Garner's *Politically Correct Bedtime Stories* have either active transitive verbs or verb phrases or passive verb phrases. Underline the verb or verb phrase in each sentence, and in the space below write *active* or *passive*.

1. On the way to Grandma's house, Red Riding Hood was accosted by a wolf.

2. Grandma, I have brought you some fat-free, sodium-free snacks.

3. Her screams were heard by a passing woodchopperperson.

4. On the following morning, his subjects lined the streets for the big parade.

5. So the wolf blew down the house of sticks.

Part II: Underline the subject in each of the following sentences from *Politically Correct Bedtime Stories*.

6. After a moment's thought, the emperor agreed to this request.

7. Of course, no such rarefied fabric existed.

8. The frightened pigs ran to the house of sticks, with the wolf in hot pursuit.

9. At this, the wolf chuckled condescendingly.

10. The other two goats bounded up to the bridge and sized up the fight.

Part III: Underline the verb or verb phrase in each of the following sentences. Then put square brackets around each direct object, parentheses around each indirect object, and curly brackets around each complement. Not all verbs have objects or complements, however. These sentences come from Jung Chang's *Wild Swans: Three Daughters of China*.

11. She called him "Father."

12. He gave her his own name.

13. My mother's closest friends were her pets.

14. The other children ostracized her completely.

15. Dr. Xia divided his property up among the members of his family.

16. The second son inherited the medicine shop.

17. The house was left to his youngest son.

18. Jinzhou was an important railroad junction.

19. It even had its own airport.

20. The Japanese had occupied it in early January 1932, after heavy fighting.

21. Chang Hsueh-liang decamped to Jinzhou with some 20,000 troops.

22. In one of the first such attacks in history, the Japanese bombed the city from the air.

23. My grandmother had never experienced such poverty.

24. My grandmother loved these gatherings.

25. Grateful patients would also give doctors valuable presents at New Year and on other special occasions.

Name ———————————————————————

Date ——————————————————————

Quiz 3.2

Part I: All of the following sentences from *Politically Correct Bedtime Stories* have either active transitive verbs or verb phrases or passive verb phrases. Underline the verb or verb phrase in each sentence, and in the space below write *active* or *passive*.

1. No actual wolves were harmed in the writing of the story.

2. Nature has made me a troll.

3. I embrace my trollhood.

4. Our presence and supreme edibility put you in this situation.

5. For years, Rapunzel's hair had been exploited for the transportational needs of others.

Part II: Underline the subject in each of the following sentences from *Politically Correct Bedtime Stories.*

6. The tinker might have argued with her over the concept of ownership.

7. Instead, in a degrading spectacle, he pleaded for mercy.

8. She later established the non-profit Foundation for the Free Proliferation of Music and cut off her hair for a fund-raising auction.

9. On the way to Grandma's house, Red Riding Hood was accosted by a wolf.

10. Red Riding Hood walked on along the main path.

Part III: Underline the verb or verb phrase in each of the following sentences. Then put square brackets around each direct object, parentheses around each indirect object, and curly brackets around each complement. Not all verbs have objects or complements, however. These sentences come from Tom Sullivan's autobiography, *If You Could See What I Hear*.

11.   To the sighted, Braille has always been a mystery.

12.   Dad had accused Mom then of infidelity.

13.   But Mom wouldn't forgive him.

14.   Dad had prospered enormously from his six clubs.

15.   I was panting with rage and frustration.

16.   My nails were cutting my palms.

17.   I've never seen his face, of course.

18.   Those horrible boys must be giving you a bad time.

19.   We, the blind people of the earth, have been a suppressed minority for too long.

20.   She would soon forget me.

21.   Professional pride had long since vanished.

22.   I would take any work.

23.   It was Sunday.

24.   A church bell was ringing.

25.   We didn't pursue the subject further.

Name ——————————————————————

Date ————————————————

Quiz 3.3

1. Write a sentence that includes an adverbial phrase. Put parentheses around the adverbial and a line under the subject.

———————————————————————————

———————————————————————————

2. Write a sentence whose predicate phrase includes no objects or complements (that is, whose verb/verb phrase is intransitive). Underline the verb/verb phrase.

———————————————————————————

———————————————————————————

3. Write a sentence whose predicate phrase includes a direct object. Underline the verb/verb phrase and put brackets around the direct object.

———————————————————————————

———————————————————————————

4. Write a sentence whose predicate phrase includes both an indirect and direct object. Underline the verb/verb phrase and put parentheses around the indirect object and brackets around the direct object.

———————————————————————————

———————————————————————————

5. Write a sentence whose predicate phrase includes a complement but no object. Underline the verb/verb phrase and put curly brackets around the complement.

    _____

    _____

6. Write a sentence whose predicate phrase includes a direct object and a complement. Underline the verb/verb phrase and put brackets around the direct object and curly brackets around the complement.

    _____

    _____

7. Write a sentence with an introductory adverbial noun phrase. Underline the adverbial.

    _____

    _____

8. Write a sentence whose verb phrase is passive. Underline the verb phrase.

    _____

    _____

9. Write a sentence that includes an adverbial prepositional phrase. Put parentheses around the prepositional phrase.

    _____

    _____

10. Write a sentence of your choosing. Then analyze the predicate phrase (give the tense, aspect, voice of the verb phrase, and specify what objects and/or complements occur, if any).

_____

_____

ANSWERS

Quiz 3.1

1. On the way to Grandma's house, Red Riding Hood <u>was accosted</u> by a wolf.
   passive
2. Grandma, I <u>have brought</u> you some fat-free, sodium-free snacks.
   active
3. Her screams <u>were heard</u> by a passing woodchopperperson.
   passive
4. On the following morning, his subjects <u>lined</u> the streets for the big parade.
   active
5. So the wolf <u>blew down</u> the house of sticks.
   active
6. After a moment's thought, <u>the emperor</u> agreed to this request.
7. Of course, <u>no such rarefied fabric</u> existed.
8. <u>The frightened pigs</u> ran to the house of sticks, with the wolf in hot pursuit.
9. At this, <u>the wolf</u> chuckled condescendingly.
10. <u>The other two goats</u> bounded up to the bridge and sized up the fight.
11. She <u>called</u> [him] {"Father."}
12. He <u>gave</u> (her) [his own name].
13. My mother's closest friends <u>were</u> {her pets}.
14. The other children <u>ostracized</u> [her] completely.
15. Dr. Xia <u>divided</u> [his property] <u>up</u> among the members of his family.
16. The second son <u>inherited</u> [the medicine shop].
17. The house <u>was left</u> (to his youngest son).
18. Jinzhou <u>was</u> {an important railroad junction}.
19. It <u>even had</u> [its own airport].
20. The Japanese <u>had occupied</u> [it] in early January 1932, after heavy fighting.
21. Chang Hsueh-liang <u>decamped</u> to Jinzhou with some 20,000 troops.
22. In one of the first such attacks in history, the Japanese <u>bombed</u> [the city] from the air.
23. My grandmother <u>had never experienced</u> [such poverty].
24. My grandmother <u>loved</u> [these gatherings].
25. Grateful patients <u>would also give</u> (doctors) [valuable presents] at New Year and on other special occasions.

Quiz 3.2

1. No actual wolves <u>were harmed</u> in the writing of the story.
   passive
2. Nature <u>has made</u> me a troll.
   active

3. I <u>embrace</u> my trollhood.
    active

4. Our presence and supreme edibility <u>put</u> you in this situation.
    active

5. For years, Rapunzel's hair <u>had been exploited</u> for the transportational needs of others.
    passive

6. <u>The tinker</u> might have argued with her over the concept of ownership.

7. Instead, in a degrading spectacle, <u>he</u> pleaded for mercy.

8. <u>She</u> later established the non-profit Foundation for the Free Proliferation of Music and cut off her hair for a fund-raising auction.

9. On the way to Grandma's house, <u>Red Riding Hood</u> was accosted by a wolf.

10. <u>Red Riding Hood</u> walked on along the main path.

11. To the sighted, Braille <u>has always been</u> {a mystery}.

12. Dad <u>had accused</u> [Mom] then of infidelity.

13. But Mom <u>wouldn't forgive</u> [him].

14. Dad <u>had prospered</u> enormously from his six clubs.

15. I <u>was panting</u> with rage and frustration.

16. My nails <u>were cutting</u> [my palms].

17. I<u>'ve never seen</u> [his face], of course.

18. Those horrible boys <u>must be giving</u> (you) [a bad time].

19. We, the blind people of the earth, <u>have been</u> {a suppressed minority} for too long.

20. She <u>would soon forget</u> [me].

21. Professional pride <u>had long since vanished</u>.

22. I <u>would take</u> [any work].

23. It <u>was</u> {Sunday}.

24. A church bell <u>was ringing</u>.

25. We <u>didn't pursue</u> [the subject] further.

Adding Details with Modifiers

OBJECTIVES

After completing this chapter, students will be able to

- expand noun phrases with prepositional phrases
- recognize appositives and relative clauses
- recognize participle phrases
- recognize the distinction between restrictive and nonrestrictive modifiers
- recognize adverbial infinitive phrases
- distinguish between different kinds of adverbial clauses
- add these modifiers to their own writing
- correct fragments

As a group, basic writers produce very short sentences that lack the kind of modifiers that add interest and variety to sentences. This chapter focuses students' attention on these constructions so that they can recognize them in real text and in their own writing. In addition, because they will learn where they occur in sentences, students will get some practice in including modificational clauses and phrases in their own writing. Of particular difficulty for most students is the nonrestrictive participle phrase. Because it is more literary than conversational, many students lack familiarity with it and do not know how to use it.

Modifiers may pose some additional difficulties for ESL students, particularly those whose native languages do not use subordination as a major device. Asian languages in particular make little use of relative clauses, for example, and so students with an Asian-language background may avoid them altogether. In any additional writing assignments you may give in conjunction with this chapter, it would be useful to have students make sure they include at least one of each kind of modifier. You can encourage them to combine short independent sentences into single sentences when such combination makes sense.

Name ——————————————————————————

Date ——————————————————————

Quiz 4.1

Part I: Each of the following sentences from *Blanche on the Lam*, a mystery by Barbara Neely, has at least one noun phrase that includes a prepositional phrase modifying the noun. Put parentheses around each of these prepositional phrases and then underline the entire noun phrase that includes it.

1. The bottom of her apple-green blouse crept out of the waistband of her skirt.

2. Two big drops of water splashed onto her rare roast beef.

3. The woman in the chair was asleep.

4. She wore a short-sleeved pink and green floral-print dress of the simple, very expensive variety.

5. Not even the noise of passing cars and trucks could be heard.

Part II: Put a line under each of the participle phrases or relative clauses in the following sentences from *Blanche on the Lam*. Then put a double line under the noun or noun phrase it modifies. In the space below each sentence, write whether the modifier you have underlined is restrictive or nonrestrictive.

6. There was a watchfulness in Everett that made her cautious.

7. He had a childish giggle that made her smile.

8. Grace was in the kitchen, leaning weakly against the wall.

9. White wicker chairs and small tables were placed casually around the porch and added to the touches of white that framed the doors and windows.

10. Blanche was partial to gap-toothed folks, having a significant space between her own front teeth.

Part III: A modifier has been underlined in each of the following sentences from Maxine Hong Kingston's *China Men*. Identify the modifier by writing one of the following labels in the space below the sentence:

adverbial infinitive phrase
nonrestrictive appositive
restrictive appositive
nonrestrictive relative clause
restrictive relative clause
nonrestrictive participle phrase
restrictive participle phrase
nonrestrictive adjective phrase

11. <u>Waiting at the gate for our father to come home from work</u>, my brothers and sisters and I saw a man come hastening around the corner.

12. We surrounded him, took his hands, pressed our noses against his coat <u>to sniff his tobacco smell</u>, reached into his pockets for the Rainbo notepads and the gold coins that were really chocolates.

13. We surrounded him, took his hands, pressed our noses against his coat to sniff his tobacco smell, reached into his pockets for the Rainbo notepads and the gold coins <u>that were really chocolates</u>.

14. The word <u>*poetry*</u> had hit them like a mallet stunning cattle.

15. <u>Tall and thin</u>, he was wearing our father's two-hundred-dollar suit that fit him just right.

Part IV: Underline the adverbial subordinate clause in each of the following sentences from *Blanche on the Lam*. In the space below each sentence, write the general meaning relationship that holds between the subordinate and main clause (time, cause, condition, concession, or purpose).

16. She hesitated a few more moments before Night Girl rescued her.

17. When the water was ready, she made a pot of tea and settled down at the kitchen table to think.

18. As they talked, Blanche listened for the sound of the limousine and waited for the tingling of her scalp that would tell her someone was nearby.

19. The rumble of his voice began before the door was fully closed.

20. She gave Blanche a bleak look before the door swung shut behind her.

21. He bubbled on about carburetors and other things that smelled of grease while Blanche sliced ham and tomatoes for sandwiches.

22. When she opened the last drawer, a hint of Grace's floral perfume scented the air.

23. If they're his cousins, then the Aunt Emmeline Mumsfield talked about must also be one of the family.

24. While Blanche was fastening her seat belt, there was a soft whirring from behind.

25. If Grace had been a friend, Blanche would have immediately asked what was troubling her.

Name ⸻

Date ⸻

Quiz 4.2

Part I: Each of the following sentences from *Blanche on the Lam*, a mystery by Barbara Neely, has at least one noun phrase that includes a prepositional phrase modifying the noun. Put parentheses around each of these prepositional phrases and then underline the entire noun phrase that includes it.

1. But she'd expected a certain amount of local fuss.

2. The smell of cheap liquor and cigarettes had been replaced in Emmeline's room by the pungent fragrance of eucalyptus.

3. Grace opened her notebook and went over the menus for the next five days.

4. He was cut off by a hacking cough from Emmeline.

5. The tightness around his eyes had increased.

Part II: Put a line under each of the participle phrases or relative clauses in the following sentences from *Blanche on the Lam*. Then put a double line under the noun or noun phrase it modifies. In the space below each sentence, write whether the modifier you have underlined is restrictive or nonrestrictive.

6. The woman looked around the kitchen like a bellhop checking the towels.

7. This house rose from a bed of flowers and shrubs that spoke of a builder and a once-a-week gardener.

8. She moved around the kitchen, opening cabinets in search of plates.

9. Her first stop was the Salvation Army secondhand store on Sixth Street, where she bought a pink and white seersucker bathrobe.

10. Blanche went through the house to a front window, where she watched the limousine slide down the drive.

Part III: A modifier has been underlined in each of the following sentences from Maxine Hong Kingston's *China Men*. Identify the modifier by writing one of the following labels in the space below the sentence:

nonrestrictive appositive
restrictive appositive
nonrestrictive relative clause
restrictive relative clause

11. Upon hearing about the sage of the Ming period <u>who shook himself and turned into a red dragonfly</u>, I remembered our airplane, which was not red.

12. Upon hearing about the sage of the Ming period who shook himself and turned into a red dragonfly, I remembered our airplane, <u>which was not red</u>.

13. Third Uncle, <u>Sahm Bak</u>, waited until the baby was tucked away in his parents' bedroom for a nap.

14. He left a teapot, <u>around which BaBa held his hands and caught the rich heat that arose</u>.

15. He left a teapot, around which BaBa held his hands and caught the rich heat <u>that arose</u>.

Part IV: Underline the adverbial subordinate clause in each of the following sentences from *Blanche on the Lam.* In the space below each sentence, write the general meaning relationship that holds between the subordinate and main clause (time, cause, condition, concession, or purpose).

16. Blanche hadn't paid any attention to the dining room when she'd peeked in earlier.

17. Blanche watched Grace as she went down the stairs.

18. After Grace left the kitchen, Blanche sat down at the table.

19. As she was about to round the corner onto the long side porch, one of the men spoke.

20. Because she knew the black community, Miz Minnie also had plenty of information about the white one.

21. While she finished the eggs, he carried the tray of grapefruit halves and orange juice into the dining room, then went to fetch Everett and Grace.

22. While the soup heated, Blanche cut the crusts from four slices of bread.

23. If he was afraid, he was that much closer to doing something stupid.

24. Blanche hummed as she cleared away the breakfast dishes.

25. Blanche was stuffing towels into the washing machine when Grace returned Emmeline's breakfast tray.

Name ———————————————————————————————

Date ————————————————————————

Quiz 4.3

1. Write a sentence with a noun phrase that includes a prepositional phrase. Put parentheses around the prepositional phrase and then underline the entire noun phrase that includes the prepositional phrase.

———————————————————————————————

———————————————————————————————

2. Write a sentence that includes a restrictive appositive. Underline the appositive.

———————————————————————————————

———————————————————————————————

3. Write a sentence that includes a nonrestrictive appositive. Underline the appositive.

———————————————————————————————

———————————————————————————————

4. Write a sentence that includes a restrictive relative clause. Underline the relative clause.

———————————————————————————————

———————————————————————————————

5. Write a sentence that includes a nonrestrictive relative clause. Underline the relative clause.

_____

_____

6. Write a sentence that includes a restrictive participle phrase. Underline the participle phrase.

_____

_____

7. Write a sentence that includes a nonrestrictive participle phrase. Underline the participle phrase.

_____

_____

8. Write a sentence that includes an adverbial clause of time. Underline the adverbial clause.

_____

_____

9. Write a sentence that includes an adverbial clause of cause. Underline the adverbial clause.

_____

_____

10. Write a sentence that includes an adverbial clause of concession. Underline the adverbial clause.

_____

_____

ANSWERS

Quiz 4.1

1. The bottom (of her apple-green blouse) crept out of the waistband (of her skirt).
2. Two big drops (of water) splashed onto her rare roast beef.
3. The woman (in the chair) was asleep.
4. She wore a short-sleeved pink and green floral-print dress (of the simple, very expensive variety).
5. Not even the noise (of passing cars and trucks) could be heard.
6. There was a watchfulness in Everett that made her cautious.
   restrictive
7. He had a childish giggle that made her smile.
   restrictive
8. Grace was in the kitchen, leaning weakly against the wall.
   nonrestrictive
9. White wicker chairs and small tables were placed casually around the porch and added to the touches of white that framed the doors and windows.
   restrictive
10. Blanche was partial to gap-toothed folks, having a significant space between her own front teeth.
    nonrestrictive
11. nonrestrictive participle phrase
12. adverbial infinitive phrase
13. restrictive relative clause
14. restrictive appositive
15. nonrestrictive adjective phrase
16. She hesitated a few more moments before Night Girl rescued her.
    time
17. When the water was ready, she made a pot of tea and settled down at the kitchen table to think.
    time
18. As they talked, Blanche listened for the sound of the limousine and waited for the tingling of her scalp that would tell her someone was nearby.
    time
19. The rumble of his voice began before the door was fully closed.
    time
20. She gave Blanche a bleak look before the door swung shut behind her.
    time
21. He bubbled on about carburetors and other things that smelled of grease while Blanche sliced ham and tomatoes for sandwiches.
    time

22. <u>When she opened the last drawer</u>, a hint of Grace's floral perfume scented the air.
    time

23. <u>If they're his cousins</u>, then the Aunt Emmeline Mumsfield talked about must also be one of the family.
    condition

24. <u>While Blanche was fastening her seat belt</u>, there was a soft whirring from behind.
    time

25. <u>If Grace had been a friend</u>, Blanche would have immediately asked what was troubling her.
    condition

Quiz 4.2

1. But she'd expected <u>a certain amount (of local fuss)</u>.

2. <u>The smell (of cheap liquor and cigarettes)</u> had been replaced in Emmeline's room by <u>the pungent fragrance (of eucalyptus)</u>.

3. Grace opened her notebook and went over <u>the menus (for the next five days)</u>.

4. He was cut off by <u>a hacking cough (from Emmeline)</u>.

5. <u>The tightness (around his eyes)</u> had increased.

6. The woman looked around the kitchen like <u>a bellhop</u> <u>checking the towels</u>.
   restrictive

7. This house rose from <u>a bed of flowers and shrubs</u> <u>that spoke of a builder and a once-a-week gardener</u>.
   restrictive

8. <u>She</u> moved around the kitchen, <u>opening cabinets in search of plates</u>.
   nonrestrictive

9. Her first stop was <u>the Salvation Army secondhand store on Sixth Street</u>, <u>where she bought a pink and white seersucker bathrobe</u>.
   nonrestrictive

10. Blanche went through the house to <u>a front window</u>, <u>where she watched the limousine slide down the drive</u>.
    nonrestrictive

11. restrictive relative clause

12. nonrestrictive relative clause

13. nonrestrictive appositive

14. nonrestrictive relative clause

15. restrictive relative clause

16. Blanche hadn't paid any attention to the dining room <u>when she'd peeked in earlier</u>.
    time

17. Blanche watched Grace <u>as she went down the stairs</u>.
    time

18. After Grace left the kitchen, Blanche sat down at the table.
    time

19. As she was about to round the corner onto the long side porch, one of the men
    spoke.
    time

20. Because she knew the black community, Miz Minnie also had plenty of informa-
    tion about the white one.
    cause

21. While she finished the eggs, he carried the tray of grapefruit halves and orange
    juice into the dining room, then went to fetch Everett and Grace.
    time

22. While the soup heated, Blanche cut the crusts from four slices of bread.
    time

23. If he was afraid, he was that much closer to doing something stupid.
    condition

24. Blanche hummed as she cleared away the breakfast dishes.
    time

25. Blanche was stuffing towels into the washing machine when Grace returned
    Emmeline's breakfast tray.
    time

Content Clauses and Verbals

 OBJECTIVES

After completing this chapter, students will be able to

- recognize content clauses
- vary the verbs that take content clauses as objects
- convert direct quotations to content clauses with appropriate syntax
- use the appropriate verbal (either a participle or an infinitive phrase) as direct object with specific verbs
- recognize verbals in their nonmodifier functions
- use these constructions in their own writing

As in other areas of grammar, the problems of native and nonnative speaking students will differ in relation to content clauses and verbals. Content clauses used as direct objects come naturally to native speakers because the verbs that require them cannot be readily used without the content clause; thus, knowing the meaning of particular verbs, such as *know* and *believe*, usually means being able to use a content clause with them. However, because basic writers often do not have an elaborated vocabulary, many students use content clauses with only a restricted set of verbs. Getting students to vary verb choice is the major challenge here. In particular, students tend to use the verb *feel* when *believe* or *contend* or *argue* is more appropriate. Thus, in any writing assignment you give that requires intellectual discussion, encourage students to use the verbs that suggest logical argument rather than emotion.

ESL students typically have difficulty in using participle phrases as objects of verbs, primarily because the distinction between the participle and the infinitive does not occur in most languages. They tend to use the infinitive phrase exclusively in these contexts, and thus we find in their writing such infelicities as "He stopped to do the dishes," when in fact the intended meaning is "He stopped doing the dishes." For this reason, I provide the information in Table 5.2 and the attendant discussion. If you have many ESL students in your class, you will need to spend extra time on this section of the chapter and make special assignments in which students are required to differentiate between infinitive and participle phrases as objects of verbs.

Finally, because nonstandard dialects of English often retain the subject-auxiliary inversion in indirect questions, you may wish to provide further drill and/or writing assignments on indirect questions to those students in your class whose home language is a nonstandard variety of English.

Name ───────────────────────────────

Date ──────────────────────────

Quiz 5.1

All the sentences on this quiz come from *Politically Correct Bedtime Stories.*

Part I: All the following sentences contain content clauses. Underline each content clause you find, and in the space below the sentence, write whether the clause is a subject, an object, or a complement.

1. On the way to Grandma's house, Red Riding Hood was accosted by a wolf, who asked her what was in her basket.

2. The tailor was able to convince the emperor that he was cutting and sewing pieces of fabric.

3. The emperor pretended that he could see the beautiful, politically correct robes.

4. The three little pigs rejoiced that justice had triumphed.

5. The tinker might have argued with her over the concept of ownership and stated that the lettuce rightfully "belonged" to anyone who was hungry and had nerve enough to take it.

6. Not long after this, the witch appeared at their door, demanding that they give her the child in return for the witch's having spared the tinker's life in the garden.

7. But soon it became clear that the commotion was turning into something ugly.

8. To the other women, it seemed that Cinderella was the cause of all the trouble.

9. Snow White surmised that the cottage belonged to either seven little men or one sloppy numerologist.

10. Snow White didn't know that this was really the queen in disguise.

Part II: Underline the verbal (that is, an infinitive phrase or a participle phrase) in the following sentences, and in the space below the sentence, write the function of the phrase in the sentence (subject, direct object, object of the preposition) and specify the verb or verb phrase to which it relates as subject or object, or the preposition to which it serves as object.

11. One day her mother asked her to take a basket of fresh fruit and mineral water to her grandmother's house.

12. He grabbed Red Riding Hood in his claws, intent on devouring her.

13. I have a troll's needs, and those needs include eating goats.

14. I really can't commit to that course of action without consulting my siblings.

15. And don't try to run away.

16. The prince was celebrating his exploitation of the dispossessed and marginalized peasantry by throwing a fancy dress ball.

17. Then he began mumbling into the built-in microphone.

18. The tailor noticed these traits and decided to use them to his advantage.

19. The prince has ordered me to spin all this straw into gold.

20. He began to invade the goat's caprinal space.

21. It's not fair to keep you in suspense.

22. We only wanted to save our own skins.

23. She begged the tinker to jump the fence.

24. You want to take her from me!

25. My fellow giants want to get rid of your corrupting feminine presence.

Name ―――――――――――――――――――――――――――――――

Date ―――――――――――――――――――――――――――――

Quiz 5.2

All the sentences on this quiz come from *The Age of Innocence*, Edith Wharton's Pulitzer Prize-winning novel.

Part I: All the following sentences contain content clauses. Underline each content clause you find, and in the space below the sentence, write whether the clause is a subject, an object, or a complement.

1. Archer understood that he ran the risk of having his mandate withdrawn.

2. Archer remarked that old Mr. du Lac was calling on his cousins the Dagonets.

3. He knew that there were societies where painters and poets and novelists and men of science, and even great actors, were as sought after as Dukes.

4. It's a shame you're going to miss the little oyster supper I'd planned for you at Delmonico's next Sunday.

5. He perceived that she had spoken of business to Beaufort simply to get rid of him.

6. It flashed across him at that instant that the charge in the letter was true.

7. The pity was that her gratitude put her, in the law's eyes and the world's, on a par with her abominable husband.

8. He supposed she had never thought of him as the sender.

9. I wonder how a Countess happens to live in our slum.

10.   From the office he sent a note by messenger to Madame
       Olenska, asking if he might call that afternoon.

Part II: Underline the verbal (that is, an infinitive phrase or a participle phrase) in the following sentences, and in the space below the sentence, write the function of the phrase in the sentence (subject, direct
object, object of the preposition) and specify the verb or verb phrase to
which it relates as subject or object, or the preposition to which it
serves as object. A sentence may have more than one verbal; follow the
procedure for each one you find.

11.   His heart began to resume its usual task.

12.   It was her habit to sit in a window of her sitting-room on the
       ground floor.

13.   It amused Newland Archer to picture her blameless life in the
       stage-setting of adultery.

14.   I want to give the wedding breakfast.

15.   To receive the Countess Olenska in the family circle was a
       different thing from producing her in public.

16.   Mrs. Archer liked to be well-informed as to society's doings.

17.   I don't want to be ridiculous.

18.   It will do me good to dine at Adeline's.

19.   Then he tried to see the persons already in the room.

20.   Archer remembered seeing a portrait by the new painter,
       Carolus Duran.

21.   Archer had tried to vary the wording of his thanks.

22.   To look at the matter in this light simplified his own case.

23.   At length he began to plead again.

24.   It was perfectly easy to place anyone then.

25.   On reaching home, he wrote a line to the Countess Olenska.

Name _____

Date _____

Quiz 5.3

1. Write a sentence that has a content clause for a subject. Underline the content clause.

   _____

   _____

2. Write a sentence that has a content clause as direct object. Underline the content clause.

   _____

   _____

3. Write a sentence that has a content clause as a complement. Underline the content clause.

   _____

   _____

4. Write a sentence that uses a content clause to express indirect speech. Be certain that it differs from your sentence for (2). Underline the content clause.

   _____

   _____

5. Write a sentence that has an infinitive phrase as subject.
    Underline the infinitive phrase.

    _____

    _____

6. Write a sentence that has an infinitive phrase as direct object.
    Underline the infinitive phrase.

    _____

    _____

7. Write a sentence that has a participle phrase as subject.
    Underline the participle phrase.

    _____

    _____

8. Write a sentence that has a participle phrase as direct object.
    Underline the participle phrase.

    _____

    _____

9. Write a sentence that has a participle phrase as the object of a
    preposition. Underline the participle phrase.

    _____

    _____

10. Write a sentence having a content clause as the direct object of
    a verb other than those you used in (2) and (4) above.
    Underline the content clause.

    _____

    _____

ANSWERS

Quiz 5.1

1. On the way to Grandma's house, Red Riding Hood was accosted by a wolf, who asked her <u>what was in her basket</u>.
   object
2. The tailor was able to convince the emperor <u>that he was cutting and sewing pieces of fabric</u>.
   object
3. The emperor pretended <u>that he could see the beautiful, politically correct robes</u>.
   object
4. The three little pigs rejoiced <u>that justice had triumphed</u>.
   object
5. The tinker might have argued with her over the concept of ownership and stated <u>that the lettuce rightfully "belonged" to anyone who was hungry and had nerve enough to take it.</u>
   object
6. Not long after this, the witch appeared at their door, demanding <u>that they give her the child in return for the witch's having spared the tinker's life in the garden</u>.
   object
7. But soon it became clear <u>that the commotion was turning into something ugly</u>.
   subject
8. To the other women, it seemed <u>that Cinderella was the cause of all the trouble</u>.
   subject
9. Snow White surmised <u>that the cottage belonged to either seven little men or one sloppy numerologist.</u>
   object
10. Snow White didn't know <u>that this was really the queen in disguise</u>.
    object
11. One day her mother asked her <u>to take a basket of fresh fruit and mineral water to her grandmother's house</u>.
    direct object of *asked*
12. He grabbed Red Riding Hood in his claws, intent on <u>devouring her</u>.
    object of the preposition *on*
13. I have a troll's needs, and those needs include <u>eating goats</u>.
    direct object of *include*
14. I really can't commit to that course of action without <u>consulting my siblings</u>.
    object of the preposition *without*
15. And don't try <u>to run away</u>.
    direct object of *don't try*

16. The prince was celebrating his exploitation of the dispossessed and marginalized peasantry by <u>throwing a fancy dress ball</u>.
     object of the preposition *by*

17. Then he began <u>mumbling into the built-in microphone</u>.
     direct object of *began*

18. The tailor noticed these traits and decided <u>to use them to his advantage</u>.
     direct object of *decided*

19. The prince has ordered me <u>to spin all this straw into gold</u>.
     direct object of *has ordered*

20. He began <u>to invade the goat's caprinal space</u>.
     direct object of *began*

21. It's not fair <u>to keep you in suspense</u>.
     subject of *is*

22. We only wanted <u>to save our own skins</u>.
     direct object of *wanted*

23. She begged the tinker <u>to jump the fence</u>.
     direct object of *begged*

24. You want <u>to take her from me</u>!
     direct object of *want*

25. My fellow giants want <u>to get rid of your corrupting feminine presence</u>.
     direct object of *want*

Quiz 5.2

1. Archer understood <u>that he ran the risk of having his mandate withdrawn</u>.
    object

2. Archer remarked <u>that old Mr. du Lac was calling on his cousins the Dagonets</u>.
    object

3. He knew <u>that there were societies where painters and poets and novelists and men of science, and even great actors, were as sought after as Dukes</u>.
    object

4. It's a shame <u>you're going to miss the little oyster supper I'd planned for you at Delmonico's next Sunday</u>.
    subject

5. He perceived <u>that she had spoken of business to Beaufort simply to get rid of him</u>.
    object

6. It flashed across him at that instant <u>that the charge in the letter was true</u>.
    subject

7. The pity was <u>that her gratitude put her, in the law's eyes and the world's, on a par with her abominable husband</u>.
    complement

8. He supposed <u>she had never thought of him as the sender</u>.
    object

9. I wonder <u>how a Countess happens to live in our slum</u>.
   object

10. From the office he sent a note by messenger to Madame Olenska, asking <u>if he might call that afternoon.</u>
    object

11. His heart began <u>to resume its usual task</u>.
    direct object of *began*

12. It was her habit <u>to sit in a window of her sitting-room on the ground floor</u>.
    subject of *was*

13. It amused Newland Archer <u>to picture her blameless life in the stage-setting of adultery</u>.
    subject of *amused*

14. I want <u>to give the wedding breakfast</u>.
    direct object of *want*

15. <u>To receive the Countess Olenska in the family circle</u> was a different thing from <u>producing her in public</u>.
    subject of *was*; object of the preposition *from*

16. Mrs. Archer liked <u>to be well-informed as to society's doings</u>.
    direct object of *liked*

17. I don't want <u>to be ridiculous</u>.
    direct object of *don't want*

18. It will do me good <u>to dine at Adeline's</u>.
    subject of *will do*

19. Then he tried <u>to see the persons already in the room</u>.
    direct object of *tried*

20. Archer remembered <u>seeing a portrait by the new painter, Carolus Duran</u>.
    direct object of *remembered*

21. Archer had tried <u>to vary the wording of his thanks</u>.
    direct object of *had tried*

22. <u>To look at the matter in this light</u> simplified his own case.
    subject of *simplified*

23. At length he began <u>to plead again</u>.
    direct object of *began*

24. It was perfectly easy <u>to place anyone then</u>.
    subject of *was*

25. On <u>reaching home</u>, he wrote a line to the Countess Olenska.
    object of the preposition *on*

Pulling Ideas Together

OBJECTIVES

After completing this chapter, students will be able to

- recognize coordinating conjunctions
- learn that elements of equal status are connected in coordination
- recognize correlative conjunctions
- recognize conjunctive adverbs and learn the punctuation rules that apply

With respect to coordination, all basic writers typically experience the same difficulties: Sentences with coordinated elements may lack parallel structure, and punctuation may be erratic. Chapter Six is designed to give students exposure to the various conjunctions and conjunctive adverbs, to provide them with exemplary examples of coordination, and to introduce them to the punctuation rules that apply in cases of coordination.

Name ———————————————————————————

Date ———————————————————————

Quiz 6.1

Part I: Circle the conjunction or the members of the correlative pair in the following sentences from *Pigs in Heaven* and *Blanche on the Lam*. Then underline the parts of the sentence that each coordinating or correlative conjunction connects.

1. Alice picks up an empty flowerpot from the porch step and throws it at the pigs.

2. The bird turns its head and looks straight at Lucky with a mean eye.

3. Taylor clicks her flashlight on and off.

4. Turtle and Taylor take one last stroll across Mr. Hoover's concrete dream.

5. Turtle is a TV heroine now, so police officers pay attention to her.

6. Mountains rise low and purple behind the river like doctor's-office art.

7. You can't think too much about luck, good or bad.

8. He stands up and barks twice.

9. He looks at her, takes off his glasses, and throws the notepad on the floor.

10. She still speaks Cherokee in her dreams sometimes but never learned to write it.

11. The front door jingles, and Pollie Turnbo brushes past the violets.

12. He spreads newspapers on the table and sits to peel his potatoes.

13. "Just think," she says, "we could be in Paris or Hong Kong. They have McDonald's in every country in the world."

14. He is tired but can't imagine sleeping.

15. She still feels pretty and young.

16. Taylor doesn't consider Barbie the ideal baby-sitter, but she's obviously short on choices.

17. Either Emmeline or that husband of hers is driving this girl's blood pressure right on up there!

18. Blanche had seen him both angry and agitated, but he seemed neither unduly unhappy nor harried.

19. Blanche neither moved nor spoke.

20. Both anger and fear were present in her voice.

Part II: Underline the conjunctive adverbs or adverbials in the following passages from *The Right Stuff* by Tom Wolfe. In the space below the sentence, write the meaning relationship it indicates.

21. Shepard and Wally Schirra were paired somewhere in between. It was not that they were inseparable pals or even buddies, however.

22. Naturally you needed a man with the courage to ride on top of a rocket, and you were grateful that such men existed. Nevertheless, their training was not a very complicated business.

23. An experienced zombie would do fine. In fact, considerable attention had been given to a plan to anesthetize or tranquilize

the astronauts, not to keep them from panicking, but just to make sure they would lie there peacefully with their sensors on and not *do something* that would ruin the flight.

24.   When a Navy pilot practiced carrier landings on the outline of a flight deck painted on an airfield, it was hoped that the maneuver might also desensitize his normal fear of landing a hurtling machine in such a small space. Nevertheless, he was there chiefly in order to learn to land the machine.

25.   The Air Force had sloughed these wrecks off on them like hand-me-downs. The poor condition of the F-102s wasn't the worst of it, however.

Name ————————————————————————————

Date ————————————————————————

Quiz 6.2

Part I: Circle the conjunction or the members of the correlative pair in the following sentences from several sources: *Blanche on the Lam, A Word Child* (by Iris Murdoch), *Talking Power* (by Robin Lakoff), and *Praisesong for the Widow*. Then underline the parts of the sentence that each coordinating or correlative conjunction connects.

1.   Blanche smiled and nodded.

2.   Putting on a dumb act was something many black people considered unacceptable, but she sometimes found it a useful place to hide.

3.   A huge bed of pink, white, and yellow flowers lay on the far side of the pond.

4.   He stopped pacing but began twisting from side to side, like an agitator in a washing machine.

5.   The stars were bright and silver-blue.

6.   Dinner was a quick and quiet affair.

7.   Still, it was odd that they didn't hire a nurse or companion for Emmeline.

8.   She wondered whether Everett might be insane and decided all murderers were probably crazy, at least in the moment.

9.   Blanche shook her head and opened the car door.

10.   Grace said that she and Everett were leaving.

11. It felt good to win a round with Everett and to be proven right about Emmeline's room being empty.

12. Grace looked startled but didn't speak.

13. She seemed to be listening to or for something.

14. Blanche dropped the scarf and headed for the back stairs.

15. Laura, no longer either young or slim, was a good-looking woman.

16. Tenured faculty are much more forthright, both in expressing controversial opinions and in expressing them relatively directly.

17. The relationship between professors and graduate students is the core of university business, in terms of both mission and politics.

18. For a long minute she stood gripping the railing, trying to steady herself and clear her head.

19. Bringing her elbows to rest on the table, she buried her throbbing forehead in her hands and closed her eyes.

20. The rum shop was seedy, run-down, stripped almost bare, yet somehow pleasant.

Part II: Underline the conjunctive adverbs or adverbials in the following passages from *The Right Stuff*. In the space below the sentence, write the meaning relationship it indicates.

21. Rathman was no ordinary auto dealer, however. He turned out to be a racing driver; the best, in fact.

22. There was no particular advantage to forming a clique in this seven-man corps, because only one man could win the competition, i.e., get the first flight, and it wasn't a voting situation, in any case. Nevertheless, if any such situation came

up, Al and Wally would probably tend to side with Deke and Gus.

23.   It was only thanks to a recent invention of his day, the magnetic compass, that Columbus had dared to sail across the Atlantic. Until then ships had stayed close to the great land masses for even the longest voyages. Likewise, putting a man into space the quick and dirty way without high-speed computers was unthinkable.

24.   Flight training consisted of teaching a man how to take certain actions. He was taught how to control an unfamiliar craft or how to put a familiar craft through unfamiliar maneuvers, such as bombing runs or carrier landings. On the other hand, the only actions the astronauts would have to learn how to take would be to initiate the emergency procedures in case of a bad rocket launch or a bad landing and to step in as a backup.

25.   For a moment it seemed as if it was going to come down in a few thousand enormous flaming pieces, right on everybody's bean. There was no danger, in fact.

Name ————————————————————————

Date ———————————————————

Quiz 6.3

1. Write a sentence that includes coordination using *and*. Circle the conjunction and underline the equal parts it connects. Use appropriate punctuation.

———————————————————————————

———————————————————————————

2. Write a sentence that includes coordination using *but*. Circle the conjunction and underline the equal parts it connects. Use appropriate punctuation.

———————————————————————————

———————————————————————————

3. Write a sentence that includes coordination using *or*. Circle the conjunction and underline the equal parts it connects. Use appropriate punctuation.

———————————————————————————

———————————————————————————

4. Write a sentence that includes coordination using *both . . . and*. Circle the members of the correlative pair and underline the equal parts they connect. Use appropriate punctuation.

———————————————————————————

———————————————————————————

5. Write a sentence that includes coordination using *neither . . . nor*. Circle the members of the correlative pair and underline the equal parts they connect. Use appropriate punctuation.

_____

_____

6. Write a sentence that includes coordination using *not only . . . but also*. Circle the members of the correlative pair and underline the equal parts they connect. Use appropriate punctuation.

_____

_____

7. Write a sentence that includes coordination using *either . . . or*. Circle the members of the correlative pair and underline the equal parts they connect. Use appropriate punctuation.

_____

_____

8. Write a pair of sentences connected by *however*. Use appropriate punctuation.

_____

_____

9. Write a pair of sentences connected by *nevertheless*. Use appropriate punctuation.

_____

_____

10. Write a sentence whose two clauses are connected by a semicolon.

_____

_____

ANSWERS

Quiz 6.1

1. Alice <u>picks up an empty flowerpot from the porch step</u> *and* <u>throws it at the pigs</u>.
2. The bird <u>turns its head</u> *and* <u>looks straight at Lucky with a mean eye</u>.
3. Taylor clicks her flashlight <u>on</u> *and* <u>off</u>.
4. <u>Turtle</u> *and* <u>Taylor</u> take one last stroll across Mr. Hoover's concrete dream.
5. <u>Turtle is a TV heroine now</u>, *so* <u>police officers pay attention to her</u>.
6. Mountains rise <u>low</u> *and* <u>purple</u> behind the river like doctor's-office art.
7. You can't think too much about luck, <u>good</u> *or* <u>bad</u>.
8. He <u>stands up</u> *and* <u>barks twice</u>.
9. He <u>looks at her</u>, <u>takes off his glasses</u>, *and* <u>throws the notepad on the floor</u>.
10. She <u>still speaks Cherokee in her dreams sometimes</u> *but* <u>never learned to write it</u>.
11. <u>The front door jingles</u>, *and* <u>Pollie Turnbo brushes past the violets</u>.
12. He <u>spreads newspapers on the table</u> *and* <u>sits to peel his potatoes</u>.
13. "Just think," she says, "we could be in <u>Paris</u> *or* <u>Hong Kong</u>. They have McDonald's in every country in the world."
14. He <u>is tired</u> *but* <u>can't imagine sleeping</u>.
15. She still feels <u>pretty</u> *and* <u>young</u>.
16. <u>Taylor doesn't consider Barbie the ideal baby-sitter</u>, *but* <u>she's obviously short on choices</u>.
17. *Either* <u>Emmeline</u> *or* <u>that husband of hers</u> is driving this girl's blood pressure right on up there!
18. Blanche had seen him *both* <u>angry</u> *and* <u>agitated</u>, but he seemed *neither* <u>unduly unhappy</u> *nor* <u>harried</u>.
19. Blanche *neither* <u>moved</u> *nor* <u>spoke</u>.
20. *Both* <u>anger</u> *and* <u>fear</u> were present in her voice.
21. Shepard and Wally Schirra were paired somewhere in between. It was not that they were inseparable pals or even buddies, <u>however</u>.
    contrast
22. Naturally you needed a man with the courage to ride on top of a rocket, and you were grateful that such men existed. <u>Nevertheless</u>, their training was not a very complicated business.
    contrast
23. An experienced zombie would do fine. <u>In fact</u>, considerable attention had been given to a plan to anesthetize or tranquilize the astronauts, not to keep them from panicking, but just to make sure they would lie there peacefully with their sensors on and not *do something* that would ruin the flight.
    emphasis
24. When a Navy pilot practiced carrier landings on the outline of a flight deck painted on an airfield, it was hoped that the maneuver might also desensitize his

normal fear of landing a hurtling machine in such a small space. <u>Nevertheless</u>, he was there chiefly in order to learn to land the machine.
contrast

25. The Air Force had sloughed these wrecks off on them like hand-me-downs. The poor condition of the F-102s wasn't the worst of it, <u>however</u>.
contrast

Quiz 6.2

1. Blanche <u>smiled</u> *and* <u>nodded</u>.
2. <u>Putting on a dumb act was something many black people considered unaccept-able</u>, *but* <u>she sometimes found it a useful place to hide</u>.
3. A huge bed of <u>pink</u>, <u>white</u>, *and* <u>yellow</u> flowers lay on the far side of the pond.
4. He <u>stopped pacing</u> *but* <u>began twisting from side to side, like an agitator in a washing machine</u>.
5. The stars were <u>bright</u> *and* <u>silver-blue</u>.
6. Dinner was a <u>quick</u> *and* <u>quiet</u> affair.
7. Still, it was odd that they didn't hire a <u>nurse</u> *or* <u>companion</u> for Emmeline.
8. She <u>wondered whether Everett might be insane</u> *and* <u>decided all murderers were probably crazy</u>, at least in the moment.
9. Blanche <u>shook her head</u> *and* <u>opened the car door</u>.
10. Grace said that <u>she</u> *and* <u>Everett</u> were leaving.
11. It felt good <u>to win a round with Everett</u> *and* <u>to be proven right about Emmeline's room being empty</u>.
12. Grace <u>looked startled</u> *but* <u>didn't speak</u>.
13. She seemed to be listening <u>to</u> *or* <u>for</u> something.
14. Blanche <u>dropped the scarf</u> *and* <u>headed for the back stairs</u>.
15. Laura, no longer *either* <u>young</u> *or* <u>slim</u>, was a good-looking woman.
16. Tenured faculty are much more forthright, *both* <u>in expressing controversial opin-ions</u> *and* <u>in expressing them relatively directly</u>.
17. The relationship between <u>professors</u> *and* <u>graduate students</u> is the core of univer-sity business, in terms of *both* <u>mission</u> *and* <u>politics</u>.
18. For a long minute she stood gripping the railing, trying to <u>steady herself</u> *and* <u>clear her head</u>.
19. Bringing her elbows to rest on the table, she <u>buried her throbbing forehead in her hands</u> *and* <u>closed her eyes</u>.
20. The rum shop was <u>seedy</u>, <u>run-down</u>, <u>stripped almost bare</u>, *yet* <u>somehow pleasant</u>.
21. Rathman was no ordinary auto dealer, <u>however</u>. He turned out to be a racing dri-ver; the best, <u>in fact</u>.
contrast; emphasis
22. There was no particular advantage to forming a clique in this seven-man corps, because only one man could win the competition, i.e., get the first flight, and it

wasn't a voting situation, in any case. <u>Nevertheless</u>, if any such situation came up, Al and Wally would probably tend to side with Deke and Gus.
contrast

23. It was only thanks to a recent invention of his day, the magnetic compass, that Columbus had dared to sail across the Atlantic. Until then ships had stayed close to the great land masses for even the longest voyages. <u>Likewise</u>, putting a man into space the quick and dirty way without high-speed computers was unthinkable.
addition

24. Flight training consisted of teaching a man how to take certain actions. He was taught how to control an unfamiliar craft or how to put a familiar craft through unfamiliar maneuvers, such as bombing runs or carrier landings. <u>On the other hand</u>, the only actions the astronauts would have to learn how to take would be to initiate the emergency procedures in case of a bad rocket launch or a bad landing and to step in as a backup.
contrast

25. For a moment it seemed as if it was going to come down in a few thousand enormous flaming pieces, right on everybody's bean. There was no danger, <u>in fact</u>.
emphasis

C H A P T E R   S E V E N

Agreement

 OBJECTIVES

After completing this chapter, students will be able to

- make verbs agree with their subjects, even when the subject appears at a distance from the verb
- make pronouns agree with their antecedents
- use strategies to avoid pronoun agreement problems with generic nouns

Most English speakers, both native and nonnative, who are not accomplished writers experience difficulties with agreement; even fluent writers who write lengthy sentences occasionally make agreement errors. In fact, when sentences are very short and include only one clause and little to no modification, agreement problems rarely occur. Thus, increasing complexity in the writing of your students may well result in agreement errors. Modifiers on the principal noun of the subject noun phrase, for example, often cause problems because the tendency for all English speakers is to make the verb agree with the nearest preceding noun. However, this rule won't do for writing, and so Chapter Seven aims to make explicit the rules developing writers will need.

Name _____

Date _____

Quiz 7.1

All of the sentences on this quiz are taken from Margaret Mead's classic study, *Coming of Age in Samoa*.

Part I: Underline the correct verb form in the parentheses for each of the following sentences.

1.   The midwife cuts the cord with a fresh bamboo knife and then all (waits, wait) eagerly for the cord to fall off, the signal for a feast.

2.   The weight of the punishment usually (falls, fall) upon the next oldest child, who (learns, learn) to shout, "Come out of the sun," before she has fully appreciated the necessity of doing so herself.

3.   No one who (throws, throw) the stones actually (means, mean) to hit a child.

4.   The small girls, burdened with heavy babies or the care of little staggerers who (is, are) too small to adventure on the reef, (has, have) little opportunity for learning the more adventurous forms of work and play.

5.   All the irritating, detailed routine of housekeeping, which in our civilization (is, are) accused of warping the souls and souring the tempers of grown women, (is, are) here performed by children under fourteen years of age.

6.   There (is, are) always relatives to whom one can flee.

7.   Before this time their knowledge of plants and trees (is, are) mainly a play one.

8. More difficult (is, are) the floor mats, woven of four great palm leaves, and the food platters with their intricate designs.

9. There (is, are) also fans to make, simple two-strand weaves which she (learns, learn) to make quite well.

10. Usually some older woman in the household (trains, train) a girl to weave and sees to it that she makes at least one of each kind of article.

11. A girl's chances of marriage (is, are) badly damaged if it gets about the village that she is lazy and inept in domestic tasks.

12. The older chiefs who (supervises, supervise) the activities of the *Aumaga* gaze equally sternly upon any backslidings and upon any undue precocity.

13. Old men of sixty (is, are) my companions and (watches, watch) my every word, lest I (makes, make) a mistake.

14. There is no one in my whole family who (dares, dare) to scold me or even to address me familiarly by my first name.

15. These households (includes, include) all the individuals who (lives, live) for any length of time under the authority and protection of a common *matai*.

16. Widows and widowers, especially when they (is, are) childless, usually return to their blood relatives, but a married couple may live with the relatives of either one.

17. No one living permanently in another village (is, are) counted as a member of the household, which (is, are) strictly a local unit.

18. A baby whose mother (has, have) gone inland to work on the plantation (is, are) passed from hand to hand for the length of the village.

19. The very number of her captors (is, are) the girl's protection.

20.   The first attitude which a little girl (learns, learn) towards boys
      (is, are) one of avoidance and antagonism.

Part II: Circle the personal or possessive pronoun in each of the following sentences and underline its antecedent.

21.   Then the visitors go home, the mother rises and goes about her
      daily tasks, and the new baby ceases to be of much interest to
      anyone.

22.   The careful child psychologist who relied upon experiment for
      his conclusions did not subscribe to these theories.

23.   The physical changes which are going on in the bodies of boys
      and girls have their definite psychological accompaniments.

24.   Meanwhile another way of studying human development had
      been gaining ground, the approach of the anthropologist, the
      student of man in all of his most diverse social settings.

25.   The anthropologist, as he pondered his growing body of
      material upon the customs of primitive people, grew to realize
      the tremendous role played in an individual's life by the social
      environments in which each is born and reared.

Name ———————————————————————

Date ————————————————

Quiz 7.2

All of the sentences on this quiz are taken from *Coming of Age in Samoa*.

Part I: Underline the correct verb form in the parentheses for each of the following sentences.

1. There (is, are) always relatives to whom one can flee.

2. Theoretically the supply of relatives (is, are) inexhaustible.

3. The most important relationships within a Samoan household which (influences, influence) the lives of the young people (is, are) the relationships between the boys and girls who call each other "brother" and "sister."

4. Relatives of opposite sex (has, have) a most rigid code of etiquette prescribed for all their contacts with each other.

5. Nevertheless, rank not of birth but of title (is, are) very important in Samoa.

6. The status of a village (depends, depend) upon the rank of its high chief.

7. There (was, were) no other males in the near relationship group.

8. Village feeling (runs, run) high in Tui's village.

9. Brothers and sisters and small cousins who (lives, live) in the same household, of course, (frolics, frolic) and (plays, play) together.

10. Outside the household each child (clings, cling) closely to its older guardian.

11. But at about seven years of age, the children (begins, begin) to form larger groups, a kind of voluntary association which never (exists, exist) in later life.

12. The prohibition that one small girl must never join a group of boys (is, are) beginning to be enforced.

13. The groups of small children which (hangs, hang) about the fringes of some adult activity often (contains, contain) both girls and boys.

14. No very intense friendships (is, are) made at this age.

15. Of the different groups of little girls there (was, were) only one which showed characteristics which would make it possible to classify it as a gang.

16. The borderline between small boys and bigger boys (is, are) therefore a continually shifting one.

17. The *Aualuma*, the organization of young girls and wives of untitled men, (is, are) an exceedingly loose association gathered for very occasional communal work.

18. Another factor which qualified men's relationships (is, are) the reciprocal relationship between chiefs and talking chiefs.

19. In the right sector (sits, sit) the high chief and his special assistant chiefs.

20. The better part of her attention and interest (is, are) focused on a smaller group.

Part II: Circle the personal or possessive pronouns in each of the following sentences and underline the antecedents.

21.   So the anthropologist, arguing from his observations of the behavior of adult human beings in other civilizations, reaches many of the same conclusions which the behaviorist reaches in his work upon human babies who have as yet no civilization to shape their malleable humanity.

22.   A Samoan girl of good family has two ways of making her debut.

23.   When a man dies, it is his paternal aunt or his sister who prepares the body for burial.

24.   The seventeen-year-old boy is not left passively to his own devices.

25.   Any older relative has a right to demand personal service from younger relatives, a right to criticize their conduct and to interfere in their affairs.

Name ————————————————————————

Date ————————————————————————

Quiz 7.3

1. Write five sentences whose subjects are third person (either singular or plural) and whose verbs are present tense. Include modifiers on the chief noun of the subject phrase, such as prepositional phrases, relative clauses, and so on. Make certain the verbs agree with the subjects. Underline the subject once and put a double line under the verb/verb phrase.

————————————————————————

————————————————————————

————————————————————————

————————————————————————

————————————————————————

————————————————————————

————————————————————————

————————————————————————

————————————————————————

————————————————————————

————————————————————————

————————————————————————

————————————————————————

2.   Write five sentences that include both pronouns and their
     antecedents. Circle the pronoun and underline the antecedent.
     Make sure they agree in person, number, and gender.

_____

_____

_____

_____

_____

_____

_____

_____

_____

_____

_____

_____

_____

_____

_____

_____

_____

3. Rewrite the following passage from *Coming of Age in Samoa* to eliminate the use of the masculine pronoun for generic reference.

    With such an attitude towards human nature the anthropologist listened to the current comment upon adolescence. He heard attitudes which seemed to him dependent upon social environment—such as rebellion against authority, philosophical perplexities, the flowering of idealism, conflict and struggle—ascribed to a period of physical development. And on the basis of his knowledge of the determinism of culture, of the plasticity of human beings, he doubted. Were these difficulties due to being adolescent or to being adolescent in America?

    _____

    _____

    _____

    _____

    _____

    _____

    _____

    _____

    _____

    _____

    _____

    _____

ANSWERS

Quiz 7.1

1. The midwife cuts the cord with a fesh bamboo knife and then all (waits, <u>wait</u>) eagerly for the cord to fall off, the signal for a feast.
2. The weight of the punishment usually (<u>falls</u>, fall) upon the next oldest child, who (<u>learns</u>, learn) to shout, "Come out of the sun," before she has fully appreciated the necessity of doing so herself.
3. No one who (<u>throws</u>, throw) the stones actually (<u>means</u>, mean) to hit a child.
4. The small girls, burdened with heavy babies or the care of little staggerers who (is, <u>are</u>) too small to adventure on the reef, (has, <u>have</u>) little opportunity for learning the more adventurous forms of work and play.
5. All the irritating, detailed routine of housekeeping, which in our civilization (<u>is</u>, are) accused of warping the souls and souring the tempers of grown women, (<u>is</u>, are) here performed by children under fourteen years of age.
6. There (is, <u>are</u>) always relatives to whom one can flee.
7. Before this time their knowledge of plants and trees (<u>is</u>, are) mainly a play one.
8. More difficult (is, <u>are</u>) the floor mats, woven of four great palm leaves, and the food platters with their intricate designs.
9. There (is, <u>are</u>) also fans to make, simple two-strand weaves which she (<u>learns</u>, learn) to make quite well.
10. Usually some older woman in the household (<u>trains</u>, train) a girl to weave and sees to it that she makes at least one of each kind of article.
11. A girl's chances of marriage (is, <u>are</u>) badly damaged if it gets about the village that she is lazy and inept in domestic tasks.
12. The older chiefs who (supervises, <u>supervise</u>) the actvities of the *Aumaga* gaze equally sternly upon any backslidings and upon any undue precocity.
13. Old men of sixty (is, <u>are</u>) my companions and (watches, <u>watch</u>) my every word, lest I (makes, <u>make</u>) a mistake.
14. There is no one in my whole family who (<u>dares</u>, dare) to scold me or even to address me familiarly by my first name.
15. These households (includes, <u>include</u>) all the individuals who (lives, <u>live</u>) for any length of time under the authority and protection of a common *matai*.
16. Widows and widowers, especially when they (is, <u>are</u>) childless, usually return to their blood relatives, but a married couple may live with the relatives of either one.
17. No one living permanently in another village (<u>is</u>, are) counted as a member of the household, which (<u>is</u>, are) strictly a local unit.
18. A baby whose mother (<u>has</u>, have) gone inland to work on the plantation (<u>is</u>, are) passed from hand to hand for the length of the village.
19. The very number of her captors (<u>is</u>, are) the girl's protection.
20. The first attitude which a little girl (<u>learns</u>, learn) towards boys (<u>is</u>, are) one of avoidance and antagonism.

21. Then the visitors go home, <u>the mother</u> rises and goes about *her* daily tasks, and the new baby ceases to be of much interest to anyone.

22. <u>The careful child psychologist</u> who relied upon experiment for *his* conclusions did not subcribe to these theories.

23. <u>The physical changes which are going on in the bodies of boys and girls</u> have *their* definite psychological accompaniments.

24. Meanwhile another way of studying human development had been gaining ground, the approach of the anthropologist, the student of <u>man</u> in all of *his* most diverse social settings.

25. <u>The anthropologist</u>, as *he* pondered *his* growing body of material upon the customs of primitive people, grew to realize the tremendous role played in an individual's life by the social environments in which each is born and reared.

Quiz 7.2

1. There (is, <u>are</u>) always relatives to whom one can flee.
2. Theoretically the supply of relatives (<u>is</u>, are) inexhaustible.
3. The most important relationships within a Samoan household which (influences, <u>influence</u>) the lives of the young people (is, <u>are</u>) the relationships between the boys and girls who call each other "brother" and "sister."
4. Relatives of opposite sex (has, <u>have</u>) a most rigid code of etiquette prescribed for all their contacts with each other.
5. Nevertheless, rank not of birth but of title (<u>is</u>, are) very important in Samoa.
6. The status of a village (<u>depends</u>, depend) upon the rank of its high chief.
7. There (was, <u>were</u>) no other males in the near relationship group.
8. Village feeling (<u>runs</u>, run) high in Tui's village.
9. Brothers and sisters and small cousins who (lives, <u>live</u>) in the same household, of course, (frolics, <u>frolic</u>) and (plays, <u>play</u>) together.
10. Outside the household each child (<u>clings</u>, cling) closely to its older guardian.
11. But at about seven years of age, the children (begins, <u>begin</u>) to form larger groups, a kind of voluntary association which never (<u>exists</u>, exist) in later life.
12. The prohibition that one small girl must never join a group of boys (<u>is</u>, are) beginning to be enforced.
13. The groups of small children which (hangs, <u>hang</u>) about the fringes of some adult activity often (contains, <u>contain</u>) both girls and boys.
14. No very intense friendships (is, <u>are</u>) made at this age.
15. Of the different groups of little girls there (<u>was</u>, were) only one which showed characteristics which would make it possible to classify it as a gang.
16. The borderline between small boys and bigger boys (<u>is</u>, are) therefore a continually shifting one.
17. The *Aualuma*, the organization of young girls and wives of untitled men, (<u>is</u>, are) an exceedingly loose association gathered for very occasional communal work.
18. Another factor which qualified men's relationships (<u>is</u>, are) the reciprocal relationship between chiefs and talking chiefs.

19. In the right sector (sits, <u>sit</u>) the high chief and his special assistant chiefs.

20. The better part of her attention and interest (<u>is</u>, are) focused on a smaller group.

21. So <u>the anthropologist</u>, arguing from *his* observations of the behavior of adult human being in other civilizations, reaches many of the same conclusions which <u>the behaviorist</u> reaches in *his* work upon <u>human babies</u> who have as yet no civilization to shape *their* malleable humanity.

22. <u>A Samoan girl of good family</u> has two ways of making *her* debut.

23. When <u>a man</u> dies, it is *his* paternal aunt or *his* sister who prepares the body for burial.

24. <u>The seventeen-year-old boy</u> is not left passively to *his* own devices.

25. Any older relative has a right to demand personal service from <u>younger relatives</u>, a right to criticize *their* conduct and to interfere in *their* affairs.

Punctuation

OBJECTIVES

After completing this chapter, students will be able to

- use appropriate sentence-final and sentence-internal punctuation
- use apostrophes for the possessive construction and for contraction
- use quotation marks with appropriate punctuation

Because there are no precise analogs to punctuation in the spoken language, students often have difficulty using punctuation appropriately, either omitting punctuation where it is required or inserting it where it is disallowed. Many students believe that a comma, for example, should be inserted wherever one would take a breath when reading aloud. Of course, such a strategy leads to idiosyncratic punctuation at best and unreadable text at worst.

Both grammatical rules and rhetorical rules may apply in appropriate punctuation. However, in this text, I focus on the grammatical rules alone. Students will have less to contend with, and they will be able to produce acceptable text.

Name _____

Date _____

Quiz 8.1

Part I: Some of these sentences from *The Kitchen God's Wife* by Amy Tan are correct; some have missing punctuation. Add punctuation where it is needed; write *correct* under the sentences that need no change.

1. As we walked up the pathway to the house I knew we had made a terrible mistake.

2. We all listened as Old Aunt took a little piece of truth and stretched it in all directions.

3. She was the senior wife the one who approved the spending of household money.

4. Three days before my wedding Peanut did a very bad thing she fed me news about the Wen family that soured in my stomach.

5. Three days before the wedding our house was crowded with relatives who had come from far away Old Aunt's people New Aunt's people and cousins connected to us by complicated marriages.

6. The back fence had a gate that led into an alley.

7. Down this alley and one turn to the left was a pathway with bushes that led to a small city lake.

8. I was remembering my poor little broken treasures my mother's painting the wings of a butterfly that crumbled into dust a dried flower bulb that I once watered every day.

9. New Aunt came back into the room with Peanut who stared at me with big eyes.

10. I waited until nighttime before I told Wen Fu about the baby.

11. He did his chores quietly complaining only about a shopkeeper who had cheated him.

12. When he fell I jumped on and pedaled away to get you.

13. The next afternoon we drove to the western foothills the place everyone called the Sleeping Beauties.

14. When I could finally open my eyes the first thing I saw was a woman standing in front of me.

15. After we reached the gate we jumped into a pit or stood behind a tree.

Part II: Each of the following sentences from *The Age of Innocence* has at least one word that requires an apostrophe. Underline each word that requires an apostrophe and rewrite it in the space below the sentence, inserting the apostrophe where needed.

16. Its worth everything, isnt it, to keep ones intellectual liberty?

17. He had heard the Countess Olenskas name pronounced often enough during the year and a half since they had last met.

18. He asked himself if Mays face was doomed to thicken into the same middle-aged image of invincible innocence.

19. The burden of Mrs. Manson Mingotts flesh had long since made it impossible for her to go up and down stairs.

20. You see, shes one of the family, and shes been away so long that shes rather sensitive.

Part III: The following passage from *The Age of Innocence* involves direct quotation. I have left off some of the punctuation, including the quotation marks. Add quotation marks and punctuation as necessary.

> You know, when it comes to the point, your parents have always let you have your way ever since you were a little girl he argued; and she had answered, with her clearest look Yes; and that's what makes it so hard to refuse the very last thing they'll ever ask of me as a little girl.

Name _____

Date _____

Quiz 8.2

Part I: Some of these sentences from *The Kitchen God's Wife* are correct as is; some have missing punctuation. Add punctuation where it is needed; write *correct* under the sentences that need no change.

1. On top of this I put a small biscuit tin containing all my jewelry and a little blue perfume bottle my mother had given me long ago.

2. Even her eyes which had once been a very dark black-brown had faded in color.

3. Behind her back we called her Miao-miao because she was just like a cat.

4. When my senses came together I was lying with my face to the ground.

5. After Pearl went home I cried.

6. He was always a person who controlled others with his strength.

7. And she was still angry when she told me.

8. Stores that once sold fancy dresses closed their doors.

9. When the servant opened the door she screamed.

10. Before I married I had come from a poor family.

11. This pavilion reminded me of the greenhouse on the island it made me homesick—although not for the house where Uncle Old Aunt and New Aunt lived.

12. When the rest of the city turned dark and quiet at night we turned on our radio our fan and our lamps.

13. He threw a bedpan at the doctor who saved his life.

14. Just as we reached the place where the bombs fell the rain started.

15. He did not dance at all like Min who moved her arms and legs like branches caught by a soft wind.

Part II: Each of the following sentences from *The Age of Innocence* has at least one word that requires an apostrophe. Underline each word that requires an apostrophe and rewrite it in the space below the sentence, inserting the apostrophe where needed.

16. He had come to America with letters of recommendation from old Mrs. Manson Mingotts English son-in-law, the banker.

17. Oh, thats part of the campaign: Grannys orders, no doubt.

18. Miss Wellands face grew rosy as the dawn.

19. Its too serious a question to decide at this late hour.

20. "Newland never seems to look ahead," Mrs. Welland once ventured to complain to her daughter; and May answered serenely: "No; but you see it doesnt matter, because when theres nothing particular to do he reads a book."

Part III: The following passage from *The Age of Innocence* involves direct quotation. I have left off some of the punctuation, including the quotation marks. Add quotation marks and punctuation as necessary.

I do think, she went on, addressing both men, that the *imprévu* adds to one's enjoyment. It's perhaps a mistake to see the same people every day.

It's confoundedly dull, anyhow; New York is dying of dullness Beaufort grumbled.

Name ————————————————————————————————

Date ———————————————————————————

Quiz 8.3

Write a paragraph of at least ten sentences on any topic of your choosing. Make certain that your sentences include some of the constructions discussed in this book, such as restrictive and nonrestrictive modifiers, adverbials, conjunctions, and so on. When you are done, check the paragraph over for correct punctuation, paying particular attention to appropriate use of commas and semicolons. Is every sentence really a sentence and not a fragment or a run-on?

ANSWERS

Quiz 8.1

1. As we walked up the pathway to the house, I knew we had made a terrible mistake.
2. We all listened as Old Aunt took a little piece of truth and stretched it in all directions.
   correct
3. She was the senior wife, the one who approved the spending of household money.
4. Three days before my wedding, Peanut did a very bad thing; she fed me news about the Wen family that soured in my stomach.
5. Three days before the wedding, our house was crowded with relatives who had come from far away: Old Aunt's people, New Aunt's people, and cousins connected to us by complicated marriages.
6. The back fence had a gate that led into an alley.
   correct
7. Down this alley and one turn to the left was a pathway with bushes that led to a small city lake.
   correct
8. I was remembering my poor little broken treasures: my mother's painting, the wings of a butterfly that crumbled into dust, a dried flower bulb that I once watered every day.
9. New Aunt came back into the room with Peanut, who stared at me with big eyes.
10. I waited until nighttime before I told Wen Fu about the baby.
    correct
11. He did his chores quietly, complaining only about a shopkeeper who had cheated him.
12. When he fell, I jumped on and pedaled away to get you.
13. The next afternoon we drove to the western foothills, the place everyone called the Sleeping Beauties.
14. When I could finally open my eyes, the first thing I saw was a woman standing in front of me.
15. After we reached the gate, we jumped into a pit or stood behind a tree.
16. <u>Its</u> worth everything, <u>isnt</u> it, to keep <u>ones</u> intellectual liberty?
    It's; isn't; one's
17. He had heard the Countess <u>Olenskas</u> name pronounced often enough during the year and a half since they had last met.
    Olenska's
18. He asked himself if <u>Mays</u> face was doomed to thicken into the same middle-aged image of invincible innocence.
    May's

19. The burden of Mrs. Manson <u>Mingotts</u> flesh had long since made it impossible for her to go up and down stairs.
    Mingott's
20. You see, <u>shes</u> one of the family, and <u>shes</u> been away so long that <u>shes</u> rather sensitive.
    she's (all three)

"You know, when it comes to the point, your parents have always let you have your way ever since you were a little girl," he argued; and she had answered, with her clearest look, "Yes; and that's what makes it so hard to refuse the very last thing they'll ever ask of me as a little girl."

Quiz 8.2

1. On top of this, I put a small biscuit tin containing all my jewelry and a little blue perfume bottle my mother had given me long ago.
2. Even her eyes, which had once been a very dark black-brown, had faded in color.
3. Behind her back, we called her Miao-miao because she was just like a cat.
4. When my senses came together, I was lying with my face to the ground.
5. After Pearl went home, I cried.
6. He was always a person who controlled others with his strength.
   correct
7. And she was still angry when she told me.
   correct
8. Stores that once sold fancy dresses closed their doors.
   correct
9. When the servant opened the door, she screamed.
10. Before I married, I had come from a poor family.
11. This pavilion reminded me of the greenhouse on the island; it made me home-sick—although not for the house where Uncle Old Aunt and New Aunt lived.
12. When the rest of the city turned dark and quiet at night, we turned on our radio, our fan, and our lamps.
13. He threw a bedpan at the doctor who saved his life.
    correct
14. Just as we reached the place where the bombs fell, the rain started.
15. He did not dance at all like Min, who moved her arms and legs like branches caught by a soft wind.
16. He had come to America with letters of recommendation from old Mrs. Manson <u>Mingotts</u> English son-in-law, the banker.
    Mingott's
17. Oh, <u>thats</u> part of the campaign: <u>Grannys</u> orders, no doubt.
    that's; Granny's
18. Miss <u>Wellands</u> face grew rosy as the dawn.
    Welland's

19. <u>Its</u> too serious a question to decide at this late hour.
    It's
20. "Newland never seems to look ahead," Mrs. Welland once ventured to complain to her daughter; and May answered serenely: "No; but you see it <u>doesnt</u> matter, because when <u>theres</u> nothing particular to do he reads a book."
    doesn't; there's

    "I do think," she went on, addressing both men, "that the *imprévu* adds to one's enjoyment. It's perhaps a mistake to see the same people every day."

    "It's confoundedly dull, anyhow; New York is dying of dullness," Beaufort grumbled.

Executive Editor: Marisa L. L'Heureux
Editor: Heidi L. Hedstrom
Cover and interior design: Karen E. Christoffersen
Design Manager: Ophelia M. Chambliss
Production Manager: Margo Goia

Library of Congress Cataloging-in-Publication Data

Silva, Marilyn Neva.
    Basic grammar in many voices / Marilyn N. Silva.
        p.   cm.
    Includes index.
    Summary: Explains the basics of English grammar, including parts
of speech, sentence structure, modifiers, clauses, idea
coordination, and punctuation, and provides practice exercises.
        ISBN 0-8442-5959-4 (pbk. : alk. paper)
        1. English language—Grammar.   2. English language—Grammar—
Problems, exercises, etc.   [1. English language—Grammar.]
I. Title.
PE1112.S542 1997
428.2—dc21   97-20019
                                                       CIP
                                                        AC

BASIC
GRAMMAR
IN MANY
VOICES

NTC Publishing Group
a division of NTC/CONTEMPORARY PUBLISHING COMPANY
Lincolnwood, Illinois USA